Wayland A-Z
A Dictionary of Then and Now

To Cary —

Edited by
Evelyn Wolfson and **Dick Hoyt**

for the Wayland Historical Society, Inc.

Evelyn Wolfson

Dick Hoyt

McNaughton & Gunn, Inc.
Saline, MI 48176

MA.

Photo & Illustration Credits

Cover photographs by Steven Engler

Page 5, Old Town Bridge, Wayland, MA. Photograph by New England News Company. Courtesy of Historic New England/SPNEA.

Page 99, "Kirkside," 221 Boston Post Road, Wayland, MA. Photograph by A. W. Cutting, before 1888. Courtesy of Historic New England/SPNEA.

Page 173, [Beatrice Herford reading on blanket, Wayland, MA.] Photograph by Alfred Wayland Cutting. Courtesy of Historic New England/SPNEA.

Page 117, Tower Hill Depot, circa 1915. William L. Patton Jr. Collection. Courtesy The Beverly Historical Society and Museum.

Page 189, Yucca filamentosa. Evelyn Wolfson.

All other illustrations and photos courtesy of the Wayland Historical Society, Inc.

Dedicated to the memory of

Nancy R. Ashkar

A teacher, scientist and friend, who served the Society in many ways during her years in Wayland. Always interested in inspiring young people, she used her extraordinary commitment and teaching skills to transfer her love of place to future generations. She felt that knowing one's roots gave a sense of time and place that helped relate to events and places throughout the world. The programs she developed and the volunteer help she inspired were unusual in their scope and quality. Her contagious laugh, her genuine enthusiasm for teaching and learning and her sharp and penetrating intellect made her a favorite teaching companion. One of the Society's most valued resources, a legacy of her work in the schools, is a collection of her school programs that provided primary source study units for elementary grades and independent projects for middle school and high school students. Nancy helped create the Local Studies Center, housed in the Mellen Law Office, which focuses on local history and natural history. Many of us remember the high quality slide shows she prepared from the Society's slide collection and presented to the public. When discussing this book in the spring of 2004, Nancy, as a competent and qualified scientist, suggested we focus our X, Y and Z entries on the scientific names of local plants. Nancy's ideas and accomplishments represent striving for excellence in every way.

Contents

Acknowledgements

This book could not have been written without the constant guidance and encouragement of Jo Goeselt, Wayland Historical Society Curator Emerita, who spent endless hours reading, editing, debating, offering suggestions and locating sources for every entry. Jo was always there when we needed her–as a resource and as a friend who constantly cheered us on.

We also owe a debt of gratitude to members of the Society who willingly contributed one or more essays of their own to the book–Joanne Davis, Lois Davis, George Lewis, Bob Mainer, Sally Newbury, John Seiler, Gretchen Schuler, Jane Sciacca, Larry Stabile, Betty Sweitzer, and Martie Taub. Joanne Davis, current Curator, opened the Historical Society's files to us, provided valuable suggestions and contributed essays of her own. Amelia Entin, photographic curator, gave her expert advice and time in photograph selection. We are deeply grateful to John Schlafer who installed scanner software, provided hours of expert instruction, prepared the manuscript for submission, and, along with John Callen, placed photos onto the pages. Thanks go to George Lewis who not only contributed a number of essays, but he and John Bryant gave freely of their time reading and discussing ideas.

We appreciate the time others took from their own work to help us by reading and reviewing individual entries: Rich Ames, Richard Conard, Paul Gardescu, Chris Hagger, Don Hollender, Chief Robert Irving, Cynthia Mayher, Brian Monahan, Irene Praeger, Judith St. Croix, Ken Sawyer, and Jack Wilson.

Special thanks go to Steve Engler for cover photography and design, and Rich Ames for his fine maps.

We also thank members of the Historical Society, friends and family who believed in the project and inspired us to go on.

Jerry Mitchell deserves particular praise for reading and critiquing the entire manuscript.

Preface

For history buffs, there can never be too many books about history. The challenge for authors interested in writing about history, however, is to capture the reader's imagination. *Wayland A-Z, a Dictionary of Then and Now*, is not an original idea. Many books have been published that arrange facts alphabetically, including history books. It is a format that allows readers to open the book to any page and read a few minutes, or if intrigued, a few hours. It was Thomas H. O'Connor's *Boston A-Z* that inspired us to create this book to raise money for the Wayland Historical Society.

It did not take long to come up with a list of topics that we believed might interest a general readership–topics covered in more depth than the League of Woman Voters booklet or the town website, but in less detail than in Helen Fitch Emery's *The Puritan Village Evolves, a History of Wayland, Massachusetts.* The topics, related only by their alphabet arrangement, are about historic and current people, places, events and subjects that are distinctive and unique to the character of the town. Our initial list grew as additional topics popped up while doing research and after members of the society agreed to contribute essays of interest to them. Readers will note that we have tried not to homogenize entries and have edited only to achieve a general style. We believe there is room for diverse voices in a book of this kind and that readers will enjoy the diversity as much as we do.

Some topics continue to make history in town: the establishment of new houses of worship, the performances of live theater at Vokes, or fresh challenges to zoning. Others, however, have a finite place in our town's history: Cranberries haven't been harvested for more than a century, cows will never again graze on Cow Common, and the town's trolley tracks long ago were covered by pavement.

We owe a great debt of gratitude to Helen Fitch Emery whose impeccably researched book served as a core for our research. *The Puritan Village Evolves,* published in 1981, is unquestionably the definitive history of Wayland. Many topics in *Wayland A-Z* are covered in greater detail in Mrs. Emery's book, which is a chronological history of the town from 1638 to 1980. Two other basic resources for *Wayland A-Z* were written by Alfred Sereno Hudson: *The History of Sudbury, 1638-1889,* published in 1889, and *Annals of Sudbury Wayland and Maynard,* published in 1891. *Puritan Village: The Formation of a New England Town* by Sumner Chilton Powell, published in 1963, served to a lesser extent. The title Mrs. Emery chose for her book, *The Puritan Village Evolves,* is in reference to Powell's earlier publication.

Many topics have also been freshly culled from original sources at the Historical Society's Grout-Heard House, from town hall records and from conversations with longtime residents. All entries have been thoroughly researched and vetted by experts.

We remind readers that our town has had three names since 1638, and time periods can be confusing since there is no chronological order to the entries. We have tried to put "Wayland" in parentheses when that was not the name of the town at the time. However, the time periods are not difficult to remember. The first settlement of Sudbury Plantation in 1638 was primarily on the east side of the river but included both sides. It was incorporated in 1639 as **Sudbury**. In 1780, the town of Sudbury was separated into two towns, the division being approximately the river. The west side of the river kept the name Sudbury and our town, the east side, was incorporated as **East Sudbury.** In 1835, **East Sudbury** was renamed **Wayland**. No record exists as to why the town's name was changed at that time, but some believe having two towns with such similar names caused confusion. Thus, our town's names: **Sudbury 1638 to 1780; East Sudbury 1780 to 1835, and Wayland 1835 to forever?**

We apologize that we could not include every topic that interested us, and perhaps readers as well, but time and space prevent us from going on. We encourage readers to research other topics of interest at local libraries. The town of Sudbury has all the sources mentioned and historians willing to share information. We also recommend two entertaining and informative memoirs written by longtime residents George Lewis and Lewis Russell. *Growing Up in Wayland* by George K. Lewis was published in 1997, and *Russell's Thru the Years* by Lewis Russell was published in 1998. In 2002, George Lewis and the Wayland Historical Society published *Images of America–WAYLAND*, a pictorial history of the town which contains 215 photographs of people, places and events over the years.

Wayland Massachusetts
Evelyn Wolfson and Dick Hoyt
October, 2004

Town of Wayland

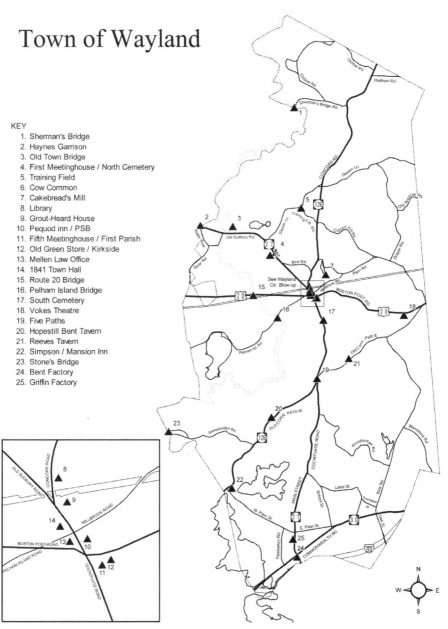

KEY

1. Sherman's Bridge
2. Haynes Garrison
3. Old Town Bridge
4. First Meetinghouse / North Cemetery
5. Training Field
6. Cow Common
7. Cakebread's Mill
8. Library
9. Grout-Heard House
10. Pequod inn / PSB
11. Fifth Meetinghouse / First Parish
12. Old Green Store / Kirkside
13. Mellen Law Office
14. 1841 Town Hall
15. Route 20 Bridge
16. Pelham Island Bridge
17. South Cemetery
18. Vokes Theatre
19. Five Paths
20. Hopestill Bent Tavern
21. Reeves Tavern
22. Simpson / Mansion Inn
23. Stone's Bridge
24. Bent Factory
25. Griffin Factory

Cochituate Village Between 1850 -1900

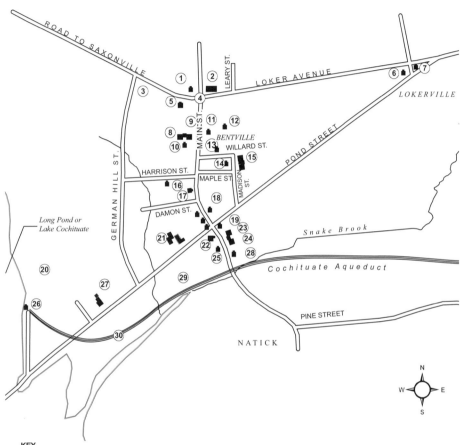

KEY

1. Knights of Labor Hall, 1887 (Grange)
2. Horsecar Barn
3. Ball Field
4. Lyons corner
5. A.B. Lyon House
6. South School House
7. Wesleyan Methodist Church, 1850
8. Beehive, 1891-1913
9. Lyon Factory
10. School, 1873
11. H.C. Dean House
12. H.C. Dean Factory
13. St. Zepherin Church
14. Beehive until 1891
15. Williams Factory
16. Engine House
17. Methodist Episcopal Church
18. Stores
19. Bent's Corner
20. Lakeview Cemetery
21. Bryant Factory
22. Bent Factory
23. Bent Boarding House
24. Omnibus Stage Depot
25. First Bryant House
26. Gatehouse
27. G.A. Damon House (later N. Griffin)
28. Blacksmith Shop (P.A. Leary)
29. City Pastures
30. Aqueduct

Wayland A-Z

A Dictionary of Then and Now

"The old life has silently passed, and the familiar features of hill, valley, meadow, and homestead, so intimately associated with it, remain in a strange, new era. But still, about the old homes, the lilacs breathe their memories in the May; and still, in many a neglected garden, or maybe by a lonely grass-grown cellar, lying open to the sky, the roses or lilacs loyally bloom on the tangled bushes, or the tulips and jonquils push up through the grass, in memory, perhaps, of some sweet Lois Maynard, who planted them and loved them, years and years ago."

Alfred Wayland Cutting, *Old Time Wayland,* 1926

A

Invoice of Personal Property and
its Appraised value on the Town's
Farm March 24th 1862

J. N. Sherman (Overseers
Thomas P. Damon { of
} Poor

Live Stock

$140.
$11.

2 Oxen $125 . 1 horse $110 =	$235.00
5 Cows $100 . 2 pigs $30	X 130.00
22 Fowls at 50 cts each	X 22.00

Carriages &c

1 Sleigh $9 . 1 Market waggon $30	39.00
1 Ox & horse Cart ————	30.00
1 Hay Waggon	20.00
1 Wheel-barrow	3.50
1 Ox Waggon	20.00
6 Tons Eng. Hay.	90.00
Corn Stalks & Straw	5.00
2 Ploughs	8.00
1 Harrow	3.00
8 Rakes	1.50
	607.00

1862 Poor Farm Invoice

3

Almshouse/Poor farm

In the seventeenth century, everyone in a small town knew everyone else's business and no one went without a place to sleep, food to eat, or warm clothing. The word spread quickly when a family was in need and town leaders reacted just as quickly to provide assistance on a case-by-case basis. For example, in 1649 the town voted to assist a local widow in need of financial help. Over the next twenty years, the town continued to provide periodic support for her, including visitation of a Dedham physician. In 1663, Thomas Rice took an indigent man into his home and the town paid for the man's keep. The following year, the town relieved another impoverished resident of his tax burden.

While the town readily supported needy residents, it discouraged transients or homeless people who wandered from town to town. Wanderers were never refused a meal or a night's lodging, but they were quickly "warned out" of town the next day. In fact, the colony enacted a law in 1692-93 that allowed towns to warn away strangers within fourteen days so that the town would not have to assume economic responsibility for them. If the town allowed three months to go by without issuing a warning, the parties then became residents entitled to town assistance.

For a number of years, needy cases were presented at town meeting and residents bid for their care. Costs increased, however, and selectmen sought a new solution. In 1831, following the example of other towns, the selectmen purchased the farmhouse of Eli Sherman at 206 Oxbow Road to house the poor. The house had been built by Ephraim Sherman in 1780 and owned by two generations of the Sherman family. Selectmen sold the house in 1845 and some time later purchased the Otis Loker farm (Cutting) on Rice Road for $3,130. The house was located on the east side of the road just north of the sharp curve in the road. (Now the entrance to a private home)

The overseers of the poor–John C. Butterfield and Charles Fairbanks of Cochituate and Luther H. Sherman of North Wayland–had the house repaired and a small farm established that would be worked by residents in exchange for room and board. A warden and his wife were hired to run the farm and household. Such farms provided a family-style environment for residents but some towns established strict rules of behavior and discipline for residents. Bad conduct, which included the use of profanity, could be punishable by solitary confinement with only bread and water, forced labor, permission required to come and go, and to accept visitors.

In addition to providing for local residents at the poor farm, the town had been feeding and providing overnight accommodations for hundreds of transient men. Some were cared for at the poor farm but others were housed at the lockup, built in 1875 to house drunks, in Cochituate. The lockup was a brick building located on the south side of Harrison Street in Cochituate. One generous overseer of the poor, John Calvin Butterfield, who lived in Cochituate, made sure that every man held in the lockup was fed. Butterfield, who lived on Pemberton Road, also served as superintendent of the Lakeview Cemetery and as local undertaker. He was a shoemaker by trade and fought in the Civil War. When he died in 1909, at the age of ninety-two, the *Natick Bulletin* called him "the grand old man of Cochituate."

Eventually, the town became so overburdened with having to meet the needs of transients–as many as 850 in 1878-79–that selectmen decided to eliminate use of the lockup and offer lodging at the almshouse only. They stipulated, however, that the overnight accommodation would include only one meal of crackers and water. Even though many indigents and drunks continued to stop in town, the word must have spread about the paltry meal they'd be given because by 1908 the number of people lodged at the almshouse had dropped to an all-time low of eleven.

The selectman also had to discourage the overseers from offering "partial" or temporary support in the form of money or groceries arguing that it resulted in "loss of self-respect and independence of character." Periodically, selectmen appointed committees to look into selling the poor farm or making recommendations about what to do about its run-down condition. In 1881, the poor farm paid its fuel and food expenses from monies received for the sale of produce raised by its seven indigent guests. Still, town records show that during 1880-81 various amounts of money were voted to cover expenses for the poor: $100 to house each of two insane and violent inmates at the Worcester Lunatic Hospital; $20 for the burial of an indigent member of the French community in Cochituate; $53 for the services of Dr. Boodey; and $53 to purchase a cow for the farm.

The pathetic condition of the farm's barn and house caused much debate at town meeting. Members could not agree whether to move the whole operation from its remote location (Rice Road was remote at the time) and rebuild in Cochituate, or make repairs at the Rice Road site. No decision had been made before state authorities came to inspect the almshouse in 1886 and declared it to be one of the worst establishments in the state. Selectmen must have been embarrassed because records reveal they excused themselves by saying monies for the poor farm had been diverted to repair the Pelham Island bridge that had been destroyed by the winter flood of 1885.

Four years later, however, the town had built a new poor house on Rice Road which stayed in operation for the next twenty years. As the number of residents dwindled over the years, it became uneconomical to support them and in 1908 the town transferred residents to an institution in Worcester. Eventually the property was purchased by the owners of Mainstone Farm.

State and federal agencies slowly assumed responsibility for housing and unemployment after World War II. Many poor farm facilities became health facilities for the sick and elderly.

Recently, federal and state cutbacks have altered or eliminated vital programs and institutions, the most serious being state mental health facilities, and towns are once again grappling with these same problems.

B

388 OLD TOWN BRIDGE
(FOUR ARCH)
WAYLAND MASS.

Old Town Bridge

Bridges

The broad meandering river that divided Sudbury Plantation provided rich meadow grass for cattle but crossing it posed a problem. Early settlers probably followed Indian fording places along the river where water flowed close to sandy banks–at Old Town Bridge, Bridle Point, Stone's Bridge, Sherman's Bridge, and Pelham Island Bridge, earlier called "Farm Bridge." But these were not dependable places to cross during periods of high water.

Since the direction of roads, the nearness of river banks, and the supply of fill were important determinants for bridge locations, Old Sudbury Road, the main path running east and west through Sudbury Plantation fixed the site for the first bridge over the river–Old Town Bridge. There was probably a foot bridge at the site until 1642 or 1643 when Ambrose Leech accepted a bid to build a cart bridge twelve feet wide and three feet above the river's high water mark. The town agreed to cut the bridge's timbers, saw the planks, take the material to the site, and help raise the bridge. (Ambrose and his assistant did help with the latter.) In exchange, Ambrose Leech was granted ten acres of meadow along with an appropriate amount of upland and rights to common land. It is reported that in 1642, Thomas Noyes operated a ferry for foot passengers across the river at that same point, probably when high water made the bridge unusable.

Old Town Bridge was replaced and repaired a number of times at considerable expense to the settlement. In addition to serving local residents and their cattle, the cart bridge was used by hundreds of travelers heading west. Unpredictable and severe flooding also wreaked havoc on the bridge and its replacements and caused such a financial strain on the settlement that selectmen appealed to the General Court for assistance. Colonial records show that in 1645 Sudbury received a tax abatement in recognition that the bridge was essential for public use. Three decades later, Watertown soldiers drove Indian warriors back over a bridge at this site during King Philip's War and marched to defend Haynes Garrison on the west side of the river. Almost a hundred years later George Washington crossed the river at this point on his way to Boston early in the Revolutionary War. The first wood-framed bridge in Middlesex County was built at this site. But, the last bridge to be built at the site, and the most picturesque, was the four-arched stone bridge built in 1848–most of which remains today and can be visited by following a short paved path off Old Sudbury Road just past the Wayland Country Club driveway.

Just west of the Old Town Bridge was Canal Bridge built over a portion of the river which flowed through an artificial channel. Although there are no records dating the construction of Canal Bridge, there is a record for repair of the bridge in 1768. It was probably built over a ditch dug into the meadow to allow water to flow through in time of flood. Canal Bridge washed away during hurricane Diane in 1955 and Old Sudbury Road was made to connect in a straight line across the river eliminating the need for both Canal and Old Town bridges.

Bridle Point was used to anchor a bridge connecting East Sudbury and South Sudbury in the 1820s. (see Bridle Point) The bridge was upgraded in 1924 when the Boston Post Road was made straight between present Buddy Dog Humane Society and Russell's Garden Center. Today, the bridge is just west of Russell's Garden Center and is referred to as the Route 20 bridge. It now carries more traffic than our forefathers could have imagined.

For many years, travelers to Pelham Island crossed the river at a fording place just south of Bridle Point via a series of appropriately placed stones. In 1775, when Bridle Point Road was discontinued as a roadway from Bow Road to Bridle Point, islanders began to cross the river at the site of the present Pelham Island Bridge. A nameless private bridge may have been built here at some time, but in 1775 the bridge used by islanders was named Farm Bridge. By then, the road was being used as a public way and islanders asked the town to accept both the road and bridge. The town accepted on condition that residents on the island keep it in good repair for ten years. The islanders must have been diligent in their repair of the bridge because it was not replaced until 1832. That bridge lasted four years and was replaced by another wooden structure. The present bridge, built of concrete in 1915, was raised high above the water but not high enough to protect islanders from periodic floods that continue to make the road and bridge impassable. Like residents of the island today, eighteenth and nineteenth century farmers often had to cross the river by boat when flood waters covered the bridge. It has been said that they fastened their boats to the elm tree in front of the Pequod House, site of the new Public Safety Building. Some twentieth century islanders remember fastening their canoes to a post at the Purity Supreme Market, now Whole Foods, before the town's fire department and later the Army Corps of Engineers provided vehicular transport through the water that flowed over the bridge and covered the road and the land on both sides of the bridge. In 2001, however, the State mandated that all bridges across the Sudbury River be replaced by ones built to state code. Repair of the Pelham Island bridge began in mid 2001 and remains a temporary bridge into 2004.

Moving farther upriver, another cart bridge called "The New Bridge," to differentiate it from "Old Town Bridge," was built on the road to Framingham. Like other bridge sites in town, there were predecessors to the bridge, one built by Samuel How(e) in 1674 at this point. This bridge, later called Stone's Bridge, was included in the General Court's layout for a highway–the South Country Path–that went from Watertown to Brookfield. The Colonial government deemed this an important route westward because floods were less likely to submerge a bridge this far upriver. The Court allowed How(e) to collect tolls on the bridge until he had recovered his construction costs. Over the years, this bridge, like others in town, underwent extensive reconstruction and repair due to heavy traffic. British spies, heading west, crossed the bridge on March 20, 1775 on their way from Jones Tavern in Weston to Worcester. Colonel Henry Knox, heading east, crossed it with men and oxen dragging cannons in the winter of 1775-1776 from Fort Ticonderoga in New York to Boston. Finally, in 1857-58 this wooden bridge was replaced by a more costly stone one which minimized frequent repairs. It should be noted, that this bridge was not named for the material used in its construction, but for the Stone family who had lived in the area from almost the beginning of town settlement. Unfortunately, hurricane Diane in 1955 washed away one entire end of this beautiful bridge and the road and bridge had to be relocated.

Another bridge, this one down-river toward Concord, served the neighbors on Sherman's Bridge

Road. Sherman's Bridge was built in 1743 after Edward Sherman, who lived on the east side of the river, and John Haynes, who lived on the west side, each agreed to give a two-rod stretch of their fields for a roadway and bridge crossing.

The two four-arched stone bridges over the river–Old Town Bridge built in 1848 and Stone's Bridge built in 1857 or 1858–have been a photographer's delight for more than a century. Town archives are filled with their handsome images. Yet, even in old age, with parts missing and grass tufts filling their crevices, they are still beautiful–beautiful enough to be visited and worthy enough to be saved.

❑❑❑

Bridle Point

Bridle Point was a little known and historically insignificant peninsula that projected out into the Sudbury River meadows from the eastern shoreline close to the Route 20 bridge. When the early settlers were trying to decide where to build a bridge across the Sudbury River, Bridle Point did not seem to be the best place to do that and the Old Town Bridge site farther north was chosen instead.

The first settlers in this area built primitive shelters along Bow Road, digging into the protective sandy slope that faced the warm sun. Nearby, a long, narrow ridge ran across the old Raytheon parking lot and terminated at Bridle Point offering another housing site. Although land was allotted for houses along the ridge, no foundations have ever been discovered. A path was laid out that reached the present Russell's Garden Center. Eventually this entire section was incorporated into the Braman estate, laid out in the nineteenth century along Old Sudbury Road. Bridle Point eventually became the anchor for the 1820 bridge (Route 20 Bridge) built to connect South Sudbury.

In 1954, approximately thirty feet of sand removed from the western half of the ridge created a large, level field for Raytheon Company to build a laboratory after convincing Wayland's voters of the wisdom of re-zoning the area "limited commercial." (see Zoning)

There is little on today's landscape to remind us of Bridle Point. Most of the hill is gone and the peninsula is lost in the brush along the river's edge. Only the ancient maps and documents honor its name.

Cakebread's Mill in Winter

Cakebread's Mill

Early New England towns needed gristmills since survival depended on eating Indian corn which was so hard and coarse it had to be ground into meal before it could be digested. Wheat, the grain preferred by Englishmen, failed as a crop in the New World, so settlers collected corn seed from vacant Indian lands and planted new crops of their own. In a very short period of time, corn became the staple crop for settlers.

The most important task for Sudbury Plantation founders was to find a competent miller. They persuaded Thomas Cakebread (aptly named), to become Sudbury's first miller. Cakebread, a resident of Watertown, had just agreed to move to Dedham when he was approached by Sudbury's leaders to join Sudbury Plantation. In exchange for his services as a miller, he was granted 100 acres of land in the vicinity of Mill Brook–upland for house and mill, and meadow land above and below the mill.

By 1639 townspeople were hard at work cutting trees on his property for lumber to build the new gristmill. Cakebread's property had an ample supply of wood and nearby Goodman's, Nobscot, and Reeves hills had granite for millstones. There is no record of the type of wheel used at the mill–whether it was an overshot, high-breast or undershot–meaning water came over the top, entered at the middle, or at the bottom. Overshot mills provided the best power but required at least a ten foot dam. Records indicate there was a dam and, most likely, a ten foot drop at the southern end of the pond. Howard S. Russell, a long-time resident of Wayland, who lived near the old mill, believed that Cakebread's mill would have been an overshot type with the water flowing onto it from above. The weight of the water would have caused the wheel to turn a horizontal shaft. By means of an interlocking gear, this turned a vertical shaft nearby and rotated a horizontal millstone, in the mill overhead, against another fixed millstone. When grain was poured into an opening for it, the kernels were ground into meal. A set of millstones that had the top stone turning at 120 revolutions per minute could grind 500 pounds of grain per hour. Millstones had a variety of different patterns cut into them, called the dress. Tradition and preference determined the shape and dress of a millstone. Often stones wore down within two weeks and had to be re-dressed, or re-sharpened, which took up to fourteen man-hours per stone to accomplish. Grinding stones lasted from ten years to a century, depending on their use.

Cakebread's mill was built almost entirely out of wood–oak, elm, hornbeam, maple, and birch. Mill parts were fastened together with leather or iron straps and kept lubricated with generous applications of tallow obtained from butchered animals. In winter, water often froze in the mill's sluiceway and Cakebread probably roofed over portions of the mill to keep it in operation. During seasons of low water the mill could not run.

Kernels of corn that escaped the grinding process, or ones that had been put through an iron corn cracker, were brought home and fed to the cattle. Dry cobs were salvaged and taken home to stoke the fire. Settlers undoubtedly learned from the Indians who dried freshly harvested corn and stored it in large baskets set into holes dug below the frost line, to store corn in their cellars–the original New England cold

15

cellar. The Indians also taught settlers how to make "Nokehick," (pronounced No-cake) by parching corn kernels. No-Cake could be eaten out of hand like peanuts, or ground up and eaten like cereal with sugar and milk. (Similar products can be purchased today in food specialty shops.)

Unfortunately, Thomas Cakebread died early in 1643 only four years after coming to Sudbury. His son-in-law, John Grout came from Watertown to operate the mill which stayed in the Grout family for several generations. The mill remained in use until 1882. A fire destroyed the building in 1890. More than three hundred and sixty years later, winter skaters can glide past the site of the original dam which the town maintains to keep sufficient water in the pond.

❑❑❑

Cemeteries

Every town has burial grounds and cemeteries that hold much of the history of the families who shaped the town. Wayland is no exception, with four different historic burial grounds, each telling part of the story. The Old Burying Ground surrounded the first meetinghouse (1643) on Old Sudbury Road. It was the final resting place of many early Sudbury residents. Names of, and epitaphs to, early settlers and succeeding generations of Goodenows, Curtises, Rutters, Parmenters, and Rices are found on some of the slate stones. Near the edge of the road leading into the Old Burial Ground (now the North Cemetery) are two slate stones with decorative tops which mark the burial sites of Jacob Reeves (1720-1795) and his wife, Abigail. Reeves was a signer of the petition to separate East Sudbury from Sudbury and served as one of the first three selectmen. In addition, he ran one of the local taverns on Old Connecticut Path. Other well known and important family names appear on grave markers throughout the cemetery, such as Draper, Heard, Glezen (or Gleason), and Noyes. Many of the earlier stones are carved with willow trees, urns, the winged cherub and death's heads, so popular in funerary art of the eighteenth and early nineteenth century. Many of the later stones are carved in marble or granite. Lydia Maria Child (1802-1880) who came to Wayland to care for her aging father is one of the most prominent persons buried here. Child, known for her anti-slavery writings, was the editor of the *Anti-Slavery Standard* in New York for a period of time, and was associated with William Lloyd Garrison.

There are two interesting anomalies in Wayland's cemetery history. Each is a small area dedicated to burials but not considered formal cemeteries. One is the small area at the far northeast corner of the North Cemetery which is an Indian burial ground that was connected to the Old Burying Ground in the early 1800s when land was purchased from the Noyes family to expand the cemetery. The other is a small burying ground just north of Old Town Bridge off Old Sudbury Road (Route 27). It is recognized by a monument dedicated to the Concord men who were killed on their way to assist Sudbury settlers who were under siege by Indians in the "Sudbury Fight" of King Philip's War in 1676. (see Memorials and Markers)

The town center was moved south from its original location on Old Sudbury Road to approximately the corner of present day Pelham Island and Cochituate roads when the fourth meetinghouse was

16

completed in 1726. (see Meetinghouses) More than a century later, in 1835, additional burial ground was needed and a site farther south on Cochituate Road was selected. The land chosen for the South Cemetery had been the site of a dwelling, or possibly a barn, as there are records that note that in October of 1839 someone was hired to fill in an old cellar at "the new burying ground." It appears that the only in-ground tomb in the lower southwest corner was built as part of estate planning because the names of the two men inscribed on the tomb were still alive in 1837 when the tomb was erected. Jotham Bullard settled in East Sudbury in 1802 and ran a prosperous farm nearly opposite the tomb on Cochituate Road. Jacob Reeves (1793-1846) lived at Reeves Tavern of which his father had been the first proprietor. (see Taverns) Each of these two men served the town, Bullard as selectmen for nine terms between 1813 and 1840, and Reeves as the town clerk. Other markers in the South Cemetery–slate, marble, and granite–are in memory of prominent families who contributed much to the development of the community: the Damons, Woods, Lokers, Wights, and Leadbetters, as well as some Civil War soldiers.

Lakeview Cemetery was established at the edge of Lake Cochituate in the thriving shoe manufacturing village of Cochituate. There are three entrances to the cemetery but the main one is on the north side of Commonwealth Road just east of Lake Cochituate. While there are death dates recorded from the 1820s, it was not until 1871 that the town purchased land from Joseph Bullard and John Calvin Butterfield and appropriated money to lay out the cemetery on the newly acquired land. Butterfield, a Civil War veteran, who came to the area before 1840 was a shoemaker and prominent resident of Cochituate Village. He served as superintendent of the Lakeview Cemetery for more than twenty years, was Cochituate's undertaker for the same period, and was one of the overseers of the poor. The picturesque design of Lakeview Cemetery was laid out on a hilly site by the lake with winding paths and roadway and a central focus of a valley or bowl with grave markers lining the slopes. The most prominent structure is the Dean family mausoleum set on the rise overlooking this central low area. It is a granite block structure with the gated entrance marked by an elaborately carved arch that springs from pairs of Corinthian columns. Another large and prominent monument marks the burial place of members of the Griffin family, one of the leading shoe manufacturing families who owned residences in Cochituate Village in the late nineteenth century. The history of other shoe manufacturing families in Cochituate Village, like the Bents and Bryants, is documented at Lakeview. So too is the history of families with both shoe workers and farmers, like the Damons and the Lokers. (see Shoe Industry)

St. Zepherin (or St. Zepherin's) private cemetery in Cochituate Village was established for the burial of Roman Catholics. St. Zepherin Church was built in 1890 in response to the large number of Roman Catholics living in the area and working in local shoe factories. Many had arrived from Canada and had established a French-speaking Catholic parish. Irish and some German immigrants joined in worship or attended other nearby parishes that worshipped in Latin and English. St. Zepherin Cemetery is midway along Bent Avenue and is marked by a large treed lot in front and many rows of granite stones behind, separated by a grid path system.

The most recently established private cemetery, run by the Jewish Cemetery Association of

Massachusetts, opened in 1999. Beit Olam, meaning "House of Forever,"consists of three acres and is entered through the North Cemetery along its south side. It serves twelve separate MetroWest synagogues with sections to meet the religious needs of Conservative, Reform, and Interfaith members.

□□□

Lydia Maria Child

When Lydia Maria Child moved to this town in 1853 to care for her elderly father, it was the beginning of her twenty-seven-year, love-hate relationship with the town of Wayland. Maria, famous novelist, an author of the first important books on women's rights, and on the abolition of slavery, and the first woman editor of a national newspaper was stuck in the Wayland she called "this little drowsy village."

The small house on Old Sudbury Road, which she later inherited from her father, was the only home she and her husband, David, were ever able to own. The Childs were always moving from rented rooms and boardinghouses, from a hardscrabble farm in Northampton and an unheated house in West Newton. David Child was a Harvard graduate and a lawyer who believed in all the idealistic causes Maria cherished. His career, however, was a long series of financial failures. Money was Maria's continual worry. All their married life, it was Maria who was the family breadwinner.

Lydia Maria Child has been called Wayland's most famous citizen, yet in her day few townspeople sympathized with the Child's political views. Maria's own brother James, who lived a mile down Old Sudbury Road, was mortified by his sister's very public abolitionist stands. Maria wrote a friend that David was "violently treated and nearly mobbed" at a Civil War aid meeting in Wayland Center when he said slaves who offered to fight for the Northern army should be permitted to do so. When her neighbor raised the Stars and Stripes to show he felt the war was being fought solely to preserve the Union, Maria hung a white flag on her garden gate.

Maria railed against the unnecessary extravagance of the new 1878 town hall and the high taxes in Wayland. She resented the fact that members of the First Parish Church insisted their ailing minister, the Reverend Edmund H. Sears, hold not one, but two services a Sunday, forcing him to retire from the Wayland pulpit.

Still Maria found a few in Wayland like the Reverend Sears and the miller William Grout, who shared her view that slavery was an injustice which should be abolished. Over the years she made warm friends with many of her neighbors and townsfolk. She loved to send little gifts such as slippers to the elderly Reverend John Burt Wight, and a favorite book of hers, *Uncle Tom's Cabin,* to her neighbor George Gleason. She delighted in sending presents to the Cutting children next door. Her letters to friends here are full of "thank you" for homemade gifts of doughnuts, crullers, bread and butter.

In her last years, after David's death, Maria found it too difficult to maintain her home in Wayland during the coldest months. Maria, who spent each winter in rented rooms in Boston, wrote a neighbor how much she missed her views of Wayland's "broad open meadows and golden sunsets." In letter after letter to Wayland friends, she spoke of her homesickness "for my humble old nest in Wayland."

□□□

Civil War

The Confederate firing on Fort Sumter, S.C., in April 1861 signaled the beginning of four long years of Civil War. Like innumerable towns, north and south, Wayland rose up to meet the challenges of the years ahead. Days after the news from Fort Sumter arrived, Wayland held the first of a series of large and enthusiastic meetings to consider the state of the country and support the war. There were speeches and songs and militia and minuteman companies were organized. As the war went on, some of the enthusiasm waned, but the resolve remained firm.

Wayland was a community of just under 1900 citizens in 1861, with farming being the main industry, although Cochituate was developing a lively shoe industry. When President Abraham Lincoln called for volunteers, Wayland responded quickly, and organized to fill quotas for soldiers and to provide support for the volunteers and their families. Over the course of the war, about 130 men connected to Wayland served in nearly thirty different regiments, a couple of artillery batteries and cavalry units and the U.S. Navy. They served in two and three year regiments and 100 day units. They saw action throughout the South, or spent their service in Boston Harbor. Their individual terms ranged from a few days to over four years. Fathers and sons, brothers, cousins, co-workers, friends enlisted and fought together. The oldest soldier was over forty-five, the youngest was not yet sixteen.

Some seventy of these men were credited to Wayland, while others enlisted with friends and relatives from other towns, or at a time when Wayland's quota was filled. At other times, recruiting was slow, and the town privately raised about $4,000 as bonus money specifically to induce foreign recruits to fill Wayland's ranks. All together, the town was responsible for about $18,000 for recruiting purposes such as bonuses. They weren't totally successful in their recruiting efforts; later in the war, three local men were drafted. Two of them had not enlisted because they felt their health couldn't stand war service, and one because he was supporting a large family and already had a son at the front. He was wounded and discharged. One of his fellow draftees never made it to the front and, after several months in army hospitals, was discharged. The third draftee was unable to keep up on the march and was captured. At war's end his family learned he had died in the Andersonville, Georgia prison camp.

A total of twelve soldiers died–six of disease, one of a combination of disease and wounds, the one at Andersonville, and four were killed in battle. Many others suffered for the rest of their lives from wounds and disease acquired during the war. Wayland had no famous generals. Several men were commissioned officers, rising to company command or staff positions, several served in military hospitals, and one commanded gunboats in the Navy.

Mostly the Wayland Warriors were the men in the ranks with the guns. Why did they go? For the same reasons soldiers have gone to war through the ages: because their friends were going, for adventure,

19

for the money, to get away from their ordinary lives. But most of them went because their country needed them, and they felt an obligation to help preserve the Union. Later on, many of them expressed satisfaction that the war became one to end slavery, but they went because their country called. When their words are read, "duty" is the one that stands out. As one of them put it, "he had been raised with the idea that patriotism is a virtue of no secondary consideration."

In the summer of 1862, President Lincoln called for 300,000 more soldiers, and Wayland held yet another rally with patriotic songs and speeches, and prominent citizens offering extra bonus money out of their own pockets. In later years soldiers remembered it as a most important moment in their lives. Of the twenty or so men who stepped forward that night, about a dozen joined Company D of the 35th Massachusetts Volunteer Infantry. Their Second Lieutenant was John Hudson from Lexington who a few years earlier had taught school in Wayland. Some of these soldiers had been his students. This was a common practice in the Civil War–whole groups of men joining together. While this made camp life more pleasant, it could mean devastating loss to a community. Wayland was lucky. They all came home alive. Five of them served in Company D to the end of the war, one of those was absent, wounded and sick for a year, and another, though on the rolls, was home recovering from six months captivity in Salisbury Prison. Two men were promoted to officers in others regiments, one deserted, and the rest were discharged for wounds or illness, including one who rose from private to company commander before receiving a near fatal wound in August 1864.

After the young men went to war, civilians formed aid and relief societies for the soldiers. Ladies' groups held regular work meetings and made blankets and quilts and items of clothing. The U.S. Sanitary Commission was the largest national civilian relief agency and most of the local supplies went through them. These groups also provided wines, jellies, preserves, bandages, and other items for the sick. Another group of citizens formed a committee to specifically meet the needs of local soldiers, and to promote the comfort and well being of their families. Wayland sent agents south after the battles of Antietam and Fredericksburg to bring supplies and to look after the welfare of the wounded. Families left behind received a stipend, and as the war progressed, aid was given to widows and children of fallen soldiers.

When the war ended in the spring of 1865, the citizen soldiers resumed their civilian ways and returned to the farms and the shoe factories and the schools of their former lives. They were changed men. They had been places and seen things that their civilian compatriots had not. For some of them, their war service always had a prominent place in their lives through their veterans organizations. Others preferred to move on and not dwell on the past.

Wayland held a general reception for the returning soldiers on July 4, 1865. A service of thanks was given for freedom and peace, and the joy of seeing the returning veterans was mingled with sad remembrances of the fallen.

Shortly after the war, Wayland, like most towns around, considered erecting a statue to honor those who served in the war. Somehow, the idea didn't get off the ground, but a group of citizens wanted to find an appropriate way to recognize the soldiers. Under the guidance of James S. Draper, prominent citizen and father of two soldiers, a memorial book was published in 1871, "Wayland in the Civil War." It contains biographical and military sketches of each soldier, quoting letters home. Because it was completed so soon after the war, it is relatively free of the hind-sight and mythology that developed as time passed.

Wayland's last Civil War veteran was George B. Howe. He had enlisted in 1864 at age 19 in a 100 day unit from Millbury and been stationed at Fort Warren in Boston Harbor. After the war he moved to Wayland where he was for years a fixture at veterans' observances and in the Memorial Day parade. He died in September 1940, as the country was once again edging towards war.

In twentieth century Wayland, names such as Campbell, Dean, Damon, Draper, Gleason, Heard, Moore, Parmenter and Rice are usually associated with streets. In the mid nineteenth century, men bearing these names (and others) marched off to the Civil War in the name of Wayland.

Claypits

The great Ice Age is credited for our town's clay deposits which were laid down on a lake floor thousands of years ago–our own Glacial Lake Sudbury.

The English who settled Sudbury Plantation in the early seventeenth century were very familiar with the useful characteristics of clay that makes excellent bricks. In England, most of the forests had been consumed for their timber and Englishmen had turned to stone and brick to build their homes, barns, and churches. But in Sudbury Plantation, there was, so to say, timber to burn. Thus, the very first crude shelters and early houses, barns, meetinghouses, bridges, and fences were made of wood. If early residents found a deposit of clay, they might have used it to chink the logs in a house wall or a crack in the chimney. That was about it.

There is a lot of clay throughout the town, usually several feet under the topsoil in a wet or boggy setting. As time went on, many deposits were unearthed: near Claypit Hill, 1/8 of a mile above Mill Pond; at Timber Neck, a high piece of land on the northern edge of the Sandy Burr Country Club near the junction of Mill and Pine brooks; on the west side of Heard's Pond; and in several other areas west of the river. During the late eighteenth and early nineteenth century, bricks were made at many of these same locations as well as a place called Smithfield, a swampy area on Concord Road northwest of the Mill Pond. Another clay pit lies west of Concord Road across from its junction with Lincoln Road.

The best-known clay pit in town was (surprise!) on Claypit Hill Road near the spot where Mill Brook passes under the road. There are depressions on both sides of the road, but the easiest to see is on the south side about two hundred feet in from the road at the edge of a marsh. There is still a large pile of excavated clay next to the pit. Archaeologists from the Wayland Historical Commission have discovered an area nearby underlain with many broken brick fragments where they believe a primitive brick-making oven once operated. The town built five school houses between 1799 and 1808. These early eighteenth century single room school buildings were built of brick–one still stands at 19 Pelham Island Road although all of the original brick has disappeared. (see Education)

New England had extraordinary deposits of very good clay. In Boston, the use of bricks soared when the city fathers decreed that no more wooden buildings would be permitted after a series of devastating house fires had occurred. Locally, only people of means could afford a brick house. Abel Gleason's handsome brick 1803 house still stands at 74 Glezen Lane across from the old Training Field. For those who couldn't afford a brick house, the exposed part of their foundation was occasionally faced with brick to improve or upgrade the appearance.

Little has changed in the world of brick building construction; it is still expensive to do and is often used sparingly in architectural design.

□□□

Cochituate Village

The area that became the village of Cochituate in 1721 had been three private colonial land grants (see Land Grants) made by the General Court. It included land between the southern boundary of Sudbury (Wayland) and the northern boundary of Natick. By the early 1700s, the twelve families living on the land had developed strong kinship ties to Sudbury and, though close to Natick, were not eager to join the "Indian Praying" town. When Sudbury began discussions to build a meetinghouse on the west side of the Sudbury River, families living along the town's southern border with Natick, played a pivotal role in that decision. The west side of the river had the greater population and the addition of twelve families appeared to solve some of the east side's problems. It added parishioners to the east side meetinghouse and 2,141 acres of land to the east side of the river. The General Court order passed on June 9, 1721 included "all land between what had been officially granted to Sudbury as a southern addition in 1640 and the northern bound established for the Indian plantation at Natick in May 1660." The boundary has remained nearly the same all these years, in spite of the very vague wording of the order. (see Separate Towns)

At the time of annexation, the area was not called "Cochituate Village," and it would not bear that name for a long time. It became a part of Sudbury's farming community, later East Sudbury and today Wayland. When Natick and Saxonville began to embrace the industrial age, residents along the town's southern boundary slowly gave up farming and joined them. What had been small family shoe shops developed into large successful factories and the little village exploded. By the 1840s, the section of today's Cochituate near the intersection of Main Street and Commonwealth Road was referred to as "Bentville," after the Bent family who owned the large factory on the southwest corner. A half-mile to the east at the junction of East Plain Street and Commonwealth Road, the area was called "Lokerville," for the Loker families who lived in the area. (see Quaint Names)

In August 1846, at a ground-breaking ceremony for the aqueduct that would take water from Lake Cochituate, then named Long Pond, to Boston, Boston's Mayor Josiah Quincy, Jr. proposed to the City Council that the name of Long Pond be changed to Lake Cochituate. The Mayor believed that an Indian name would connote wilderness and pure clean water to Bostonians. The Mayor's proposal was enthusiastically adopted and thenceforth, Long Pond became Lake Cochituate. (see Water Works)

In October of that year a post office called "Cochituate" was established on Main Street in the southern part of Wayland, changing the name Bentville to Cochituate. Although there does not appear to have been any action on the part of the town to change the name of the village, records show that James Madison Bent served on the three-member board of selectmen in 1846 and 1847 and probably instigated the change. William and James Madison Bent lived in the area and were partners in the shoe business. James Madison had been employed as an agent with the Boston Water Board and had helped with the purchase of land for the aqueduct. Perhaps he got the idea to change the village name after Long Pond had been changed to Lake Cochituate.

Cochituate's growing population increased the tax burden on North Wayland and led to a petition for separation in 1881. The petition failed to garner enough votes and was dropped. In 1890, however, another attempt was made to split into two towns. This time Natick was interested in annexing Cochituate so that it could become a city. It was taxes and not fear of Indians that made Cochituate residents reject this proposal. Tax increases to pay for schools and municipal facilities caused discontent between the two sides of town for a number of years.

The name "Cochituate" seems appropriate since the Indians in their language had always called the land around the lake "Cochituate"–meaning "place of the rushing torrent" or "wild dashing brook." The word refers to the outlet of the lake to the Sudbury River when the water is high.

The history of the village is covered in greater detail in "Shoe Industry."

❑❑❑

Conservation

The Native American men and women who lived in Wayland and surrounding towns were perhaps our first conservationists. They depended heavily upon the presence of wild birds, mammals and fish for their food, trees for shelter, utensils, and weapons, plants for food and medicine, and animals for clothing.

The English settlers brought with them many well-established ideas and customs about living with nature. Among the first laws passed in Wayland were those that aimed at protecting Wayland's trees by imposing heavy fines for destructive practices. Other laws recognized differences in the quality of soils when it came time to assign land for farming. Regarding wolves and crows, the settlers were less forgiving than today's residents might be. In general, however, Wayland's early residents saw the wisdom of the Native American way of life.

The word "conservation," as it is used today, has only been in common use since the early twentieth century. It gained widespread use during the Great Depression and the New Deal era when it entered the vocabulary of newspapers and school curricula, and became part of the newly formed government agencies like the Civilian Conservation Corps. Boys Scouts and Girl Scouts popularized conservation as a part of their programs and acquainted Wayland boys and girls with the value and pleasure of getting to know the out-of-doors.

The establishment of the Sudbury Valley Trustees in 1953 by seven Wayland residents created a new urgency to the protection of wildlife and the preservation of open space, one in which every citizen could participate. The Wayland landscape was disappearing as suburbanization consumed town farmlands and wooded lots. SVT not only began to acquire tracts of "wild" undeveloped land, but also urged that conservation ideas be emphasized in school systems and offered public presentations on such topics as the value of wetlands and their relation to public water supplies.

A decade later, the Commonwealth of Massachusetts passed an Act authorizing individual towns like Wayland to establish, at their town meetings, an official body to assume responsibility for conservation. At Wayland's 1961 annual town meeting, town residents voted to establish a Conservation Commission of seven members, appointed annually by the selectman, and authorized to spend public funds for conservation purposes. It was not surprising that the new commission and the leadership of the Sudbury Valley Trustees soon saw the benefits of a close working relationship between the two organizations. It was not difficult to find volunteers to carry out a wide variety of jobs for both organizations.

The new Conservation Commission soon wrote and published a modest pamphlet entitled "A Conservation Program for Wayland" (1963) and followed this with a larger and more detailed report in 1966 with maps and graphs laying out specific programs to be gradually undertaken throughout Wayland. Although protection of water resources was of prime importance to the Commission, the master plan included protection of woodlands and wildlife, recreation and open space. In addition to advice from members of the Board of Health, Selectmen, and the Planning Board, the Commission appointed subcommittees to research, analyze, and compile data for: Brooks and Wetlands Protection, Forest and Trails, and Soil Survey Evaluation. The Brooks and Wetlands Committee identified the boundaries of wet areas from aerial photos and delineated their resource values. The Forest and Trails Committee investigated the need for a town forest and compiled a map of recommended acquisitions of wooded areas and trails "which would connect with existing recreation or conservation lands to span the length of Wayland." The Soil Survey Evaluation Committe mapped the soil types found in Wayland and described their suitability for various types of development, "including particularly their limitations relative to septic tank disposal systems." With the assistance of a professional planning consultant, the Commission produced a map portraying wetlands and lands recommended for protection or acquisition. In addition, the planner prepared a detailed analysis of all primary brooks, "which emerged as the basic obvious framework for a meaningful conservation plan. Without the protection of town brooks, other protective measures and land purchases seemed futile."

Eventually a Watershed Protection District zoning proposal was drafted and submitted to the Selectmen and the Planning Board which called for the acquisition of, or granting of, conservation restrictions on 1,351 acres of land. The general public was then invited to meetings during which selectmen explained the proposal and solicited advice and criticisms. The plan was accepted by the Planning Board and submitted to the selectmen to be included in the Warrant for the 1967 town meeting. The Master Plan map has served as a guide for acquisition of important private parcels of land which the town has successfully acquired over the years. Many acres have been purchased from private owners, often with the aid of the Sudbury Valley Trustees who provide immediate funds until reimbursement is approved by town meeting. Soon after the Conservation Master Plan was prepared, the Great Meadows National Wildlife Refuge acquired more than 15% of the land within the Sudbury River flood plain. The Federal Government continues to acquire additional tracts of wetland with high wildlife protection capability.

To familiarize residents with the town's conservation areas, the Conservation Commission's Outdoor Education Committee published a guide to all areas acquired before 1977. This self-guided book included the history, natural features, birding opportunities and maps of the areas. Outdoor Education Committee members sponsored weekend walks on many of the areas including sessions for children only. In 1978, Virginia Steel, a longtime member of the Committee, created a series of waterproof maps with illustrations and text for cross-country skiers. Members of the Conservation Committee continue to sponsor weekend walks throughout the town. By 1980 the town had spent $866,340 on the purchase of conservation land. After reimbursement from state and federal funds the net expenditure was $384,172. Since 1980, the Conservation Commission has acquired 228 acres of land which is assessed today at $3,916,200.

❑❑❑

Cow Common

Today, there are no fences around Cow Common to keep cattle from straying. And the lush meadow grass is long gone. But one can still walk, more than 350 years later, some of the original "common land" where settlers first set their cattle to graze.

Since cattle were the foundation of farming in early New England, men sought land grants that included good grassland to feed their animals. In 1638, when Peter Noyes, Edmund Browne, and Brian Pendleton of Watertown petitioned the General Court for "straitness of accommodation, and want of meadow," they had chosen the Musketaquid, or Sudbury River Valley, ten miles west of Watertown. The Indian word Musketaquid meant "grassy ground," which clearly described the meadow grasses that had attracted Sudbury proprietors. The petitioners were granted "five square miles astride the river," approximately 3,000 acres, just upstream from Concord.

But Sudbury would be unlike Watertown where farms were kept individually. Sudbury's proprietors established an open field, or communal system of farming whereby river meadow for harvesting hay was apportioned based on the number of persons in a family, or according to an assessment of the wealth and property each family had brought with them, or in relation to some combination of both of these. An investment could be for public service like the miller Thomas Cakebread, or for the Reverend Edmund Browne who also received a salary. Meadow rights entitled proprietors to a share in the common lands of the community–fields to raise crops and pasture to graze cattle. The first fifty families, or proprietors, had proprietors' rights to common land use. To cover town expenses, families paid taxes based on the amount of river meadow they owned. Thus, the community's largest investors had the most at risk and paid the highest tax.

Sumner Chilton Powell in *Puritan Village: the Formation of a New England Town,* stated "the committee did not distribute all of the available river meadow but kept the major part in reserve, as a type of town bank account, on which they later drew to 'gratulate' town officials for time and service rendered. Out of the estimated 3000 acres, the committee allotted only 848."

For example, river meadow was allotted to Richard Sanger, a blacksmith who was persuaded to join the settlement in 1646. Sanger, eighteen years of age, came on the good ship "Confidence" in 1638 as the servant of Edmund Goodenow. Sanger set up a blacksmith shop not far from the gristmill. In 1649, he returned to Watertown.

Traditionally, the amount of river meadow which a farmer owned as a proprietor also determined how many animals he could graze on the cow common. But the common land was so extensive at the time, selectmen decided to wait until the herds grew too large for the area before enforcing "sizing" limits. The northern boundary of the original "cow common" approximates that of the northern boundary of today's fields. A second cow common was opened on the west side of the river in 1647 to accommodate farmers living on that side.

Within a decade new settlers and a second generation of young men were without river meadow and some had no land. The town was growing fast and the limited availability of land and meadow became a very large issue. In 1649, Edmund Goodenow, deputy to the General Court, petitioned the Court for land for the town and Sudbury was granted a two-mile strip adjacent to Sudbury's western boundary. But apportioning the new land soon divided the town. At a town meeting called in 1651 someone proposed a radical change–"When the two miles shall be laid out, that every man shall enjoy a like quantity of land." The proposal was in exact opposition to the communal farming system established by Noyes, Pendleton and Browne. Individual ownership of land in the two-mile grant would take able-bodied young men away from work in the town's six open fields and destroy the open-field system of communal farming. To the great surprise and disappointment of the town's founders the proposal for division of the two-miles strip passed at that meeting.

Not surprisingly, the issue divided the town. For the next two years, from 1655-57, Sudbury's policy toward the land caused violent town meeting disputes. Most proprietors had come from open-field communities in England and wanted to continue the practice. John Rudduck, also a proprietor, was the exception. He had been raised in an English town where men owned their own land individually. When the debate to divide the two-mile strip erupted, Rudduck abandoned his support for the open-field system he had bought into and became a strong proponent for change. Town meetings became so well attended during the debate that a motion was made to build a new, larger meetinghouse. Once again the town became divided over the issue. Selectmen and the more conservative faction in town believed the town could not afford to build a new meetinghouse and preferred adding to the old one. The debate continued for three years. The new group of "expansionists," the same group who wanted the two-mile strip divided equally, pressed for a "yes" vote to build a new meetinghouse. They argued that if the two-mile strip were divided equally and farming begun in a competitive way, each citizen would have money to pay for a new meetinghouse. Said Sumner Chilton Powell "the social, political, and economic philosophy of Sudbury was at stake."

Selectmen drew up a proposal designed to please everyone but maintain the basic concept of rank and proportion. The original meadow-grant list defined the social and economic status of town founders and selectmen were determined to maintain due respect. The selectmen's proposal, however, was voted down. The following day the "expansionists" petitioned for another meeting and forced a "yes" or "no" vote–"to every man an equal portion in quantity." The vote passed in the affirmative and selectmen were defeated again.

Selectmen still had control of the Cow Common, which required meadow rights. Rudduck as a proprietor could graze his cattle on the common. But few of the new land owners had rights. Where would they graze their cattle?

Peter Noyes, his son Thomas, Edmund Goodnow, and Walter Haines raised a new question for debate in January, 1655-56: "was the town herd of cattle too large for the Sudbury commons?" The men devised a formula:

> "For every two acres of meadow–one beast: a cow, a bull a steer,
> or heifer above a year old, a horse or a mare above a year old–each
> was to be considered 'one beast', but all cattle under a year old were
> to be allowed on the commons, without sizing until further reason doth
> appear for sizing them."

Rudduck opposed the sizing regulation because at least thirty-two young men would have no chance of grazing their animals on the common. He also argued that the cow common could support many more animals than proposed. The town became so bitterly divided on the issue that a committee had to be appointed by the General Court and a Puritan Church Council named to settle the argument. Their findings did not favor Rudduck and his group of "expansionist" young men. Shortly thereafter Rudduck left the settlement. He and Edmund Rice, Sudbury deputy to the General Court, petitioned the Court for another land grant. By 1656 they were discussing entrance requirements and citizenship rights for the new town of Marlborough, which was incorporated four years later.

Shaken by the loss of so many young townsmen and their families to Marlborough, Sudbury town officials set about dividing up the two-mile land grant equally. Each proprietor, regardless of his status in the community, received 130 acres. Slowly farmers cleared their land and moved their cattle from the common land to their own. By the early seventeen hundreds, most Sudbury families had made the transition to individual farms.

The sixty-five acres of the present Cow Common include the narrow lots of land bought by farmers on the opposite side of Old Sudbury Road (Route 27) when the common land was sold by the proprietors. These farmers had their arable land on the higher east side of the road and their meadow and grazing land close to the river on the west side. Ditch banks defined their property boundaries. If you have seen these long depressions in the fields, think now of why they were put there and how long ago they had to have been dug out. Ditch banks are currently being mapped using aerial photos of the land.

Cranberries

Could Sudbury settlers, who came to harvest the rich meadow hay of the Musketaquid Valley, have known that beneath their precious hay grew ruby-red cranberries? That small red fruit high in Vitamin C with a blossom that looks like a crane? Aren't cranberries associated with Cape Cod? And didn't their popularity arise from their place on the Thanksgiving table? Maybe. But, maybe not. "Ocean Spray" creates the image of "Cape Cod only." And, Thanksgiving makes them appear a tradition. But cranberries had grown in many places for a much longer time. The truth is that cranberries did and do grow on the Cape. However, it isn't just because the area is so well suited for their growth. It is because land owners have protected the bogs and marshes where cranberries like to grow. In the early 1800s, the bulk of the cranberry crop came from large natural inland meadows, much like those along the Sudbury River. In 1843, for example, a single twenty-five-acre bog in Franklin County reported a yield of 1,050 barrels of cranberries. But that was before most of the inland meadow land had been drained and filled. For Sudbury settlers, a surprise fruit crop hiding beneath the hay must have been a welcome delight. After the hay was harvested in late summer and early fall, whole families descended upon the meadows to pick the little fruits before the first frost turned them to mush. Where the fruit was thickest, farmers often didn't mow at all, but just clipped off the top of the hay to facilitate picking. Or they did not mow as closely as in other places. Then, the fruit was raked before being gathered by hand. Cranberries became a reasonable source of income for local farmers as evidenced by the rake that was donated to the Historical Society by the Campbell family of Pelham Island Road.

It is doubtful, however, that Sudbury settlers, or other newcomers discovered cranberries. Or, that they ate the little fruits before being tested. Their testers and teachers were probably local Indians.

28

Haying on a Dairy Farm

Dairy Farms

The story of farming in Wayland began when the first settlers came in 1638 for the rich meadow grasses for their cows. There have been many changes in agricultural practices since. By the nineteenth century farming had gone beyond subsistence and many farmers were producing for the local market. By the mid nineteenth century most farmers owned a number of cows, up to fourteen for the more prosperous farmers, and produced enough butter to satisfy their own needs as well as sending some to market. From the late 1860s, this shift from subsistence farming to production for outside markets was seen in milk production as well.

While the number of farms remained high–over 100 by 1870–there were about ten farmers who seemed to have taken over the dairy business. For instance, Jude Damon had forty-four cows on his farm on Old Sudbury Road. A neighboring farm, owned by Jonathan Maynard Parmenter and Henry Dana Parmenter, had eighty-four cows. (see Parmenter, Jonathan M.)

With the advent of the railroad and the construction of the Depot in 1881 and the freight house two years later, the Boston market was easily reached by the daily trains that passed through and milk production rose accordingly. The Parmenter brothers had over 160 acres of farmland–pasture and agricultural fields to grow crops to feed the cows. By the end of the nineteenth century they had two sizeable barns on Bow Road for their herd, which they drove to Troy, New Hampshire for summer pasturage. Isaac Damon, who had a farm in Cochituate, also took part of his herd to New Hampshire for summer grazing. This meant that the farmers literally walked their herds to New Hampshire. Just to give an idea of the volume of the dairy business in 1875, 129,843 gallons of milk were produced. This nearly doubled to 219,852 gallons produced in 1880. That number was reported to have doubled again by 1885. Much of the milk was shipped to market via the newly opened railroad.

In the 1870s the first country retreats were developed in Wayland for Bostonians. Some of these out-of-town owners continued farming on their properties. William Powell Perkins had purchased the Cutting-Cushing farm on Old Connecticut Path in 1868 and in 1871 purchased four Guernsey cows and one bull that had been brought on order from the Isle of Jersey by his friend, James Codman of Brookline. The interest in Guernseys was for the rich golden color of the cream and butter produced by these cows. Perkins, who made Mainstone Farm his summer estate, established the first Guernsey herd in Massachusetts and only the second in the United States. He named the first of his foremost herd Pearl, Pearl 2nd, Topaz and Jewel. The bull was named Jasper. It is interesting to note that nearly 100 years later, the descendants of Perkins herd were still pastured at Mainstone and producing premium milk that was distributed locally and to a dairy in Weston.

Other country retreats on which dairy farming was carried out belonged to Francis Shaw and to Henry Whitely Patterson, both in the early 1900s. Shaw's estate was high on the hill overlooking Cochituate Road near the Old Connecticut Path intersection. (see Estates) His barn, located near Cochituate Road at its intersection with the present Woodridge Road, housed another Guernsey herd. The farmer's house was across the driveway. Henry Patterson had fifty-five acres of land north of his house, the 1803 brick Abel Glezen house on Glezen Lane at Training Field Road, which Patterson greatly enlarged. Soon after World War I, Patterson's dairy farm was sold to Albert H. Beck, a successful investment banker from New York. In the 1940s this same dairy operation on more acreage than Patterson's original farm, became the Watertown Dairy under the proprietorship of Hyman Shick.

Dairy farming practices evolved with changes in pasteurization, and experimental farming with crops cultivated to feed the herd. Some local farmers engaged in experimental farming that enhanced their product. An important part of farming was the ability to raise food for one's own dairy cows. Grass was grown and harvested as hay and while the harvesting was improved, the cutting, drying and storage changed little over time. Harvesting was done at first by a team of oxen, then by horses, and eventually by tractors. The old Samuel Maynard Thomas farm on Old Connecticut Path was purchased in 1944 by Frank Schofield who moved his family and thirty cows from Concord to his new farm. Schofield adopted some of the new practices to develop an outstanding grass farm where he rotated hay fields and pastures, grew alfalfa and clover and filled his silos with surplus grasses. In the early 1950s his farm was among the top seven in a Green Pastures contest run in Middlesex County. Schofield used a minimum of commercial fertilizer and depended upon manure produced on his farm and poultry manure from neighboring farms. He also grew acres of corn for ensilage. Eventually the Wayland High School was built on Schofield's farmland.

Other dairies are remembered by place names of today. On land that had been farmed for generations, Isaac Damon maintained a dairy herd, which today is recalled in the Damon Farms (or Daymon) neighborhood off Commonwealth Road. Samuel Cutler had extensive lush land on which to raise his dairy herd near the Sudbury River and Heard's Pond. Today his farmland has been preserved for passive recreation and is known as the Heard Farm Conservation Area. Access is off Pelham Island Road at the end of Heard Road.

The most substantial changes in dairy farming came in the 1940s and 1950s with new standards established for milking. Many farmers decided to give up milk production due to the elaborate changes they would have to make in the equipment necessary to upgrade the milking parlors where they actually milked the cows and the milk processing rooms where the milk was readied for shipping to processing dairies. The exceptions were the Watertown Dairy which stayed in business until the last quarter of the twentieth century. Mainstone Farm continued to produce milk into the early 1960s as did the Harringtons who maintained a large herd on a small farm at Plain and Millbrook roads until the late 1960s or early 1970s. Dorothy and Walter Harrington milked up to eighty-five cows daily. The milk was shipped to Clarke's Dairy in Weston for processing and distribution. No dairy cows remain in Wayland in the twenty-first century. The cattle at Mainstone Farm, the Belted Galloways, are beef cattle raised mostly to sell to other farmers looking to augment their stock of the same breed.

Draper, James Sumner

For more than a century, the name Draper was associated with selfless service and dedication to the town. Deacon James Draper (1787-1870), a cheerful man with a sunny disposition strove to improve the town's appearance. He gathered elm saplings from around the Abel Heard home on the Island–the house and one old elm tree remain standing at 187 Pelham Island Road–and planted them around the First Parish Church, the Old Green Store and the town green. After Deacon Draper's death, his son James Sumner Draper wrote, "On the tablets of memory his name will represent sterling integrity, persistent energy and broad beneficence."

James Sumner Draper (1811-1896), was born and educated in town and carried on his father's legacy to make Wayland a better place to live. He worked tirelessly to create the town's first public library, promoted new schools, and helped to establish rail service from Boston to Hudson. Draper served the town as a teacher, librarian, farmer, and land surveyor. He was associated with the Unitarian denomination, though more of a Spiritualist. By the age of twenty-one Draper had become an outspoken advocate of women's rights and an ardent anti-slavery protester. He organized and supervised the church choir and taught Sunday school, entertaining the children at an annual 4th of July party at his home. He had a fine singing voice and taught children many of his favorite hymns.

Later Draper became a Whig and a member of the Free Soil Party (1847-48) which came into existence because of rising opposition to the extension of slavery into territory newly acquired from Mexico. The party was absorbed into the new Republican Party in 1854. Draper became a National Republican and later a Unionist during the Civil War.

Draper served as town librarian for twenty years and was interested in making books available to everyone. Wayland center had a private library, the East Sudbury Social Library, established in 1796 and a collection of "moral and religious books" housed in the homes of various librarians, and, for a time, in the vestibule of the First Parish Church. A 300 volume collection, housed at the First Parish Church, was shared by the six school districts and available to all residents. After the first free public library was started in 1850, Draper and others still did not feel books were conveniently available to everyone. In 1871, the town responded to Cochituate's need for more town facilities and Draper joined the committee to make library books available, "so that the citizens of the southern part of town can avail themselves of the benefits of the library by receiving and exchanging books at some suitable place in Cochituate Village."

Draper owned three properties on Plain Road–one he built in 1834 at 110 Plain Road, another built in 1856 at 104 Plain Road, and the family home he inherited from his father at 116 Plain Road, as well as farmland across the road.

One of Draper's most lasting and generous gifts of time and energy to the town occurred in 1846 when the Reverend Francis Wayland offered to donate the sum of $500 for the establishment of a free library, provided townsfolk would donate an equal amount. Raising the money in a small town with a population of only 1,100 people was a great challenge but Draper willingly assumed the task. No effort involving a permanent home for books was impossible to him. Although he secured several donations between $5 and $20, most of the money he collected was in dollar bills and coins. In the end, the Reverend Francis Wayland's gift was matched with a small amount in excess. (see Library)

Draper was later appointed by the selectmen to chair a committee to investigate allegations that the 1873 Cochituate School had not been built according to contract. The selectmen had discharged the building committee members and had appointed a five-person committee chaired by Draper to investigate. It was learned that the building committee, in an effort to save money had failed to provide for adequate ventilation of the building.

Draper's map, "Plan of the Town of Wayland in 1775," (later reprinted as "Plan of the Town of Wayland in 1776" copied by G. B. Smith, December 17, 1881), was drawn presumably in time for the 1875 centennial celebration of the beginning of the American Revolution. It is a reconstruction of how Draper thought the town appeared, through his research, in 1775. It has remained a valuable tool for researchers studying residents and land ownership.

When the 1841 town hall, built on land donated by Deacon Draper, James Sumner's father, was deemed inadequate, James Sumner joined a committee to find a new site. The site of the present Grout-Heard house was chosen and by 1878 a new Gothic-style town hall stood in its place. (see Town Halls, Grout-Heard House) Draper prepared a seventy-nine-page pamphlet for the dedication of the new town hall. In recognition of his tireless efforts on behalf of the town, his gifted ability as a speaker, and his enjoyment of ceremonies, Draper was chosen President of the Day.

Draper's legacies are many. He wrote a memorial volume of the history of the town's service in the Civil War which included letters and diaries and records of the experiences of Wayland's servicemen. He was also a surveyor and cartographer and an amateur poet. In addition to the centennial map, Draper prepared "Map of the First Roads & House-Lots in Sudbury," which was incorporated in Alfred Sereno Hudson's *The History of Sudbury, Massachusetts 1638-1889*. These maps, reprinted numerous times, remain important research tools.

❏❏❏

Dudley Pond

The map, "Plan of the Town of Wayland in 1775," prepared by James Sumner Draper, labels the body of water next to Lake Cochituate as Johnson's Pond, not Dudley Pond. There were Johnson families living on the west side of the pond and a Dudley family living on the east side. The explanation for the name change is yet to be determined but today's Dudley Pond has an interesting and varied history. It was formed from a detached ice block left behind during the last glaciation of New England–sometimes referred to as a kettle hole. As it melted, the topographic depression filled with water. The pond is fed by rainfall and by an inlet on the southeastern shore. A slow flowing aquifer beneath ground level may be feeding water to the pond. Runoff from an outlet in the extreme northeast corner of the pond's shoreline forms Dudley Brook which empties into the Sudbury River.

Any pond larger than ten acres is designated a "Great Pond" by the Commonwealth of Massachusetts which owns Dudley Pond's eighty-four acres. Thus, all residents of the state have the right of free access to the pond. Management and administration of the pond, however, were transferred to the Town of Wayland in 1916 under a long-term lease of ninety-nine years.

Once connected to Lake Cochituate by an eighteen-inch underground pipe, Dudley Pond served as a standby drinking water supply for Boston until 1947. In 1926 the concrete pipe connecting the pond to the lake was disconnected because the pond had become more polluted than the lake and was no longer a desirable source of drinking water. The pipe was finally sealed off in 1935. (see Water Works, Lake Cochituate)

During 1882-83, two large homes were constructed in the Dudley Pond area. The first one to be built was owned by Michael Simpson, president of the nearby Roxbury Carpet Company and Saxonville Mills. It was situated at the southwest corner of the pond on the corner of Old Connecticut Path and West Plain Street. Simpson's home later became a popular dining and dancing establishment. (see Simpson Estate/Mansion Inn) The second house belonged to James Madison Bent who constructed what he called a "cottage" on a bluff on the south shore overlooking the pond. Mr. Bent moored his small steamer, the "Hannah Dexter," by a wharf that led up one hundred steps to his cottage.

Between 1900 and 1915, Dudley Pond was a popular fishing campsite and summer resort. A group of sizable developments, financed and managed by outside speculators, were laid out in 1913 and reached a peak in 1918. D. Arthur Brown and John F. Stackpole, chief developers of the area, advertised in the newspapers of neighboring towns, but most sales were made to residents from the Boston area. Wayland Manor, one of the earliest developments, had 301 lots on the eastern shore of the pond. Some of the lots were as small as one twentieth of an acre. Woodland Park, laid out in 1914, was the largest development created by Brown and Stackpole. It had 969 lots, many as small as 1200 square feet, or one thirtieth of an acre. Lots were even sold through lotteries at Boston's Orpheum movie theater.

The land along the north shore of the pond included a network of roads and paths around what is now Maiden Lane. Woodland Park was followed by Shore Acres, Lakewood, Castle Gate North, and Castle Gate South. From 1913 to 1928, people continued to build cottages and purchase lots around the pond. The clean water and exceptional bass fishing remained an important attraction. However, the period of Prohibition in the 1930's changed what had been a quiet, rural, and pristine summer resort area. Gangsters began to use the cottages for illicit activities–posting signs in front of some camps indicating that rental could be had by the hour–with women. On one occasion, gunfire erupted into a full-fledged riot which caused great consternation among local residents who then forbade their children from going near the area.

Many cottage owners did not foresee their summer houses becoming year-round residences until the Great Depression in 1929. Few cottages had heat and the roads were unsuitable for driving during icy, snowy, and muddy conditions. There were no formalized health regulations around the pond and septic systems typically consisted of dry wells made by burying fifty-five gallon drums in the yard. These crude systems often overflowed. Unfortunately, by the time residents became concerned about the growth of thickly settled and poorly planned developments in town, and began to formulate zoning ordinances in the 1930s, it was too late to re-zone the area around the pond. (see Zoning)

In 1959, the Wayland Redevelopment Authority, in an attempt to improve congested areas of town, began to look for Federal financial assistance. In 1960, selectmen applied for assistance from the Urban Renewal Authority and received a $410,000 grant for study and preliminary work. To secure the funds, fifty percent of the dwellings around Dudley Pond had to be declared unfit for human habitation. During the next three years, the committee inspected homes and access roads around Dudley Pond and recommended that 265 homes be removed to allow for larger lot sizes or road improvements. The idea was to combine all of the land and give it to a developer to build houses on regulation size lots. No provision was made to find new areas for the people living in the 265 houses which would be dispossessed. When the five member Citizen's Advisory Committee appointed by selectmen held the first formal hearing, 300 angry residents turned out to protest their homes being condemned.

Residents suggested they improve their properties themselves and collected signatures on a petition from more than one-half of the town's residents stating that urban renewal was unnecessary and unfair. It was obvious the urban renewal activity was not wanted in town. In 1963, the Wayland Redevelopment Authority, issued a report asking that it be dissolved in a proper legal manner and that urban renewal activities be abandoned within the town. The $410,000 granted to the town by the state was returned. Town officials began to see that the people being impacted were real human beings, that their often ramshackle houses, once summer camps, were "homes" to them. After a very tumultuous time, with a lot of bruised personalities, the town vowed a slower, small-scale program of incremental improvements.

Pond water remained fairly clean and biologically balanced for a few years after it was opened to the public for recreational use in 1947. During the late 1950s and early 1960s, however, indications of a speeded-up eutrophication process became evident and pond water became choked with weeds and pond lilies. Freshwater jellyfish began to disappear, along with large bass and pickerel. Motorboats were prevalent and many boaters took sport in running over the many muskrats that swam in the pond. Soon the muskrat population diminished, and growth of pond lilies exploded.

After many years of complaining to town selectmen and the police department about boating abuses on the pond, neighbors took responsibility for pond activities and formed the Dudley Pond Association, which came from an earlier Dudley Pond Improvement Association. They organized an ongoing program to control litter, weeds, noise and to monitor safety, protect property, and improve water quality. Informal swimming continues at Mansion Inn Beach during the summer and skating during the winter. Today, the modernized neighborhoods of Dudley Pond are sought-after places to live.

E

Rutter School Children, Circa 1883

East Sudbury 1780-1835

Occasionally the question arises–"Why is the original settlement of Sudbury Plantation named Wayland and the not-quite-as-old-side named Sudbury?" The brief answer is, "the side of the river most eager to separate gave up the most, including its original name."

In 1779 a petition was circulated, signed by almost every head of household on the east side to separate, or divide the town of Sudbury using the river, more or less, as a dividing line. East side inhabitants had lost their feeling of unity with their neighbors across the river. They wanted to go it alone. They wanted it so badly that they gave up their beloved town name, kept the smaller land area and agreed to live with an irregular western town boundary.

Although most east siders considered themselves farmers, there were tavern owners, a blacksmith, a wheelwright, a miller and a minister. Most families were descended from Puritans who emigrated from England in 1638-39, with a few who had come earlier and a few later on. The majority had been born in Sudbury. Although little is known about the education of either men or women, records show that the Reverend Josiah Bridge and Deacon William Baldwin were Harvard College graduates.

At East Sudbury's first town meeting on April 24, 1780, five selectmen were elected instead of the previous seven-man board: Phinehas Glezen, Jacob Reeves, Isaac Loker, Richard Heard and Joseph Curtis. Glezen, Reeves and Loker had served as selectmen prior to separation and, with the exception of Isaac Loker, had been leaders in town. Heard and Curtis had been instrumental in the separation of the town. Heard was intent upon making Pelham Island part of East Sudbury. East Sudbury's 770-775 inhabitants had elected this first governing board because they honored and trusted them. Selectmen, although not considered wealthy, represented the local elite because they had experience in town government, family status, and property.

In 1780, the Boston Post Road went west as far as the town green, then turned northwest along Old Sudbury Road crossing over the Sudbury River, using the Old Town and Canal bridges. There was no road directly westward in the direction of the present Boston Post Road. The one acre town green, larger than today, would have extended southward to the edge of Mill Brook and westward to the intersections of Pelham Island and the Boston Post roads.

Even the portion of the Boston Post Road approaching today's intersection from the east took a different track until Dwight B. Heard's development was started in the late 1890s. The road ran closer to the present First Parish Church, leaving room for several houses and a tannery between the road and Mill Brook. Dwight Heard's development was south and east of the present church on land inherited from his grandfather Horace Heard. Young Heard moved his grandfather's house to its present location at 4 Winthrop Place and created a subdivision with eighteen lots–one half to three quarters of an acre each. A new combination high school and grammar school was located across from the subdivision on Cochituate Road. The Boston Post Road was probably moved to its present location at that time.

Homes and businesses had sprung up around the town center. Elijah Bent built a tavern, the Pequod

House, in 1771 on the lot where the Public Safety Building now stands. The tavern was a popular spot for locals to gather and catch up on the latest news. Across the street, where the Mellen Law Office now stands on the town green, stray animals milled around inside the town pound waiting to be claimed by their owners. The fourth meetinghouse which had been moved from its original site at the Old Burial Ground and rebuilt in 1726, stood at the corner of Cochituate and Pelham Island roads.

For the next fifty-five years, the town of East Sudbury went about its business building schools, taking care of the poor, and scheduling town meetings. In 1835, the Town of East Sudbury petitioned the General Court to change its name to Wayland–probably to avoid confusion between East Sudbury and Sudbury and to achieve separate identity, although the reasons were never recorded.

The origin of the new town name of Wayland is yet another story. (see Wayland, the name)

❏❏❏

Education

The public school system of today was given its real foundation in 1647 when the General Court of the Massachusetts Bay Colony passed an act that ordered each town to hire one reading and writing teacher for each fifty families. When a town grew to one hundred families it had to establish a grammar school "to instruct the youth so far as they may be fitted for the University." Teachers were usually men, though "dame schools," a combination of day care and schooling, were held in private homes where a homemaker gave instruction for a fee. Regular tax-supported schools were also held in private homes with the expense borne by "the inhabitants in general" as the population was too scattered for a central schoolhouse to be practical.

The struggle to raise money for schools was as difficult then as it is today. The town needed to be prodded by the General Court to make funds available and arrange for schools. All children, servants as well, were to demonstrate competency in reading and writing. In 1680, shortly after King Philip's War, the selectmen who examined children and servants "about their improvement in 'reading and catechism,'" reported that "tho' there be no stated school in this town…two school dames on each side of the river teacheth small children to spell and read." Selectmen were to approve the effectiveness of their education. "Mr. Thomas Walker, and two or three others about this town teach all that need, to write or cipher."

A vote was taken in 1702 to build a school as near the center of town as convenient. In 1711 it voted again to build the school house, this time at "ye gravel pitt," not far from the Causeway on River Road, midway between the two town centers. The first minister, Edmund Browne, had left a legacy of £50 in 1678 to build a school house and upgrade the quality of Sudbury's reading and writing (elementary) and grammar (college preparatory) schools. Later, under pressure to pay for demolition of the third meeting house in 1724, that money was diverted by town vote. Eventually more schools were built because a fine was assessed when sufficient facilities were not provided and qualified teachers were not hired. The school master was to be an actual school master, not to be substituted by the town minister. A "Reverend Committee" of local ministers had to approve the schoolmaster. At the beginning of the eighteenth century Sudbury was just barely meeting Massachusetts requirements.

Records show that in 1717 Mr. Samuel Parris, previously connected with witchcraft hysteria in Salem Village, now Danvers, was hired to teach school four months of the year at the school house on the west side of the river. The rest of the year he taught at his home on the east side of the river - the Noyes-Parris house, still standing today. The town divided into two precincts in 1722 and schools were built on both sides of the river. By 1735 two school masters were employed in each precinct. One year later three fifths of the school budget was spent on schools on the west side and two-fifths on the east, apportioned according to the number of children on each side of the river.

Although records concerning education during the American Revolution were not kept, or are not available, records do exist after the separation of the town in 1780 when the east side of the river became East Sudbury and the west side Sudbury. In 1781 educational needs in East Sudbury were resolved by the establishment of six school districts. The district system became firmly established between 1799 and 1808. During that time six schools, five of them brick, were built. Some schools were built amid much controversy. For example, it took twenty-six meetings to decide to build the brick school in the North district on Concord Road.

The North District brick school was built in 1805 on the west side of Concord Road at its junction with Lincoln Road and was rebuilt on the east side of Concord Road in 1825. The Northwest District brick school was built in 1804 on Old Sudbury Road near Baldwin's Pond but replaced with a wooden school closer to Bow Road in 1841. In 1854 it was moved to Bow Road and became the Center Primary School and is a private residence today. The Center District brick school built in 1808 on Pelham Island Road across from the town green is the only early brick school still standing. It was later sold by the town to a family who converted it to a residence, which it remained for nearly a century. After World War II it was sold again for commercial use and a wing was added on the east side of the building. The brick exterior was largely preserved until 2004 when it was completely covered during remodeling by new owners.

The East District "Rutter" school (1799-1840) was located near the intersection of Old Connecticut Path and Rice Road. The South District "Lokerville" school was built in 1806 on the south side of East Plain Street at the intersection of Commonwealth Road. In the Southwest District, a brick school was first located in 1803 on the east side of Old Connecticut Path. Called the "Thomas" School, it was replaced by a wooden one in 1858 on the opposite side of the street, just south of the present high school and is now a private residence.

Typically, schools were small and plain with all grades being taught in one room. The teacher's desk sat on a raised platform at one end of the room. There were three sizes of desks and benches. Older pupils sat in the back on the tallest benches. The older boys were in charge of keeping the fire going and bringing in wood for the fireplace and later the stove. They also filled the water pail with fresh water daily, either from the well or a nearby spring. Germs and diseases were likely to spread quickly since all the children drank from the same dipper. Each school had its own outhouse, often slightly apart from the school.

In 1839 Wayland Academy, a private school, conducted classes in the chapel of the Congregational Church on Cochituate Road. Music and languages were taught at the Old Green Store, later known as Kirkside. By 1841 there were over one hundred pupils in the Academy which by now held its classes upstairs in the new town hall. Although it was popular, the Academy lasted only a few years.

In 1854 the school system underwent a complete change. District schools were replaced with graded schools. Students fourteen years and older were assigned to a high school which was built on Cochituate Road in town center in 1855–presently the property of the Trinitarian Congregational Church. The new high school was established "not without considerable difficulty and hard words." Some families on the outskirts of town objected to the school's location because their children would have to walk two or three miles to school. A short trial period showed that children from the remotest parts of town could benefit from a high school education after arrangements were made for neighborhood transportation. Classes were suspended twice, once in 1859 and again in 1862 because the town was unwilling to vote the funds for high school support. During the mid 1860s and through the 1870s the high school struggled, with limited success, to have a "greater number of mature and advanced scholars." Often during this period high school students studied in neighboring towns. Thus, there was no graduating class until 1891.

The Cochituate Village population increased rapidly between 1865 and 1870 and a new school was built in 1873 to accommodate the large number of students. The Cochituate School was located on the west side of Main Street, just south of the corner with West Plain Street. Fifty-six primary students occupied one of the two rooms on the first floor, and sixty-four intermediate students occupied the second room. The upstairs was reserved for older students. By 1885 crowded conditions caused the administration to reserve both downstairs rooms for primary students and move the intermediate students to the second floor auditorium, known as Village Hall or Schoolhouse Hall.

In the 1890s state public building inspectors ordered changes at the Center High School and at the Rutter, Center Primary, and North school houses. A new center school was needed but citizens were unwilling to pay for one. In March 1896 a new resident, Francis Shaw, contributed supporting funds and helped push a vote to build a school in the center that would accommodate primary, intermediate, and high school students. After the former high school was sold to the Odd Fellows of Wayland, it was moved a few feet north so the Center High and Grammar School could be placed behind two large oak trees. A ground-breaking ceremony was held in 1896 and the school first occupied in 1897. There were four classrooms on the first floor, each of which held two grade levels. The second floor had a small auditorium and two unfinished classrooms–one later made into a small science laboratory with additional funds from Shaw.

After the Center School was completed, attention turned to the Cochituate School. In 1907 school reports indicated the school had many deficiencies: poor ventilation, poor heating facilities, poor lighting, dampness and an overall dilapidated appearance. A decision was made to replace the 1873 wooden building with a new larger brick school which opened in 1911. The building was overcrowded by 1925 and an addition was made to the building.

By the mid 1930s the Center and Cochituate schools were both severely overcrowded. With the aid of a federal grant, a new high school was built in town center in 1935 . The town transferred a portion of the thirty-five acre park and playground that had been donated to the town in 1911 (behind the Odd Fellows Hall and Trinitarian Congregational Church) to be used for a high school. A gymnasium wing and library-cafeteria were added to the north side of the building in 1948. Today the former school forms the nucleus of the present Town Building.   In 1948 the Cochituate School was also enlarged.

Continued postwar population growth dictated a need for elementary schools, especially in the new neighborhoods with large numbers of preschoolers. A school site committee identified six school sites which would help facilitate orderly school expansion. In 1954 Happy Hollow School opened and in 1957 Claypit Hill and Loker Schools opened. Later additions to all three schools in the 1960s permitted the transfer of all elementary students from the Center School.

To prepare for progression of a larger student population from the lower grades, a new high school site was purchased in 1956 on Old Connecticut Path. A campus-style facility of six buildings was ready for occupancy in 1960. The new forward looking design was even featured in *Life* magazine. Spaces were provided for small, medium and large group instruction. An addition was made in 1967.

Planning began in 1971 to incorporate kindergarten into the schools and these children were fully housed in the elementary schools by 1972.

A new junior high school was built at the north end of Cochituate Village and ready for occupancy in the fall on 1972. It later became a Middle School when sixth grade pupils were included. The old Center School was recycled as administrative office space and finally torn down in 1978.

Once again, as has happened several times in Wayland's past, the School Committee sees a need for major renovations at the high school level to meet educational challenges and a growing population. In 2004 plans are being made to replace the high school with a new modern facility.   Today the Wayland school system is among the best in the state.

Estates

There is little doubt that the agricultural community of Wayland, convenient to the city of Boston, attracted well-to-do businessmen and manufacturers who purchased estates and small summer retreats. Where but in Wayland are views looking east over the valley of the Charles River and west over the Sudbury River Valley so spectacular?

The evolution of estates began when men started to clear land for planting crops on small farms. Along Old Connecticut Path from the present Coach Grill to the intersection with Cochituate Road (Route 27), it is easy to imagine that the fields sweeping up to the crest of the hill were once filled with trees. By 1713, Robert Cutting had begun to farm this land. Successive generations of Cuttings added to the acreage and it remained in the Cutting family until 1851.   It was purchased by John Cushing who paid $8,800 for 205 acres in 1852. By the time Cushing, a wealthy China trade merchant, died in 1862, he had built stone walls along the farm's boundaries. His descendants sold the property, known today as Mainstone Farm, to William Powell Perkins in 1868.

WilliamPowell Perkins, a member of an old Boston family, grew up in a large brick house on Beacon Hill and spent his summers at the family estate in Brookline. A confirmed bachelor, Perkins bought the farm in Wayland for $10,000. It appears he had no plan to develop it and did not intend to live in the house. However, the great Boston Fire of 1872 was a financial disaster for Perkins and he sold his estate in Brookline for $250,000 and moved into the farmhouse at the bottom of the hill with his gardener, George Washington Hancock and his family, while awaiting changes to the house on the hill. Perkins, who was known to his family as "Uncle Powell," had convinced Hancock, who had been his head gardener in Brookline, to move to Wayland with the promise of full charge of the horticultural work.

The house on the hill was originally two stories high and had four rooms on each floor. Perkins engaged WilliamFullick of Cochituate in 1874 to enlarge the house and add a mansard roof. Enlarging the main house meant that the Hancock family could live in a new ell during the winter. In summer the family moved to the farmhouse at the bottom of the hill making room for Uncle Powell's nieces and nephew and their maids who came to live in the main house in summer.

By the mid 1870s the farm, as we know it today, was taking shape. Gardener Hancock landscaped the area by planting trees, creating terraces up the hill, establishing Lombardy poplars along the main driveway, and maple trees along Old Connecticut Path. Hancock's tree-lined driveway and the trees along the road remain today. Dairying became an increasingly important farm specialty in the area and Perkin's farm was no exception. He purchased four Guernsey cows and one bull and started the first Guernsey herd in Massachusetts. (see Dairy Farms)

Through the 1870s Perkins added other land to his farm and in 1880 purchased the house at 68 Old Connecticut Path at the corner of Pine Brook Road, along with its barn and surrounding acres, for his trusted gardener and caretaker George Hancock and his family.

Perkins' sister Miriam died in 1871, and her husband Mr. Loring passed away in 1874 at the time the Mainstone farmhouse was completed. Of the Lorings five children, only Gertrude Loring married. She married Nathaniel Perez Hamlen and they had four children. The other Loring children–three girls and one boy–never married and had few financial resources. They were dependent upon Uncle Powell and his half-sister Eliza Perkins. These unmarried nieces, known to the next generation as "the Aunts," provided company for Uncle Powell who lived a semi-isolated life in Wayland and seldom went into the city.

After Uncle Powell died in 1891, Mainstone Farm, valued then at $100,000 was left in trust to his nieces and to Nathaniel Hamlen and his four children. Nathaniel's wife had died fifteen years earlier in childbirth. After all of the nieces died, the farm was run by Paul Hamlen and has descended to generations of Hamlens. The farm was greatly enlarged and, although still a "gentleman's farm," it became well-known for the dairy products from its Guernsey cows. About 1912-13, a big old barn was moved down the hill to be near the farmhouse, but it later burned. Today, Mainstone Farm is the last of the large farms remaining in private hands.

The most imposing of the early estates in Wayland was that of Francis Shaw. Shaw was part of an elite Boston social set intent upon purchasing country houses in areas like Wayland. Shaw set his sights on Wayland in 1890 and over the next several years quietly bought up farms near the intersection of Old Connecticut Path and Cochituate Road. He called his property Five Paths. Although Shaw had a house in Boston, his Wayland property allowed him to establish residency in town. Wayland welcomed this wealthy newcomer who would pay hefty taxes. Not only would Shaw be taxed for 849 acres and a new twenty-two room house, but the tax on his personal property like stocks and bonds would reduce the rate for all other taxpayers. Shaw built his house on the crest of Reeves Hill to take advantage of the spectacular views, especially westward. He hired unemployed shoe factory workers to clear the land for the house and gardens. The house had its own efficient water system fed by three springs. It was equipped with a tower and an electric pump which pumped water to other buildings on the property. Shaw became a benefactor of the town when he pledged $3000 toward construction of the Center School. Later, he pledged another $5000 to help cover over-run costs and also provided landscaping. The school eventually cost a total of $25,000. It opened in 1897.

In late 1909, Francis Shaw sold 219 acres of his land, from the Five Paths intersection to the Sudbury River and along Cochituate Road to the boundary line at the present Sandy Burr Country Club, to his friend Edwin Farnham Greene. The Greenes had a home on Beacon Hill and were leading figures in the cultural and social life of Boston. Edwin F. Greene was Treasurer and Chief Executive Officer of Pacific Mills. He commissioned the architect Samuel Mead, who designed the Wayland Library, to create a summer mansion for the family in Wayland.

A formal Georgian brick mansion called "Greenways," was built in 1910 overlooking the Sudbury River. The house had eight bedrooms and five bathrooms on the second floor, along with five small servant rooms and a bathroom on the top floor. The Greenes occupied the house from late May to November. Since it was common for new property owners to build a mansion and keep the old farmhouses on the property, the Greenes kept the 1690 Noyes-Parris house down the hill from the mansion for guests.

Mr. Greene and his friend Edmund Sears, a prominent citizen, purchased thirty-three acres of land behind the Odd Fellows Hall and next to the Trinitarian Congregational Church from Jonathan M. Parmenter. They donated the land to the town in 1911 for use as a town park and playground. (see Recreation)

The Greenes sold the mansion and property to Frank and Virginia Paine in 1926. Frank Cabot Paine was the youngest of seven children of Charles Jackson Paine a former Civil War general who made millions of dollars in railroads and other investments and became a famed yachtsman. His son, Frank Cabot, grew up to be a noted yachtsman and naval architect. Frank was an enthusiastic game hunter and traveled to Africa where he acquired enough trophy heads to adorn the music or "head" room–later called the Great Room. On one trip to Africa, Frank and Virginia brought back an orphaned baby monkey, Simmy, who lived at Greenways for thirty-two years and is buried in a pet cemetery at the back of the property.

According to Tom Paine's book *Growing Paines,* when the family looked at the house it had paneling from English houses, but when they moved in the paneling was gone. A dispute followed but the paneling was never returned, only reproduced. Frank Paine died in 1959 and Virginia Paine died in 1987 at the age of ninety-four.

Both the Greenes and the Paines maintained the farm landscape, so important to them, to enjoy the sweeping Sudbury River vista and spectacular sunsets.

Shaw died in 1935 and his mansion was torn down in 1942. At least one of the architectural elements from earlier houses that had been incorporated into Shaw's home, the Bulfinch-designed staircase, was removed and reinstalled at the Somerville Historical Society.

In the mid 1990s the Sudbury Valley Trustees and the Town of Wayland partnered to develop a plan to preserve most of the land for conservation and recreation. Some limited development included independent condominiums for seniors and single-family houses. The main house was converted to an assisted living facility and a hospice care unit, both administered by Parmenter Visiting Nurse Association and Community Center.

It is clear that the presence of early "estates," which stretched from the Weston line to the Sudbury River, slowed development enough through the years to preserve a moderate amount of open space into the twenty-first century.

46

*Fifth Meetinghouse/
First Parish Church*

Fence Viewers/Field Drivers

In colonial times, fence viewers were citizens appointed to examine "partition fences" and determine if they were adequate. These fences were to be at least four feet high and built of wood or stone, but a brook, ditch, or hedge of sufficient width or depth might also serve as a fence. As early as 1671, ditching was used to "fence" the great river meadows and, where necessary "to have a ditch made from the upland to the river . . ."

Early records indicate those fence viewers had the power to enforce their orders. The condition of the fence and the barrier effectiveness of the brook or ditch were an important part of their job. In 1641, "It was ordered that those men who were deputed to look after the fences shall have power to distrain for every rod of fence not lawful, half a bushel of corn, the one-half to him that looks to the fence the other half to the town." Later, a table of fees was set to inspect a fence and if not paid in thirty days "the amount would be doubled."

Today, the job of fence viewers is defined as follows: "Occupants of adjoining land enclosed with fences shall maintain partition fences between their enclosures in equal shares. Fence viewers can order a partition fence even though neither parcel is fully enclosed with fences. Where an occupant refuses to keep his part of a division fence in repair, fence viewers take action." At present two or more individuals are elected annually at town meeting by the Town Clerk casting one ballot for each.

The annual town report today also lists Field Drivers: one or more elected annually by the Town Clerk casting one ballot for each. They shall "impound horses, mules, asses, neat cattle, sheep, goats and swine going at large in public ways within the town and not under the care of a keeper." Dog owners need not worry!

Fifth Meetinghouse/First Parish Church

When townspeople decided to build a fifth meetinghouse early in the nineteenth century–discussions began in May 1806–they wanted it for religious purposes only. Alfred Wayland Cutting said the meetinghouse should "be an outward expression of the beauty and dignity of its purpose of being." Town meetings, traditionally the most significant civic use of the meetinghouse, would have to go elsewhere. Why would these thrifty Puritans be willing to financially support separate facilities eighteen years before separation of church and state in Massachusetts? Perhaps because they knew it was coming, they just didn't know when. The outward appearance of the 1815 Fifth Meetinghouse was one of a church, but legally, it remained a municipal meetinghouse until the separation of church and state in Massachusetts in 1833. East Sudbury residents, however, would hold public meetings in the Old Green Store next door to the church. (see Old Green Store/Kirkside)

Debate over which side of Mill Brook to locate the Fifth Meetinghouse went on for seven years.

Townspeople living south of the new town center wanted it on its present site and those living north of the new town center wanted it on the north side of Mill Brook, which today runs under Route 20. At last, at the April 1813 town meeting, a motion was made to have citizens from the south end of town purchase an acre of Mr. Wyman's land for a meetinghouse and carriage sheds. In exchange, the north end of town would accept the site preferred by the south end of town. The motion passed and debate ended. The land from William Wyman was deeded to the "Citizens of the town of East Sudbury."

There appears to have been little debate about the architecture of the meetinghouse. A master carpenter from Newburyport, Andrews Palmer, was hired as designer and builder. Work began in June 1814 and was completed in 1815. Horse sheds, double the present number, formerly bordered two sides of the church lot, extending to Cochituate Road. Mr. Palmer adapted an Asher Benjamin design for a rectangular church with a three-door entrance, Palladian windows and gables. (Benjamin had written the first original work on architecture in America in 1797.) The cupola rises 110 feet into the air. Amazingly, the distance from the roof line to the top of the cupola is the same as the distance from ground level to the roof line. The bell, weighing 1019 pounds was cast by the foundry of Paul Revere and Sons. The original receipt for the bell still exists. Since the bell was first hoisted into the belfry in 1814, it has been taken down only once for repairs–in 2003.

Inside the building is a large space–all white and with a minimum of ornamentation. In 1815, this space was even larger because the upper floor level of the sanctuary, where the congregation now worships, wasn't there. Instead, the main floor seating was at the first level with galleries supported by fluted columns on three sides. The pulpit formerly stood upon six slender columns high above the floor, approached by winding stairs on either side. The family pews, of the old square type, were introduced for the first time in the fifth meetinghouse. They were entered by a door from the aisles and had seats on three sides so that nearly one-half of the congregation–usually the children–sat with their backs to the minister.

What happened thirty-five years later in 1850 to alter the interior so drastically? By then, simple tastes had changed and the building was remodeled. Two stories were created by flooring over the space between the galleries. The pulpit was removed to the basement and another of mahogany veneer substituted. The window behind it was closed up. The old white interior woodwork was "grained" in imitation of hardwood, and the walls were elaborately frescoed in imitation of columns, arches, alcoves, and panels. The original windows had to be altered to the present three window sashes atop one another on the second floor and only one on the first floor, rather than the original two-over-two double-hung sashes. In addition, the choir loft was built at the rear and ceiling decorations, still visible, added. It was covered in rich yellow-brown, light ochre, and tan paints. A slate roof was added at the same time the top of the cupola was gilded and a town clock installed to go with the Paul Revere bell.

Toward the end of the nineteenth century, some parishioners apparently reacted against the sham and pretension of the prevailing taste of the period and the old pulpit and windows behind it were brought back. The woodwork was then restored to its original white.

There have been inevitable changes, mostly unseen, in this 190-year-old building. In addition to those already mentioned, a noticeable tilt to the belfry in the 1920s required placement of structural steel in the attic to strengthen it. In 1929 there was a fire that charred some attic timbers but, fortunately, caused minimal damage. An addition at the rear of the church, in 1992, is in keeping with the style of Asher Benjamin.

The landmark belfry withstood the storms of winter all these years but in 2003 it was time for an overhaul. The complete rebuilding of the cupola was done at ground level and was ready to be reinstalled when it was discovered that the supporting posts required replacement. The presence of powder post beetles had weakened some parts of the structure which will require constant watchfulness. On Wednesday, March 31, 2004, the newly gilded cupola was hoisted onto its refurbished foundation and can be seen once again from afar.

❑❑❑

Fifties

The 1950s–that was the decade that put Wayland on the map! That was the time when new construction in town just exploded. Damon Farms (Daymon), Happy Hollow and Woodridge areas were all being built. By July 1953, more than a hundred sites on Glezen Lane, Mansion and Draper roads were in the planning stage. The 1950 census listed the population at a little more than 4,000. Ten years later the town had grown by more than 6,000 reaching a population of 10,444.

In 1954 residents reluctantly gave up their phone system, run by a small band of telephone operators who knew everyone in town. Townspeople exchanged phone numbers like "182 ring three," for Olympic 3 (OL3 or 653) in Cochituate, and Elmwood 8 (EL8 or 358) in Wayland. For the first time, people in the Cochituate area could phone the north end of town, and vice versa, without paying for a toll call.

Town fathers decided street numbers were needed to guide the fire department in locating a house on fire. As a public service, the *Town Crier*, in just five and a half pages, published every house number in town. The paper came out once a month, printed a copy for every home, and contained only Wayland news. The subscription price was a dollar a year, paid on the honor system.

The new Cochituate Fire Station opened in 1953. 1954 construction included the Happy Hollow School, the first bank branch in town–Newton Waltham Bank in Cochituate, and Parmenter Health Center. Wayland's first industrial facility, Raytheon, was being built by early 1955. In late 1957, town departments began moving into the new one-story brick town hall building at the northeast corner of the Boston Post and Cochituate roads in the center of town. That building was replaced in 2003 by the current Public Safely Building.

Those who moved to town in the early fifties remember a town with an all-volunteer fire department, a single-person police force and an annual town budget of less than a million dollars. They can recall when people collected their mail each day from the white clapboard post office on Pelham Island Road. House-to-house delivery didn't begin until May 1955.

Newcomers in the 1950s remember when the town hall was a Gothic monster sitting next to the library, when St. Ann Church (St. Ann's) was a wooden church on the current Post Office site, and when the landfill, then called "the dump," was located across the road from the present facility.

Back then, little girls wore dresses to school. Sneakers were worn just for gym and the school lunch cost twenty-five cents. The school bus stop had no supervising adults. Kids lined their lunch boxes up in the order they arrived at the bus stop to insure their place getting on the bus. In those days, children made their own Halloween costumes. There wasn't the wide array of extracurricular activities now offered–just Little League and Scouting.

As young families with young children moved to town, a babysitter crunch developed. While the preschool and elementary populations were huge, Wayland High School classes were only about one-quarter their current size. The going rate for babysitters was fifty cents for teenagers and a dollar an hour for the few adult sitters.

Nineteen hundred and fifty-five was a very different world, but as early as August 1955, town officials announced that lawn watering must be severely curtailed as there was a serious water shortage. Some things never change!

❏❏❏

Five Paths

It has often been said that a home in Wayland will not be called "the old so and so place" until a family has occupied it for several generations. Perhaps the same can be said for old paths and roads. Old-timers often refer to the intersection of Old Connecticut Path and Cochituate Road as "Five Paths." The fifth path was probably Bridle Point Road, one of the settlement's earliest pathways. It began at the easterly end of Bow Road, ran westerly along the ridge once occupied by Raytheon, and later, Polaroid facilities, turning south to cross Route 20, then along the present easterly entrance to Russell's Garden Center, over Mill Brook, which runs between Pelham Island Road and Sandy Burr Country Club, continued southerly up the golf course, past the Noyes-Parris house and out to Old Connecticut Path, now a private driveway. A branch of it led down to Rice's Spring, near Charena Road, probably used by Edmund Rice's family and their visitors.

Families who settled along Sudbury's southwestern border, before the incorporation of Framingham, were called "Sudbury Out-dwellers" or "Sudbury Farmers." They worshiped at the first meetinghouse on Old Sudbury Road and paid taxes to Sudbury. Travel to the meetinghouse was along Old Connecticut and Bridle Point paths.

Bridle Point Path was probably the "fifth path" to intersect Old Connecticut Path and Cochituate Road. Today the intersection is difficult to visualize as the Hultman Aqueduct dramatically changed the intersection when it was made to pass through town in 1940.

52

Grout-Heard House on the Move in 1962

Grout-Heard House

Across from the Wayland Depot at the junction of Cochituate Road with Old Sudbury and Concord roads (Routes 27 and 126) stands a large yellow house behind two towering beech trees. From its solid appearance, one would never guess that it has been moved twice. Now known as the Grout-Heard house, it is the present home of the Wayland Historical Society. Members of two families–the Grouts and the Heards–played prominent roles in Wayland from its earliest settlement.

In 1639, soon after the first settlers of Sudbury arrived, Thomas Cakebread of Watertown was granted one hundred acres of land in the vicinity of the Mill Brook to persuade him to build a gristmill and to serve as the town miller. When Cakebread died in 1643, his son-in-law, John Grout, moved here to take over the mill and property.

Jonathan Grout, grandson of John, probably built the original house on this site around 1740. The earliest construction may have had only four rooms with a large central chimney. A lean-to was probably added sometime later. Jonathan's marriage in 1743 might have been an appropriate reason for the construction of this homestead. The original house was sold in 1744 to Richard Heard, Jonathan's brother-in-law. Soon afterward, it passed out of the family to Elijah Bent and Bent's son-in-law, David Curtis. As the Minutemen headed for Concord Bridge in April of 1775, they would have passed Elijah Bent's store in the house.

In 1787, Silas Grout, a blacksmith and descendant of the first John Grout, living in East Sudbury (Wayland) since 1783, bought this house. The next year, Silas married and brought his new wife, Susanna Clapp, from Sherborn where he had previously lived. It was probably at this time that the rear rooms of the first floor and a second floor over them were built. Silas Grout modernized the façade by moving the old smaller windows to the rear and replacing them with larger windows. Silas Grout operated his blacksmith shop just south of the house very close to the road.

Jerusaha Grout, one of the five children raised by Silas and Susanna, married Newell Heard, owner of the Old Red Store across the street in 1822. The house became a two-family house as Newell and Jerusha Heard and their two children continued to share it with Jerusha's unmarried brother and sister, William and Susan. An ell was built on the south end of the house sometime after 1820. Their mother Susanna, widowed in 1820, also lived there. John Augustus Heard, Newell's and Jerusha's son, was born in 1828. At the age of seventeen, he left for Boston and learned the trade of daguerreotype photographer, gaining some renown. In 1851, he married Sarah Hawkes in Boston and the couple had two girls, Grace and Blanche. Sarah brought the family to Wayland around 1868, after the death of John's parents, Newell and Jerusha. She served as Wayland's librarian from 1885-1901. John continued to have a studio in Boston and in 1875 he was employed by Dr. A.B. Gould to go to South America where he was to assist astonomers by photographing the planets. For several years, John was an official photographer of the Argentine government. He returned to Wayland in 1877 and died a year later. He is buried in the North Cemetery.

The house remained on this site until it was moved in 1878 to Old Sudbury Road to make way for the construction of a new town hall. A prominent landowner, selectman, and chairman of the committee to build the new town hall, Hodijah Braman, apparently wanted it built on that particular plot of land in the center of town. He offered to transfer some of his land to Sarah Heard on favorable terms as a new site for her house. Braman's large 1873 Victorian house, stood on a rise on Old Sudbury Road behind the two remaining fieldstone gate posts, with Sarah Heard's house adjacent to it on the north.

Sarah Heard continued to live in her house on Old Sudbury Road after it was moved. Her two daughters became school teachers in Concord and Arlington but were regular visitors to the old homestead, especially during the summer. In 1955, Raytheon Corporation built a facility on Old Sudbury Road and bought the Heard house, which they soon donated to the newly incorporated Wayland Historical Society. (see Zoning) The house was not moved until 1962. Some wondered whether, and where, the house should be relocated. The 1878 town hall, which had been built on the original house site, had been demolished in 1958 and the site was vacant. All that remained were two sets of granite stairs–one leading to the library in the old town hall and the other to the main entrance. A stone wall bordering the sidewalk also remained. After completing a fund drive to pay for the move, the Grout-Heard house was prepared to go home–but not without incident.

The house was sited on a rise of land which presented a problem in lowering it to street level. The sills in the old kitchen and sheds were too rotten to consider moving and there was a question of whether the two-story bow window added around 1900 should be kept intact since it was not an authentic eighteenth century feature. It stayed. Along the route, strong objections arose because tree trimming on private property was necessary to make way for the move.

One positive note was that the cellar hole remaining from the old town hall was larger than needed for the house, so a cement block foundation could be built without additional excavation. The present site is a few feet back from its original placement, according to local historian George Lewis who staked out the new location. Thus, the old house and all the memories associated with two families had come home.

Horse Car & Trolley Line

□□□

Haynes Garrison

The remains of the Haynes Garrison are on the west side of the Sudbury River and not in Wayland. However, the site is often visited by local students and others interested in King Philip's War. Had the Haynes Garrison been unable to protect the town's earliest settlers against Indian attack on April 21, 1676, King Philip's plan to wipe out every settlement eastward until he reached Boston might have succeeded. But Philip suffered a significant setback in Sudbury and it was here that he was made to turn back.

King Philip, also known as Metacom, Metacomet, or Pometacom, became Great Sachem of the Wampanoag Federation in 1662 after he inherited the power and influence of his father and brother. Philip succeeded in organizing the Indians of New England to fight against the English. He knew that if the Indians did not go to war, they would have had to submit to English authority. King Philip had no trouble convincing the Wampanoags to join him. However, he had to temper his men while he made careful plans and gained the support of surrounding tribes. Philip's plan seemed simple: ready all the tribes and strike all at once. He even allied himself with the fearsome Narragansetts, one of the most powerful federations in New England, after Roger Williams convinced the Narragansetts to combine their energies and turn against the English in concert. Canonchet, Great Sachem of the Narragansetts, and King Philip made detailed plans to have adequate food supplies, weapon repair, bullet molding capability and stored gunpowder available at strategic villages along their route. Whenever Plymouth Colonists became suspicious of Indian activity, Philip met with them at Plymouth and assured them that nothing was brewing. He even signed treaties to appease them.

When Philip and Canonchet were satisfied that the English were no longer worried about an uprising, they purchased guns from the French and Dutch and resumed their earlier plan to attack all the settlements at once and retake all of their lands in New England. They chose a date in the spring of 1676. Unfortunately Philip's plan had to be abandoned because as soon as his warriors were armed they ignored his leadership and began their attacks in June and July 1675 on Swansea, Taunton, Middleborough, Rehoboth, and Dartmouth. By April 1676 they had reached Sudbury.

On the night of April 20, 1676, a large number of warriors spread throughout the area on the west side of the river prepared to attack the Haynes Garrison on Water Row. One group waited near the causeway on the west side of the river, prepared to cross into east Sudbury once Haynes Garrison had been destroyed.

That same night, while Philip and his warriors were skulking around Haynes Garrison, Capt. Samuel Wadsworth and between thirty-five and fifty militiamen were marching toward Marlborough. The Indians did not try to stop the group because they planned to ambush Wadsworth and his men on their return to Sudbury.

The following day, April 21, Philip and his warriors (estimated to have been between five- hundred and one-thousand) attacked all at once the Haynes and Goodenow garrisons. Goodenow Garrison was located on the road to Landham, which would later become the Boston Post Road at its junction with Old County Road. Some warriors managed to cross the river to the east side during the attack, but scattered when Hugh Mason arrived with reinforcements from Watertown. Many Indians, driven back across the river, spread themselves out over Goodman and Green hills.

Additional reinforcements, eight brave men from Concord who came to assist Sudbury, were ambushed in the meadow on the east side of the river, with only one man making it safely back to the Garrison. In the meantime, Capt. Samuel Wadsworth, having arrived at Marlborough, heard that Sudbury was under attack and quickly exchanged some of his exhausted men for fresh recruits and headed back. But Philip and his men were waiting to ambush Wadsworth on the westerly side of Green Hill. The militia fought valiantly and eventually made it to the top of the hill with the loss of only five men. They prepared to battle again the following day but during the night the Indians set the entire hill on fire. Wadsworth and his men retreated down the hill toward South Sudbury, near Hop Brook and the Noyes Mill–today's Mill Village. Wadsworth was killed and the few soldiers who survived the retreat took refuge in the mill which, for some unknown reason, Philip did not attack.

By the end of the day, Philip had abandoned his plan to wipe out settlers all the way to Boston and turned back. Still, he and his warriors continued to harass settlements to the west and south until August of that year when Philip was killed in Rhode Island by one of his own men–the brother of a man Philip had killed for desertion.

Today a plaque on the Boston Post and Old County roads marks Goodenow Garrison and a plaque plus the remains of the foundation of Haynes Garrison remain on Water Row, off Old Sudbury Road. The scene has changed little and the legends about Indians hurling a flaming hay cart down the hill toward the house while soldiers and families shuttered inside seem easy to imagine.

King Philip did not succeed in taking back any of the former Indian lands in New England, and after his death the war ended. Indian power had been destroyed and the future of Indians in New England was set.

❏❏❏

Heard Family

The Heards are one of the largest and best-known families to have lived in Wayland. Although there are now only one or two known direct descendants of the original Zachariah Heard living in town, the family has left its name on Heard's Pond, Heard Road, Heard Farm Conservation Area, the Grout-Heard House, and a large number of headstones in our cemeteries.

It all started with Zachariah Heard, born in 1675, who is known to have lived in town as early as 1707 where it is recorded that he was a highway surveyor. He lived near Mill Pond close to the corner of Glen and the Boston Post roads. He and his wife Silence had five children but only one boy whom they named Richard.

On April 9, 1746, Richard Heard married Sarah Fiske, born and raised on Pelham Island. The couple had four boys and three girls. Through the boys in the family, the Heards became associated with Pelham Island, an area first claimed by Herbert Pelham and for whom the pond was first named. (see Land Grants) The house built in 1793 by Thomas Heard still stands on Erwin Road as a private home.

The Heards multiplied rapidly in the late eighteenth century and their descendants were the men and women who built today's Wayland Center Historic District. The Heard men became the storekeepers, inn keepers and postmasters of pre-Civil War East Sudbury. They also continued to farm the area west of the

Sudbury River known as "The Farm" or "Heard's Island." These broad fields eventually became the Heard Farm Conservation Area and today provide many residents with unusual beauty and tranquility.

Later, some Heards moved from Wayland to other parts of the country. One, Dwight B. Heard, left after high school. He was employed by Hibbard, Spencer and Bartlett Company of Chicago, one of the largest wholesale hardware companies in the country and the precursor of True Value Hardware Stores. In 1893, Dwight married Maie Bartlett, daughter of one of the company founders. After Dwight developed lung ailments, the couple traveled to the west seeking a dryer, warmer climate. In 1895, they settled in Phoenix, Arizona.

In 1899, Dwight returned to Wayland having inherited his grandfather's land holdings south and east of the First Parish Church. He had his grandfather's house on Cochituate Road moved some distance eastward and up a steep hill to its present location at 4 Winthrop Place–quite a feat in those days! He then proceeded to lay out Wayland's first genuine real estate development with eighteen lots–one half to three quarters of an acre each along Winthrop Road and Winthrop Terrace. The portion of the Boston Post Road approaching today's intersection from the east took a different track until the development was started. It ran closer to the present First Parish Church, leaving room for several houses and a tannery between the road and Mill Brook. The Boston Post Road was probably moved to its present location at that time. A new combination high school and grammar school was located across from the subdivision on Cochituate Road.

Heard returned to Phoenix where he and his wife Maie founded the Heard Museum. Today the museum is one of the world's preeminent institutions dedicated to Native American art and culture.

❑❑❑

Horse Cars and Trolley Lines

Today, it is easy to undervalue the great importance of horses in the daily functioning of nineteenth century Wayland life. Horses were used by farmers as draft animals to pull wagons filled with freight, make store deliveries, and haul passengers by the street railroad. The more prosperous householders used their own animals or hired them from the livery stables. George F. Keep, who ran a livery stable in Cochituate, had horses and eight carriages for rent. In 1860, 162 horses were reported in Wayland and by 1877, according to the town report, the number of horses, had perhaps peaked at 392. Visible evidence of the use of horses remains along Cochituate Road north from Millbrook Road to the front of the Grout-Heard house in the form of five granite hitching posts topped by iron rings.

In 1885 a group of Natick men decided to build a horse car line and obtained a charter for the Natick and Cochituate Street Railway. They built stables at the present site of the Cochituate fire station on a lot sold to the company by James N. Hammond and opened for business that July. Horses pulled two closed cars in winter and two open cars in summer. The open cars were named "Lake Cochituate" and "William Bent," the latter for the founder of one of Cochituate's larger shoe companies. George Keep became a superintendent of the line, which by the spring of 1886 had seven cars and a comparable number of horses. By 1887, there were three large, open cars for summer use and three closed cars for winter use, each pulled by two horses. These horses were large animals, each weighing about a half ton.

The terminus in Cochituate was at Lyons Corner where the fire station and Finnerty's Restaurant now stand. When the horse car line opened, it reduced travel time by other means between Natick and Cochituate by ten minutes. The trip took one half-hour and cost ten cents. T-rails, flush with the ground on the outside, were used in open areas. Flat rails, smooth and slightly grooved, were used in thickly settled places and on grades and corners.

In May 1892 the Natick and Cochituate Street Railway began to electrify their line and convert to trolley cars. By July, the trolleys were ready to roll. The first trip, a free ride led by Selectman Edwin Marston, carried fifty-two passengers. Town selectmen and the Railway Company then agreed upon a five-cent fare. Later that month, Cochituate celebrated the opening of the new railway with fireworks and a parade.

In 1893, talk began about extending the line from Cochituate to Wayland Center within a year. The Natick and Cochituate Street Railway was in the midst of building extensions to Wellesley and Newton and did not apply to the Wayland selectmen for a franchise for another three years. On March 23, 1897, the selectmen gave the street railway company permission to build a track from Lyons Corner in Cochituate to the railroad track in Wayland Center to be completed by September. The railway company was also allowed to build a track on the Boston Post Road to the Weston Line as well as a track from Lyons Corner along West Plain Street to Old Connecticut Path, then to the Framingham town line on its way to Saxonville.

Further, the franchise specified that the track should run on the westerly side of Main Street in Cochituate to the intersection of Old Connecticut Path and Cochituate Road and cross there to the easterly side of Cochituate Road until it reached the Boston Post Road. The track would then run up the middle of Cochituate Road to the Massachusetts Central Railroad tracks. One section of track would pass through the private estate of Francis Shaw whose property ran from School Street to beyond the intersection of Old Connecticut Path and Cochituate Road. The company, however, was unable to work out arrangements with the landowner. The street railway did lay track to Saxonville within their allotted time and trolleys were in operation by July 1897. Many Cochituate residents took the opening day ride to celebrate in Saxonville.

Two years later on March 15, 1899, the Natick and Cochituate Street Railway again applied for a franchise to run an extension from Lyons Corner in Cochituate to the railroad track in Wayland Center. This time the alignment of the track was changed and made to run on the easterly side of Cochituate Road from Lyons Corner to Fiske's Corner at School Street and on the westerly side of the road where it crossed the Shaw property. Engineering difficulties around the Old Connecticut Path and Cochituate Road intersection caused delays and the project was not completed until the last week in July 1899.

One impetus for building the line was to transport Cochituate pupils to the new Center School that had been built across the street from the First Parish Church. Prior to trolley service, they traveled by horse-drawn wagon or barge.

Unfortunately, passenger service by trolley between Cochituate Village and Wayland Center was never profitable. Attempts to carry freight and express items to increase profits were likewise unsuccessful. After a period of declining ridership, the trolley company received permission to convert to buses, and all trolley service to Wayland and Cochituate ended in 1924. Some of the track along Cochituate Road was taken up at the time town water pipes were laid in the late 1920s. Generally, the era of trolley lines between rural towns and villages lasted only into the 1920s in eastern Massachusetts.

❑❑❑

Houses of Worship

The town's first houses of worship served both religious and civic purposes. The first three meetinghouses were built at the original settlement site on Old Sudbury Road. The fourth and fifth meetinghouses were built in the town's center. (see Meetinghouses) The town supplied all financial support including money for the minister's salary. These hardy Puritans, determined to "purify" the practices of the Anglican church, avoided using the word "church" for almost a full century. Everyone was required by law to attend religious services twice on Sunday–both morning and afternoon. Early meetinghouses served as houses for worship, for town meetings, and also held stores of ammunition. It was a gathering place for people to socialize, debate and vote, as well as worship. When the fifth meetinghouse was dedicated in 1815–at the location of today's First Parish Church on the corner of Cochituate and Boston Post roads–it was to serve solely as a church, some eighteen years before separation of church and state was mandated in Massachusetts. (see Meetinghouses)

As early as the 1820s, some members of the First Parish, unhappy at the congregation's movement toward Unitarianism, became dissatisfied and in 1828 organized the Evangelical Trinitarian Church and built their own small chapel. The chapel soon proved too small and a church with carriage sheds was built in 1835 on the west side of Cochituate Road. The organizers first formed as the Evangelical Society of East Sudbury or the Evangelical Religious Society. But it soon changed its name to the Evangelical Trinitarian Church in East Sudbury and in 1896 to the Trinitarian Congregational Church in Wayland. An early Covenant of the church (unfortunately undated) calls it the First Congregational Church Society.

The next church building in town was in Cochituate Village. Begun by a Wesleyan Methodist Society group in 1846, parishioners met in the south schoolhouse until a church was built at the present intersection of East Plain and Commonwealth roads. Construction of the church, however, caused much debate. Some members wanted to build on Main Street. Others, most probably members of the Loker family who lived in the area, wanted it in "Lokerville" where it was finally built. In 1850, however, the church blew down in a wind storm and was made to face Cochituate when it was rebuilt "to secure the attendance of a member who had objected to the orientation of the first building." One can only assume that the first church faced Lokerville.

Sixteen years later, a group that included twenty-two of the village's most influential members broke off from the Wesleyan Methodist and organized the Episcopal Methodist Society. Their church was completed in 1866 on a half-acre of land purchased from Mr. Charles R. Damon on Main Street at the corner of Damon Street. In 1869 Mr. Damon gave the site for the parsonage which was later replaced by an educational building and the Ladies Social Union. More renovations followed in the mid 1890s and 1950s. In 1962, a new fourteen-room wing was added to the church and in 1966 a church-sponsored preschool opened in the

63

building.

The old Wesleyan Methodist Church in Lokerville continued to be used on occasion by Baptists and certain revival and non-denominational groups. Eventually the original building fell into disrepair and, in 1902, after the death of Jefferson Loker at the age of ninety-three, the building was put up for auction. Loker, who had been a neighbor and a devoted church member, had donated a mahogany table and two collection boxes to the old church. Just before his death he bequeathed these items to the new Episcopal Methodist Church. At the auction, Edgar B. Loker bought the old building, moved it to his property, and made it into a hen house. The church site became an informal park.

When French and Irish immigrants came to work in the Cochituate shoe factories in the 1870s the village did not have its own Catholic Church. Many of the French-speaking residents, comprising 22% of Cochituate's population in 1880, came from Canada or had Canadian-born parents. The new parish activities began in 1879-80 and services, held upstairs in the Lokerville schoolhouse, began in French in 1881. They also attended services in Saxonville, Natick, Waltham and Marlborough. The Albert Dean home on the corner of Main Street and Shawmut Avenue was purchased to house Father Rainville, the first priest assigned to the Cochituate parish. In August 1889 ground was broken for St. Zepherin (St. Zepherin's) on Willard Street behind the priest's residence. It was dedicated on April 27, 1890. A new church was built in 1960, with the old one remaining as a parish hall, or social center, until it was demolished in 1989. The present rectory was built in 1965. A new parish center was built in 1991 and the original St. Zepherin church building demolished at this time. Major renovations were made to the church in October 1998.

By the turn of the twentieth century, the Catholic population in Wayland Center had formed a parish and begun to meet upstairs over Lovell's Store, the lovely old white-columned building originally built in 1841 as a town hall. (Town Halls) They built their own church, St. Ann, on the Boston Post Road in 1905 near the site of today's post office. In 1959, a generous parishioner donated a fifteen-acre site on which to build a church less than a mile south of Wayland Center on Cochituate Road. In 1961, a thirteen-room rectory was completed and less than two years later, ground was broken for construction of a new Colonial style church next door. The old church on the Boston Post Road was razed in 1967 to clear land for a new post office.

Beginning in the late 1950s, a group of local residents met to discuss their interest in having an Episcopal church in town. In 1961 the Church of the Holy Spirit was incorporated as a mission. Services were held in schools, the First Parish Church, and Parmenter Health Center for several years. In 1963, Nathaniel Hamlen donated land on Rice Road for a church. A year later, the Reverend Donald W. Noseworthy, the first rector, dedicated the completed church building.

Peace Lutheran Church was organized in 1964 and a church built on a three-acre site on Concord Road. It was one of seventy-four congregations of the American Lutheran Church begun that year across the country. The congregation, which has always worshiped in this church, is part of the national church.

In the summer of 1978, a Reform Jewish congregation rented space at the First Parish Church in Wayland Center to celebrate holiday occasions and Shabbat services. The congregation quickly grew and in 1980 members of Temple Shir Tikva purchased a permanent home at the former site of Rosebud Gardens. (see Rosebud Gardens) The original building, extensively renovated, was dedicated in May 1981. Ten years

64

later, a two-phase expansion project began. In 1992, an updated sanctuary for worship and a function/meeting hall were added to the existing building which was renovated for offices and classrooms. The original building was demolished in October 1997 and replaced by a new education center, dedicated in September 1998.

The Wellesley Park Assembly of God began in the campgrounds known as Wellesley Park in 1932 and moved to a new facility in Wayland on Loker Street in 1984. Confusion over its name–Wellesley Park–when located in Wayland prompted the congregation to change the name to Celebration International Church. Sunday worship is regularly attended by people from more than twenty nations.

The Islamic Center of Boston was started in 1979 in a public school facility in Cambridge. In 1988, the Islamic Center purchased a twelve-room house on 1.75 acres of land at 126 Boston Post Road. In the early nineties, a new building was constructed to provide additional classrooms and a larger prayer area. Parking facilities were later expanded after the center acquired an adjoining plot of land. Construction of an additional 14,000 square feet of building space began in 2004 after the original twelve-room house was demolished. The center serves the Muslim community west and north of Boston as well as families from New Hampshire and Falmouth. The center's membership includes many ethnic groups and represents Muslims from all over the world.

The Conservative Jewish congregation Or Atid, meaning "light of the future," celebrated a groundbreaking ceremony in September 2001 at 97 Concord Road, site of their new synagogue. Organized in 1991, families had met in the First Parish Church in Wayland, sent older children to religious school at Temple Israel of Natick, and in 1992 celebrated high holiday services at the Unitarian Church in Weston. On September 1, 2002, congregants, family, friends and neighbors marched with Or Atid's Torah from the congregation's first home at First Parish to its new permanent home. A week later, the quest for a permanent home over, 120 families worshiped in their spacious new facility.

The eleven different houses of worship within the town's fifteen square mile boundary are a tribute to the great diversity of our community.

Ice Cutting on Mill Pond

Icehouses

Our colonial ancestors did not think very much about ice, except perhaps as a nuisance or a hazard to life and limb. There was plenty of ice in Wayland, but no consideration was given to its potential for preserving perishable foods or drinks or, perish the thought, personal recreation. But those ideas did take root over the eighteenth and nineteenth centuries. Some early house builders left a tiny space in a new cellar wall for a jug of milk or a crock of cheese, knowing the natural coolness would keep them fresh. Underground root cellars would serve the same purpose for potatoes, carrots, and beets.

The growth of commercial dairy farming, with distant markets, led to the consideration of pond and river ice as a coolant, and the construction on the farm of a separate building to hold ice over the warm weather season. A whole new industry sprang up with its own tools and techniques. A storage facility, however, was a necessity.

An entire building of ice could solidify, however, so farmers thought of placing layers of sawdust between the cakes of ice to keep it from melting too fast. There was plenty of sawdust in a region where every town had a sawmill. Although an icehouse on the farm was very handy for family uses, it was soon apparent that there was a commercial use for stored ice elsewhere. There was a period in New England history when ice was cut and shipped in specially designed ships to ports in the American South, the Caribbean islands, and elsewhere at enormous profit.

Wayland had two important icehouses: a very large one on Dudley Pond and a smaller one at the Mill Pond. The Dudley Pond ice house was located at the end of Mathews Drive. It was a huge windowless structure, solidly built of wood. Ice men like Harry Wyatt served the local Cochituate, and perhaps the Natick, markets. The Mill Pond icehouse was built from what was left after the 1890 fire at the old Cakebread mill. Arthur Atwood developed the ice business there. He also supplied the town's needs for wood, coal, and oil.

The icehouses are long gone, but residents today enjoy pond ice for recreation. The Mill Pond is plowed in winter for skating and is lighted at night. Dudley Pond's skating is more informal. But nobody cuts and stores the town's ice today.

The Cochituate  Jeep

Conveyor Of News From The Folks At Home To Their Service Men And Women Everywhere

No. 2   February 24, 1945   MAIL ADDRESS
P. O. Box 70, Cochituate, Mass.

Correction

Sorry to have made errors and omissions in the honor roll of our first edition, it was unintentional and hope you will bear with us.

On the Honor Roll, the surnames of Francis J. Hartin and his brother Bill were listed as "Martin."

The name of Harold C. Hurlbut, husband of the former Alice Forbes, should have been included, as well as Wm. Burgin, C. Russell Thomas, Wm. V. Young, Robert Merritt, John Hampstead.

Discharged From The Service

Several men who have been discharged from the service were not listed on the Jeep Honor Roll. They are as follows:

Kenneth A. Baker
Roy F. Hallenbrook
Gurney O. Nichol
Chester R. Rafus
Arthur A. Therrien
George Toohill
Charles Maher

Cochituate boys who registered elsewhere and are in the service, but not on the Honor Roll are:

Charles Waters
Rowland W. Ashley
Ralph M. Bent
Richard W. Bishop
Chester H. Dusseault
Francis L. Fisher
Alle Petrocelli
Raymond Snell
Percy H. Steele
John O'Connor
Raymond MacMillen
Paul Thomas
Henry Stanley
Wm. A. Hammond
Wm. A. Hammond, Jr.

To You And You

Climb aboard the Jeep
The townsfolk want a peep
A bit that's new
From all of you
Just be a pal—'twill boost morale.

GERTRUDE PERODEAU

71

Jeep and Village Bugle Newspapers

During World War II when the idea of publishing a newspaper for local servicemen was first considered, it apparently didn't occur to townspeople that there might be just one such publication. Back then, Wayland and Cochituate were two separate villages within the town, and both published their own newspaper just for their own servicemen.

Wayland's *Village Bugle,* begun in September 1942, was the first to start. Previously, a local paper, the *Wayland Chronicle,* published its last issue in June 1942 after the editor, Rev. John Slade Franklin, went into the service. Franklin had started the *Chronicle* in October 1936 and published six other newspapers in nearby towns. The need to provide Wayland boys with news from their hometown was apparent. The legal-length of four pages was prepared and mailed to Wayland servicemen every two weeks for more than three years. Occasionally a woodcut of a Wayland Center landmark by local artist, F. Wenderoth Saunders, was featured on the front page.

Cochituate, on the other hand, had neighboring newspapers that carried Cochituate news. So, Cochituate's *Jeep* wasn't started until much later, in February 1945. It was mailed free to servicemen and could be ordered by mail for $1.50 for six months, or purchased for ten cents per copy. Every edition carried its signature sketch of a jeep, drawn by an eleven-year-old boy at the Convalescent Home for Children. The *Jeep* was a smaller format newspaper with more pages. Because it used a print process, it carried lots of photographs. There were photos of a record snowstorm, of Cochituate Center buildings, and many photos of men and women in uniform. Early in its career, the *Jeep* began the practice of giving away a war bond with each issue. The names of all Cochituate residents in the service were placed in a cookie jar. A photo of the winner appeared in each issue along with a photo of the person–a cute little girl, a blue star mother–who had drawn the winner's name. Soon local businesses and townspeople began donating additional war bonds for the drawing. Sometimes as many as thirteen war bonds were listed in a single issue and the photo of each winner was published. In the end, enough war bonds were contributed to award one to each of Cochituate's 263 men and women in the service.

Both the *Bugle* and *Jeep* had many columns of news "from" local servicemen and generous helpings of town events. High school news, football and baseball scores, weddings, births, and news of the civilian defense effort were all presented in a relentlessly cheerful style. Both papers were mailed free to all local servicemen and organized by a large crew of volunteers. It was an operation that ran on a shoestring. The *Bugle* operated out of the Mellen Law Office on the town green. Mrs. John Upton compiled, edited and typed the paper which was mimeographed gratis in the Boston office of Charles T. Morgan. Cochituate stores served as contacts for the *Jeep.* Both papers carried news of the VJ Day (Victory over Japan) celebration ending World War II on August 14, 1945: bells rang and the fire alarm sounded at both ends of town. Wayland Center neighbors fired off blanks from a "45." In Cochituate, cars and bikes drove the streets decorated with colored streamers. Lacking ticker tape, Cochituate's Main Street was carpeted with bits of paper. Stores were closed for two days and the local churches held services.

By the time the Cochituate *Jeep* ceased publication on February 8, 1946, most of the people in the service had been discharged. The number of servicemen and women had dwindled to eighty-five. By its last edition on December 14, 1945, the *Bugle* listed only eighty-seven who had not been discharged. But the need for a local newspaper did not really die. Less than three years after the last edition of the Bugle was printed at the Mellen Law Office, the early editions of the *Wayland Junior Town House Crier* were published in December 1948. Eventually the current *Wayland Town Crier* became the local newspaper.

K

Marker at Stone's Bridge

Knox Trail

Travelers along Stonebridge Road and the portion of Old Connecticut Path (Route 126) that goes through Wayland, pass two Henry Knox monuments–one at close proximity to the site of Old Stone's Bridge and the other on the south side of Old Connecticut Path at the junction of Old Connecticut Path and Cochituate Road (Route 27). The stone monuments that mark the 300 mile route taken by Knox and his men are important reminders of the heroic trek made that winter of 1775-76 from Fort Ticonderoga to Boston.

After the defeat of the American Army at the Battle of Bunker Hill on June 16, 1775, the British became firmly entrenched in Boston and General George Washington lacked the artillery needed to drive them out. While searching for a solution, he met Henry Knox, a twenty-five-year-old Boston bookseller with extensive military knowledge. They devised a plan to move artillery 300 miles from Fort Ticonderoga, far to the northwest on Lake Champlain, to Boston. The Fort was then firmly under American control and no longer in fear of attack. With the British so strategically placed in Boston, time was of the essence. Young Knox, eager to help, agreed to lead an expedition to the Fort in December 1775, determined to bring the cannons to Boston.

Knox, his brother William, and a servant traveled to Fort Ticonderoga prepared to bring to Boston fifty-nine pieces of artillery that had been selected and dismantled for the journey. On the morning of December 6, 1775 the caravan set off from the Fort to Lake George. There they loaded small boats and floated them down the lake. Five days later they arrived at the south end of the lake before the surface of the lake froze over. They transferred everything to forty-two strong sleds pulled by eighty yokes of oxen. There were forty-three heavy brass and iron cannons, six cohorns (a cannon of small caliber on its own wheels), eight mortars, two howitzers and sixteen smaller pieces. For the next fifty-six days, Knox and his men braved the winter elements as they dragged the artillery over snow-covered mountains and across icy rivers.

Once in Massachusetts they followed Indian trails from Alford to Worcester. From Worcester the trail continued on much of what is Route 20 today. But, each mile closer to Boston the journey became more and more dangerous. Fearing that British spies might be lurking along the latter portion of the route, Washington sent orders to seek local guides and take secret paths through the communities of Marlborough, Southborough, Framingham, Sudbury, which then included Wayland, and Weston. A Cutting family journal–the Cutting family lived at Mainstone Farm when Knox came along Old Connecticut Path–indicates they heard the caravan coming and invited the men up the hill for a meal.

On January 24, 1776, Knox finally delivered the cache of artillery to Gen. Washington in Boston and his heroic expedition ended. After General Washington assembled the artillery and set it up on Dorchester Heights, the British Commander, Lord William Howe, realized that the only way he could save his army was to evacuate the city. So, without firing a shot, the American Army marched into the deserted city the second week in March 1776.

Four months later, the Declaration of Independence was signed in Philadelphia. Henry Knox's epic story and the part he played in our country's fight for freedom were being told in and out of Boston. Knox served as Washington's artillery chief throughout the Revolutionary War. Washington commissioned him major-general, and later appointed him Secretary of War.

In 2001, Philip Lord, Jr., curator of the State Museum of New York traveled the length of the Knox trail photographing all the markers. Much to his surprise he discovered at Stone's Bridge in Wayland a smaller marker than anywhere else on the trail. Lord learned after researching the question that when Massachusetts state officials had been rearranging storage in the maze of tunnels beneath the State House in 1967, they had come upon a granite marker inscribed "Knox Trail–Fort Ticonderoga, N.Y. to Cambridge, Mass." Word circulated about the find among town historians. Wayland Historical Society's curator heard about it and contacted the State's Bicentennial Commissioner requesting the stone be donated to Wayland. She explained that the monument originally placed at Stone's Bridge in 1927 had mysteriously disappeared a long time ago and a replacement, even a smaller one, would be welcomed. Thus, the lost marker found a home in Wayland. After more research, Lord concluded that the marker found in the State House must have been the smaller stone sample made by the stone-carver who did all of the markers for the state in 1927.

Using the diaries of Henry Knox and a twelve-year-old boy who had accompanied his father on the journey, historians were able to determine the probable route taken by the General. Since neither diary mentioned the specific route taken through Massachusetts, it required diligent research. Historians believe the route that has been marked through Massachusetts is a reasonable one considering that it had been such a well-kept secret.

Monuments along the Massachusetts portion of the Trail begin in Alford, Massachusetts on the New York State line and continue to Boston. That portion of the trail marked through Metrowest begins in Marlborough on the Boston Post Road at Prospect Street; in Southborough on the south side of Commonwealth Road (Route 30) at American Legion Post; in Framingham on Edgell Road, at town common; and in Wayland at Old Stone's Bridge and on Old Connecticut Path at its junction with Cochituate Road.

A historic map of the Knox Trail titled MetroWest Knox Trail Heritage Corridor may be obtained at the Wayland Historical Society, MetroWest libraries and town halls along the route, or by calling MetroWest Growth Management 508-620-7330 .

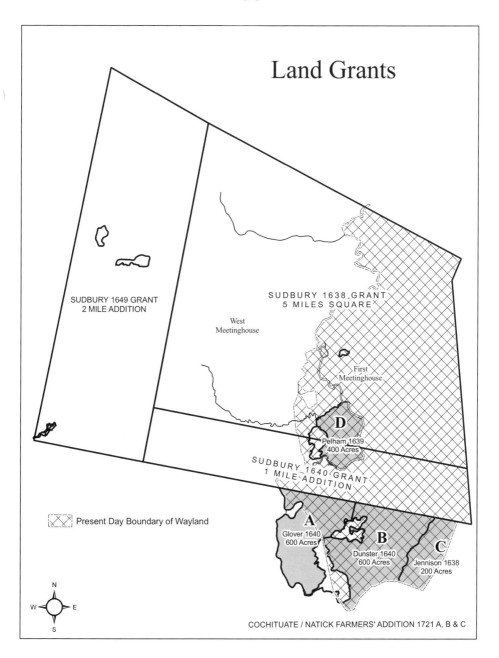

Land Grants

SUDBURY 1649 GRANT
2 MILE ADDITION

SUDBURY 1638 GRANT
5 MILES SQUARE

West
Meetinghouse

First
Meetinghouse

D

Pelham 1639
400 Acres

SUDBURY 1640 GRANT
1 MILE ADDITION

Present Day Boundary of Wayland

A

Glover 1640
600 Acres

B

Dunster 1640
600 Acres

C

Jennison 1638
200 Acres

N
W E
S

COCHITUATE / NATICK FARMERS' ADDITION 1721 A, B & C

Lake Cochituate

The lake's first fishermen called their encampment on the bluffs of the lake "Cochituate," meaning "place of the rushing torrent." They fished the clean, clear waters of the lake and hunted in the surrounding forests. When English settlers came, they did the same. But they also gave the lake a name. They called it "Long Pond," for the three main ponds and two connector ponds that divided the long body of water. A portion of North Pond is in Wayland and extends from the Wayland/Saxonville line to the Wayland/Natick line along the easterly side of the lake. The town maintains a municipal beach off Parkland Drive and a boat ramp adjacent to the Beach. Residents purchase annual beach permits and the Department of Park and Recreation offers swimming programs for all ages. A car-top boat access is located off Commonwealth Road immediately west of the entrance to Lakeview Cemetery. The Massachusetts Division of State Parks and Recreation operates Cochituate State Park on Commonwealth Road (Route 30) in Framingham. Wayland and Natick land along the southeastern side of the lake beyond Commonwealth Road (Route 30) lies within the boundary of the park.

The lake has long played a role in the town's history. Sometime before 1848 a steam excursion boat plied the waters of the lake. Though little is known about the boat, it is said that it cruised the lake carrying upwards of sixty people. A century later, another steam boat, the "Carrie Nation," (probably named in jest after the woman who led the temperance movement at the turn of the century) paddled up and down the south lake in present-day Natick. It carried about twenty-five passengers, mostly men, who played cards, drank, and fished. One day, however, it blew up. Fortunately, all the passengers swam ashore safely.

In 1845, Boston city officials approached the town to purchase the waters of Long Pond for a public water supply for Boston. The town agreed. Boston politicians, eager to sell the new water source to the city's residents, renamed Long Pond, "Lake Cochituate," which they believed sounded like a wild and pure source of water. The Massachusetts Water Commission built a granite dam at the outlet and a gatehouse on the eastern side of North Pond. The gatehouse, which still stands near the edge of the lake at the end of the car-top boat access area, served to control the flow of water into the aqueduct connecting the body of water with Boston. It drew water from a depth of eighty-nine feet, the deepest part of the lake. Ten years later a second dam was built 500 feet downstream from the first one.

In 1858, the Boston Water Commission requested the towns of Wayland, Natick and Framingham to join them in applying to the legislature for permission to raise the original dam two additional feet to assure an emergency supply of water for Boston. The towns agreed, and were paid in proportion to the amount of lakeshore within their town. Wayland received $1,000. That act of the legislature allowed the city of Boston to take by eminent domain properties not more than five rods in width, or 16-1/2 feet. It also provided for damages caused by water flowage onto private property and an indemnity to the three towns for any damages done to highways or bridges caused by high waters. The water used to raise the level of the lake was to come from Dudley Pond through a connecting tunnel built between the two in 1863.

Although it cost the city of Boston $27,130 to raise the level of the dam, the Dudley Pond connector did not work as well as planned and was later sealed up.

While residents of Boston enjoyed their new source of drinking water, towns around the lake lost their swimming rights on the lake, along with activities on the shore. Although the loss of fishing rights must have been a great hardship for residents who depended on fish as a source of food, most people were too busy working to complain about the recreational losses. Finally, in 1947, the Massachusetts District Commission, which by now had secured sufficient drinking water for the residents of Boston from Quabbin Reservoir, placed Lake Cochituate under the administration of the State Department of Natural Resources and recreation resumed on the lake.

In the summer of 2002 State biologists began a program to eliminate three non-native invasive aquatic plants that had invaded Middle and South ponds: Eurasian Milfoil, Variable Milfoil and Curly-leaved Pondweed. North Pond has been closed to motorboats for a number of years and nets placed between the ponds to prevent the plants from spreading any further. The program has included the installation of additional nets and hand pulling of the weeds by trained volunteers.

Cochituate State Park at 93 Commonwealth Road is for day-use and features boating, swimming, wind surfing, and boat launching including picnic facilities, rest rooms, and parking. While the lake continues to be a valuable source of recreation, remedies are being sought to improve water quality on the lake. The swimming beach is often closed due to bacteria in the water caused by the large number of geese that visit the park.

Thanks to the dedication of members of the Lake Cochituate Watershed Association and various volunteers, there are no "nine-eyed carp" or "glowing frogs" in the lake's waters. With the Association's vigilance, it is hoped there will never be any.

❑❑❑

Land Grants (Individual)

Sudbury Plantation became the nineteenth town to be incorporated as part of the Massachusetts Bay Colony when the General Court ordered that "the newe Plantation by Concord shall be called Sudbury." This grant had been made to settlers collectively and was not to encroach on private grants previously made by the legislature to individuals who had provided important services to the Massachusetts Bay Colony.

Important in Wayland's history are four individual land grants, three of which became the Cochituate region of town. Only Herbert Pelham's grant was near the center of the settlement, just west of the Sudbury River. The other three, made to Elizabeth Glover, Henry Dunster and William Jennison, were on the south side of town adjacent to Framingham and Natick. Land grants were often referred to as "farms."

Herbert Pelham, the first treasurer of Harvard College, was granted 400 acres for one hundred pounds paid into the common stock of the Colony and for other services. His land, which was surrounded by water in spring, was long referred to as the "Island." Pelham did not live there, choosing to live in Cambridge instead, so town officials refused him the right to vote, even by absentee ballot. He returned to England, and after his death in 1673, left the land to his son Edward. It passed from the family in 1711 and was eventually purchased by Samuel Stone, Jr. and Jonathan Fiske. Stone and Fiske settled on the island, dividing it into two farms–Stone on the west and Fiske on the east. Samuel Stone built a house on his side in 1715, just in time for the birth of one of his daughters, Tabitha. Seven years later, Jonathan Fiske built a home on the eastern half in time for the birth of his daughter, Sarah. (see Heards)

Years later, Thomas Bent, who married Mary Stone, acquired the western half of the island from his father-in-law, Samuel. Sarah Fiske married Richard Heard and they became owners of the east side of the island. Eventually Heards came to own the whole island when, in 1779, the Bent family sold their farm to Richard Heard. Heard descendants have lived there continuously, though some of the land has since been developed for houses and a large portion preserved for recreational use.

The three individual land grants on the south side of town extended from Framingham in the west to Watertown in the east. The most westerly grant belonged to the Reverend Josse Glover. In 1638, the Reverend Glover and his family sailed from England to deliver and establish in Cambridge a printing press, the first in British North America. He also brought a printer named Stephen Day. Josse Glover died during the voyage, leaving Stephen Day to set up the printing operation, and his widow Elizabeth Glover to raise five children alone. Glover had been a good friend to the Colony and shortly after the family arrived in Cambridge his widow was granted 600 acres of land–later found to include 960 acres, some of it in Framingham–on the south side of the Sudbury settlement.

Adjacent to the Glover grant, and to the east of it, was Henry Dunster's 600 acre grant. Dunster, the first president of Harvard College (1640-1654), took office after Nathaniel Eaton, the headmaster, was ousted for inflicting harsh punishment on the students. The General Court which had appropriated £400 to establish the college ordered that it be named in honor of the Reverend John Harvard who died and bequeathed his library of 400 books and half his estate, £779, to the college. Dunster ordered construction of the college's first building, established a stiff curriculum, and designed the college arms with the motto, *Veritas*, on three open books. Dunster's 600 acre grant extended to the present Rice Road, adjacent to Capt. Jennison's grant. In 1641, Dunster married the widow Elizabeth Glover who died only two years later, leaving Dunster as guardian of her children and administrator of the Glover estate. When Dunster later remarried, he chose another Elizabeth, thus confusing future genealogists who find that "Dunster and Elizabeth had two children." That would be the second Elizabeth!

The most easterly grant, that of Capt. William Jennison, had been made in 1638. Jennison, of Watertown, had been a Company Commander during the 1636 Pequot War. He was granted 200 acres of land which extended from the present Rice Road to Weston (then Watertown). Jennison returned to England in 1651 and his brother, Robert, inherited the property. Robert later gave it to his grandsons.

It is not surprising that records of the Dunster, Glover and Jennison families are somewhat obscure since none of them lived on their lands. Fortunately, several Sudbury citizens left behind deeds that record

83

the dates of purchase and sale of their lands. In 1642, and again in 1653, Edmund Rice of Sudbury leased the Dunster Farm. Six years later, he bought it. Rice also leased the Glover farm in 1647 for a period of ten years. Almost forty years later that farm was sold by the Glover heirs to three Sudbury parties: Thomas Brown, Thomas Drury and Caleb Johnson. Rice had purchased the Jennison farm in 1657.

Edmund Rice became a prominent Sudbury citizen and left many descendants. The Rice name is mentioned in both Sudbury and Wayland histories, which is not surprising. Rice married twice and had twelve children, some of whom were born in Marlborough where he and several sons moved.

❏❏❏

Library

On August 20, 1851, the Reverend Doctor Francis Wayland spoke to citizens gathered at the First Parish Church for a library celebration: "This gives me a higher idea of New England character than anything I before have witnessed. Your inhabitants have assembled without distinction of age or sex, to celebrate with joyful festivities, not any great history, not any great political event, but the founding of a library."

For the town, this was no ordinary event. It was the culmination of many years of effort, beginning in 1796, to establish a free public library. The Reverend Doctor Francis Wayland was president of Brown University and a major contributor to the establishment of Wayland's library. His words suggested the determined struggle that had gone on in the intervening years.

In 1796, the Reverend Josiah Bridge, pastor of the First Parish Church, together with other prominent citizens, organized the East Sudbury Social Library. It was not free to all people of the town, but only to the thirty-two "proprietors" who paid a $4.00 membership fee and an annual assessment of 25 cents. The budget was $128.00, with a book account of $8.00 and a $2.00 yearly stipend for the librarian. The first collection boasted thirty-six volumes. By 1832, there were 227 volumes, housed in the homes of various librarians and, for a time, in the vestibule of the First Parish Church.

As early as 1815, the Reverend John Burt Wight, an intellectual and a politically active pastor, established the East Sudbury Charitable Library with a collection of "moral and religious books." The collection, kept in the church, was supported by private contributions but available free to anyone. A circulating collection of 300 volumes was shared by the six district schools, and was later added to the Wayland library collection. In 1835, the town of East Sudbury changed its name to Wayland, some say to honor Dr. Wayland who was a close friend of Judge Edward Mellen. (see Wayland, the Name) Dr. Wayland, who was proud of his namesake town, offered $500 to be matched by the citizens of Wayland for the purpose of founding a library. In his letter to Judge Mellen on January 9, 1848, Dr. Wayland wrote, "I therefore propose that if the citizens of the town of Wayland, within 30 days from this 10th of January, will raise by subscription or otherwise the sum of $500 for the purchase of a Town library, I will add to it the same sum as soon as I am informed that the said subscription is completed."

Thanks to the tireless efforts of James Sumner Draper who collected money from 208 citizens, including donations of 25 cents, the town exceeded the "matching" request by collecting $553.50. This amount, and Dr. Wayland's $500, was accepted at town meeting in 1848. The Wayland Free Public Library, as it is known today, was opened in August of 1850 in the small front room of the 1841 town hall at 21 Cochituate Road, later known as the Collins Market building. (see Town Halls) It proudly declares itself to be the first public library in Massachusetts and second in the United States. This honor is claimed by several other local libraries, including the Boston Public Library. Although the debate continues, the Wayland Library was certainly one of the first. In 1850, it was not legal for a town library to be supported by tax monies. The town needed to find a way around this problem. The Reverend John Burt Wight, Wayland's representative to the General Court, introduced legislation and lobbied vigorously for the 1851 passage of the Library Act which made it legal for tax monies to be used in the establishment and maintenance of public libraries.

The first library was later expanded to include the whole lower floor in what had been a classroom in the old Town Hall. The library was opened to the public every Saturday afternoon and evening. Although any resident of the town over the age of fourteen could take out a book, families could only borrow three books at a time. A list of books borrowed in those early years shows that one of the favorites was "Diseases of Horses," a good source book in an agricultural community. In 1879, the library moved across the street to the new Gothic/Victorian-style town hall. On this site–now the home of the Wayland Historical Society–is a boulder with a bronze plaque commemorating the first free public library in Massachusetts and the second public library in the United States dated 1850.

Wayland resident Warren Gould Roby in an 1898 bequest gave the sum of $25,000 and a gift of land to the town to build a new library. The architect was Samuel Mead of Weston, a member of the firm of Cabot, Everett and Mead. He designed the building in the popular Italian Romanesque style with a Mediterranean red tiled roof and a beautiful rotunda. The frieze of bas reliefs of dancing children around the rotunda was copied from a frieze by Della Robbia and Donatello, in the Cantoria Museum of the Opera del Duomo in Florence. The library moved to its new home in 1900. It remains the oldest building built for public use in Wayland.

On the walls of the rotunda are three oil portraits: over the east fireplace is Warren G. Roby (1834-1897) and over the west fireplace is John B. Wight (1815-1883). A small oil portrait to the right above the Reverend Wight is Margaret Ulman. On the balcony walls are four life-size Indian ink portraits: on the east wall, James Draper (1787-1870), north, Francis Wayland (1790-1865), west, Edward Mellen (1802-1875), and south, Lydia Maria Child (1802-1880).

One hundred and ninety years ago, John Burt Wight, who worked long and hard for the establishment of public libraries, made the statement which remains the guiding principle of the library today: "Happiness depends on the general diffusion of useful knowledge by the free use of well-chosen books."

$\mathcal{M}$

Monument at Old Town Bridge, 1908

Meetinghouses

During the seventeenth century everyone was required by the General Court to attend Sunday religious services. Thus, an early order of business was to design and build a meetinghouse. New England colonists, determined to "purify" the practices of the Anglican church, avoided using the word "church" for almost a full century. They worshiped in meetinghouses which were also the centers for social activity in the community. Town meetings were held in the local meetinghouse, munitions were stored there for defense against Indians, and townspeople from all corners of the settlement met there to debate and socialize when they came to town. The town supplied all financial support including money for the minister's salary. A burial place was started around the first meetinghouse, as had been the custom in old England.

Sudbury's first meetinghouse was built in 1643 at a cost of £6 at the site of the Old Burial Ground on Old Sudbury Road. Thirty feet long and twenty feet wide, the finished building had a thatched roof, dirt floor, and four windows. Considerable importance was given to the arrangement of seats, when these were added two years later. Seats were privately purchased and arranged according to social position and circumstance. As a general rule, men sat at one end of the pew and women at the other end. They kept their feet warm in winter by wrapping them in fur bags or by shoving them beneath the bellies of their dogs which they brought to services.

A drum beat called settlers to Sabbath meetings until the community hired its first sexton in 1654 and purchased a bell to ring the call. Religious services were conducted by the Reverend Edmund Browne who preached two hour-long sessions (measured by an hour glass placed on the pulpit), with a mid-day intermission. There was no reading of Scripture (except as preface to the sermon), no recitation of the Lord's Prayer, and no playing of musical instruments during services. These were considered "popish practices" reminiscent of the Church of England. However, the lack of instruments did not stop the congregation from singing. A literate man would stand up and loudly read the first line of an old Scottish or English tune. (All of the words to all of the songs were scriptural, at least for a while.) He would then wait for another gentleman, the human pitch-pipe, to sound the first note of the tune and hold it until the congregation joined in. Line by line, note by note, they proceeded through their songs.

In 1653, after a three-year controversy over whether to enlarge or rebuild the meetinghouse, a new one was built at the same site "on the bank by the roadside." Ten feet longer than the previous one, this meetinghouse served the community for another thirty-four years. A third meetinghouse, built in 1688, a little farther up the bank at the site marked today, was considerably more sophisticated and costly. It was square, covered with clapboards, had a hip roof, and was topped by a short bell turret. By town vote, the seating rule in this meetinghouse, with some exceptions, was determined by the amount of money a person contributed to the building costs. Pews were arranged to seat seven men on one side of the aisle and seven women on the other side.

Seemingly undaunted by the distance from their meetinghouse and mill, and their exposure to danger, but motivated by the opportunity for open land, more and more settlers moved to the west side of the river.

Within a couple of decades, they began to complain about the great distances they had to travel and the difficulties of getting to the meetinghouse during snowy winters and spring floods. Finally, on January 15, 1707 a number of west side inhabitants submitted a petition to the General Court requesting permission to build a second meetinghouse on the west side of the river. East side inhabitants filed an opposing petition. Eventually, the General Court had to appoint a committee to visit Sudbury and decide if a second meetinghouse was warranted. The Court turned down the request, but a few months later, west side inhabitants tried again. This time, they included a map that showed house locations to prove there would be enough families on both sides of the river to support two ministers. The General Court agreed and approved a second meetinghouse to be built on the west side of the river and that there be a West Precinct. For some unexplained reason, Sudbury chose not to follow the traditional rules governing "precincts," whereby each precinct is responsible for building its own meetinghouse, paying the settlement and salary of a new minister, and assuming other municipal functions. Instead, they ignored the precinct designation and continued to function as one town. Town Historian, Helen Fitch Emery, speculated: "Perhaps it was because town leaders understood that typically separations were led up to by the creation of a separate church precinct . . ."

At the same time, an alternate proposal surfaced to relocate the existing meetinghouse to a location central to both sides of the river. After much debate, this suggestion proved impractical and attention returned to finding a west side location. Six years passed, however, and a site had not been agreed upon. Frustrated, west siders petitioned the General Court to be set off as a separate township. The petition was not allowed but the Court appointed a committee to go to Sudbury and help find a location for the second meetinghouse. It took two more years before a meetinghouse was finally built on the west side in 1723. Its successor, built in 1797, still stands at the same location at the junction of Old Sudbury and Concord roads in Sudbury.

The same day, June 9, 1721, that the General Court passed orders that the west side meetinghouse be built and the east side one be repaired, another petition was presented to the Court. The petition asked that farmers and farmlands lying between Sudbury's southern boundary and Natick be included in the town. These twelve "Natick" families, as they were called, lived on land that had originally been private colonial land grants to Elizabeth Glover and Henry Dunster in 1640, and William Jennison in 1638. The twelve Natick families already had strong kinship ties to Sudbury and had no desire to join Natick, which was still an Indian town. For the town, the addition of twelve families helped to even the number of houses on the two sides of the river and add 2,141 acres of land to the much smaller land area east of the river. This is the area of Cochituate today. (see Land Grants)

At the time the General Court authorized a meetinghouse on the west side of the river, it had also ordered repairs to the east side meetinghouse. However, records and documents indicate that the Natick families had agreed to join the town only on condition that the existing meetinghouse be relocated a mile south near present day Pelham Island and Cochituate roads. When it became apparent that leadership in the town favored repairing the old meetinghouse rather than moving it south as had been promised, the

Natick families threatened to leave and return to Natick, though they had never been a part of it. As a result, the General Court was asked to intervene. In the end, it was decreed that a new meetinghouse be built in the East Precinct within eighteen months at a location one mile south of the Old Burial Ground. Although the exact completion date of the fourth meetinghouse is unknown, it was probably finished in the spring of 1726 because that year town meeting voted to hold its meetings from thence forth alternately at the west and east meetinghouses.

Israel Loring, who had served for sixteen years as the town's minister, became the minister for the new West Precinct. He began to refer to the West Precinct as the First Parish, his reason being that it had been organized six months before the East Precinct. Years later, outraged by Loring's assertion, James Sumner Draper, a well-respected public spirited citizen, reminded residents of both Sudbury and Wayland that the First Parish had a long history in the town and that the creation of a West Precinct had not caused the church on the east side to lose its identity. (see Draper, James Sumner)

In the early years of settlement, the minister, not the church, owned church records. While most ministers left their records behind, Loring took most of the books dating back to early settlement. He was known as an arrogant chauvinistic man who wanted the part of town he served to hold first place. Accordingly, the early records ended up in the West Precinct.

Many years after the fourth meeting house on the east side had been built at its new location, it was described as "a rather undistinguished, square-built structure." It had been built the same size and in the same style as the West Precinct meetinghouse and, plain as it was, it served East Sudbury for almost a century.

The fifth and final meetinghouse is a story unto itself. (see Fifth Meetinghouse)

___ ❑❑❑ _____

Mellen Law Office

Wayland's town green features one of the few surviving examples of a typical two-room law office of the early nineteenth century. This small white building which faces the Public Safety Building was built by Samuel Hale Mann in 1826. Mann, who lived across the street, practiced law in the building for four years before illness forced him to sell both the house and office to Edward Mellen.

Edward Mellen, who read law with Samuel Hoar of Concord, opened an office of his own in the building in 1831. Sixteen years later, he became justice of the Court of Common Pleas in Worcester, and, in 1855 made Chief Justice of the same court. While on the bench, Mellen often boarded in Worcester while his wife, two daughters and two sons, remained in Wayland. Four years after his appointment as Chief Justice, the court was abolished and replaced by the Superior Court. After leaving the bench, Judge Mellen opened an office in Worcester where he practiced law until illness forced him to return to Wayland in 1872. Teachers and students were freshly inspired when the Judge made school visits in town. Mellen tiptoed from seat to seat peering over shoulders to see what book lay open. A fine Latin scholar, the Judge often translated at the desks of students studying Virgil or Cicero.

Mellen was a graduate of Brown University and became friends with Dr. Wayland, president of the University. Mellen became an advocate of higher education and served on the Wayland School Committee. He also became involved in the founding of our town's library after he was asked by Dr. Wayland to accept a donation of money for town purposes. (see Library)

Mellen died in 1875 after a long illness. An example of one of the many testimonials from colleagues at his memorial service read: "His public addresses, not less than his pleas in court, were free from sophistry, and were presented in a manner that attested to the sincerity of the speaker. Court and hall were moved not by florid display, but by the power of compact logic."

Thereafter, the law office had several tenants, including another lawyer. But, its best-known tenant was the publisher of the *Village Bugle*, a small biweekly newspaper full of local news that was sent to servicemen during World War II. (see *Jeep/Village Bugle*) The *Village Bugle* sign that hung above the front door is now at the Wayland Historical Society. The building once housed a decorating business and a real estate office.

The law office remained in the possession of the Mellen family, passing through marriage of a Mellen granddaughter to the Sears family. In 1971, Sophie Bennett Sears, who lived on Pelham Island Road, donated the building to the town for the "protection and beautification of the center." The town let out bids to move the office away from an elm tree that was slowly uprooting it but keep it on the town green.

Currently, the office is the home of Wayland's Local Studies Center, an affiliate of the Wayland Historical Society. The building houses a rich collection of environmental education materials available to Wayland citizens upon request. The building is maintained by Historical Society volunteers and town employees.

ꗷꗷꗷ

Memorials and Markers

Memorials in Wayland? What memorials? Where are they? These questions may never surface but if asked, here are some answers. Most of the memorials and markers were erected in Wayland during the twentieth century. They commemorate significant events and important sites in town and, with the exception of eight Concord soldiers, memorialize Wayland people.

One of the most visible memorials marking an important event is on the lawn of the First Parish Church on the southeast corner of Boston Post (Route 20) and Cochituate roads (Route 27). It consists of two old millstones donated by Nellie Rice Fiske chairwoman of the Wayside Inn Chapter of the Daughters of the American Revolution. The bottom stone was given to her by Henry Ford when he was developing the Wayside Inn during the 1930s. It came from an old grist mill in Sudbury. Mrs. Fiske donated the upended stone with the bronze bas-relief of Washington, from the Rice Grist Mill (1750-1878) on Rice Road. As a result of a campaign by the Wayside Inn Chapter of the DAR, the Boston Post Road was designated as the George Washington Memorial Highway in 1932 commemorating the 200th

92

anniversary of Washington's birth. It is presumed that Washington traveled this route on his way to take command of the Continental Army in Cambridge in 1775. A rededication of the memorial was held in 1999 commemorating Washington's death.

Old Connecticut Path has at least five memorials or markers commemorating significant events scattered along its length through Wayland. Starting from the east where Old Connecticut Path veers to the left from the Boston Post Road at the Coach Grill restaurant, there is a marker designating this as the route of an ancient Indian trail. It was traveled by the Reverend Thomas Hooker and his Puritan flock in 1636 on their way to settle a new colony in what is now Hartford, Connecticut. Farther along, on the right in front of what was once the Reeves Tavern (see Taverns), there is a badly eroded mile marker giving the number of miles as seventeen to the Boston marker near Faneuil Hall. This marker is embedded in a low stone wall close to the road in front of the former Reeves Tavern. At the intersection of Cochituate Road and Old Connecticut Path on the southwest side, a granite stone marks the route taken by General Henry Knox on his trip to Boston from Fort Ticonderoga in the winter of 1775-1776. (see Knox Trail)

On the left of the Grout-Heard house driveway on Cochituate Road is a mile-marker "19 Miles Boston 1768" which was originally on Old Connecticut Path, perhaps near Mansion Inn. Opposite Wayland High School on Old Connecticut Path is another mile-marker, "18 miles from Boston- E. Taylor 1771." This was moved across the street from its original location near the high school entrance when the road was straightened to remove a dangerous curve.

On the lawn of the Grout-Heard house to the right of the beech trees is a large boulder with a bronze plaque: "In Commemoration of the establishment of the Town of Wayland of the First Public Library in Massachusetts and the second in the United States–August 7, 1850." Farther south along Cochituate Road in the park beside the Trinitarian Congregational Church property is a stone marker surrounded by juniper, "Center School Park–site of the Center School Grammar and High School 1896-1978."

The earliest war victims are memorialized at the site of Old Town Bridge off Old Sudbury Road, just past the entrance to the Wayland Country Club. A tall square monument carved in Acton granite sits beside the old road. On the side facing the river it reads: "Old Town Bridge - Foot Bridge and Ferry until a Cart Bridge in 1643. First frame bridge in Middlesex County. First four arch stone bridge in Massachusetts. Over this the Indians were forced in King Philip's invasion. Washington crossed here in passing through the Town." On the side facing the road it reads: "Near here are buried James Hosmer, John Barnes, Samuel Potter, Daniel Comy, Joseph Buttrick, David Curry, Josiah Wheeler, William Hayward, and others of Concord, who were slain by the Indians, April 21, 1676 while going to assist the settlers of Sudbury - erected by Wayside Inn Chapter DAR October 4, 1908."

Four World War I veterans are honored by having "Squares" named for them throughout the town. Tall metal signposts bear their names–at the intersection of Concord and Old Sudbury roads, Charles H. Alward, killed in France in 1917, was the first of the four men to die in the War. The American Legion Post, named for him, was once located at West Plain and Main streets at the current Finnerty's Restaurant site. The Joseph R. Loggia signpost is at the intersection of the Boston Post and Cochituate roads in Wayland

Center, the Albert R. Ringer at the intersection of Cochituate Road and School Street, and the Spencer Richardson near his home at the end of West Plain Street and Old Connecticut Path.

Charles Kirby Whittier was the first to lose his life in World War II. A granite obelisk in his memory stands at the intersection of Concord and Waltham roads. He served in the merchant marine in convoys across the North Atlantic. His ship was torpedoed and he was lost at sea. Fifteen other Wayland servicemen are memorialized by a bronze plaque attached to a boulder in the small park at the intersection of East Plain Street and Commonwealth Road (Route 30): "In Memoriam to those who made sacrifices for their country in World War II."

Following World War II, Wayland had two honor rolls listing all local residents who had served: one was located by the fire station and branch library in Cochituate and the other on the village green in Wayland Center dedicated on May 30, 1945. When a 1963 committee appointed by the Selectmen to update and restore the honor rolls reported they had finally determined to "erect one lasting memorial" in front of what is now the Public Safety Building, the honor rolls were retired. In their place, a monument and flagpole were dedicated on November 11, 1970 to honor all Wayland men and women who served their country. The monument and flagpole had to be removed for construction of the 2003 Public Safety Building. It was replaced by a new flagpole with a granite base upon which is carved, "In honor of the citizens of Wayland who have served their country." A large new veterans memorial honoring all who have served since the Revolutionary War will be erected in 2005 near the Wayland Town Building.

In front of the Cochituate Fire Station stands a memorial to all the firemen who lost their lives in the line of duty. The firemen of Wayland erected this to honor their heroic fire fighting comrades.

Memorials to Wayland people are scattered throughout town. The Rice Family Association placed a boulder with background information about the early ancestors on Old Connecticut Path just north of the entrance to Charena Road. The Rice homestead and Rice's Spring were nearby just off Old Connecticut Path, both shown on early maps. Deacon Edmund Rice settled in Sudbury Plantation in 1638. The boulder sits among lilac bushes at the side of the road. Another family memorial was placed in the North Cemetery on the right side of the maintenance building. It reads, "This memorial plaque is dedicated to the memory of the many Parmenters who were buried nearby in the early years of Sudbury. It is erected by the Pioneering Parmenters of North America, descendants of Deacon John Parmenter and John Parmenter Jr., two of the original founders of Sudbury. Dedicated this 27 day June 1993."

At the side of the basketball court at the high school is a stone memorial tablet to Austin S. Hale, "A friend of Youth of Wayland, 1881-1964," flanked by two benches with small brass plaques in memory of David Kelton and Neil MacLean, Wayland High School graduates who died in a tragic car accident on Stonebridge Road in 1995. In front of the Arts Building at Wayland High School is a long ornate memorial bench with a plaque for Jane Simpkin, a 1983 graduate who was killed when United Air Lines flight 173 flew into the World Trade Center on September 11, 2001. On the west side of Lake Cochituate's North Pond, a nipple of town land juts out into the lake that can be reached by following Snake Brook Trail off Commonwealth Road. A memorial bench made of split logs to which a bronze plaque is attached was placed on top of the hill by the daughters of Judy Larocque, a Wayland High School graduate who was killed when American Air Lines flight 11 hit the World Trade Center.

On the triangular plot formed by the intersection of Plain and Claypit Hill roads, locally termed a "heater piece," is a dark rock with a small bronze plaque. It honors the Reverend Edmund Hamilton Sears, a pastor of the First Parish Church. Sears wrote the words for "It Came Upon the Midnight Clear." This memorial was placed by the children of the First Parish Sunday School on December 24, 2000 near the spot where Sears once lived, in a house no longer standing.

Another "heater piece" at Glezen Lane and Training Field Road contains two stones. Near the northeast corner of the triangle the brass plaque reads: "In memory of Ephraim Curtis noted Indian Scout, First settler of Worcester 1673, son of Henry Curtis, Early Grantee of Sudbury. This marker placed here by the Curtis family of Worcester 1937." Close to the center of the triangle another stone with a brass plaque: "This half acre was part of the 8 acres plus 114 rod Sudbury Training Field - Laid out in 1714, sold in 1804 - successor to the circa 1640 Training Field. Given to the town of Wayland by Philip and Flora Donham in 1957."

A bronze sculpture of dog and sled, and an inscribed tablet honors the memory of Sarah Pryor in Cochituate's Hannah Williams playground. In 1985 while walking near her home, Sarah disappeared and an intensive search failed to find any trace of her until thirteen years later. This tragedy has been unsettling for the whole town.

At the former Mainstone Farm property on Rice Road, there is a bronze plaque honoring Paul Hamlen, who donated Hamlen Woods to the Sudbury Valley Trustees as park land. On the Traditions/Greenways land, close by the Sudbury River, there is a plaque mounted on a large stone naming the contributors who helped the Sudbury Valley Trustees purchase the property.

At the time of the Massachusetts Bay Tercentenary in 1930, annual town meeting in March voted to observe the 150th Anniversary of the separation of the town from Sudbury to East Sudbury (1780), while at the same time observing the State's Tercentenary. Wayland scheduled a number of events in celebration of the occasion. Townspeople had hoped the State would furnish several town markers, but only one was placed at that time. It is on Old Sudbury Road in front of North Cemetery. It marks the passing of three hundred years since the founding of Boston by Puritan settlers in 1630.

Mourning Rings

Two rings now in the possession of the Wayland Historical Society provide a fascinating story about a nearly forgotten eighteenth century custom and an unlikely coincidence played out in Wayland.

The story begins with the death in 1760 of Beulah Rice Bent, a woman with two well-known Wayland names. Two years after Beulah's death, her daughter, Elizabeth Bent, married Micah Rice. Two rings were in Elizabeth's possession when she married–a large gold one and a small copper alloy one, each engraved with a death head. As was the custom in those days, these gloomy ornaments were given to all the chief mourners at funerals and nearly all people of any social of standing had one. One of these rings may have originally belonged to her father, Hopestill Bent, husband of the deceased, who later operated the Bent Tavern in his home on Old Connecticut Path now located just east of the present Wayland Town Pool.

Elizabeth Rice's daughter, Levinah, married Joseph Rutter, whose farmhouse on Bow Road stood about where 27 Bow Road is now. This old place had been in the Rutter family descending from father to son through successive generations from John Rutter, carpenter, who came from England in 1638. Eunice Rutter, their daughter, took the rings out to the barn to play and lost them in the hay. The family helped her search for them but only one was found.

Over the years, the farm changed owners twice more until Leonard Drury bought it. Drury's daughter, Emma, born in 1844, wore a strange ring to school one day. Emma stayed after school to do some blackboard work. Her teacher, Lydia Rutter Draper, immediately noticed it and asked where it had come from The story was that this ring was found in the soil of a garden planted where the Bow Road barn, now removed, used to be.

Lydia said that it matched one her mother, Eunice, owned and sometimes wore. She had been told that her mother had lost the mate to it in the barn on Bow Road when she was a child. Since this was where Emma Drury now lived, it appeared to be the very same ring which Lydia's mother had lost and could not find. Emma was persuaded to accept a new, prettier ring in exchange for the older more gruesome one.

The telling of the story of these rings came first from Lydia Rutter Draper. She returned to her native town of Wayland in 1860 and became the teacher of the High School where Emma Drury was a pupil. Later in life after she had married Alfred Sereno Hudson, author of *The History of Sudbury, Massachusetts. 1638-1889* and *The Annals of Sudbury, Wayland and Maynard. Middlesex County, Mass.*, 1891, Lydia wrote:

> "One day Emma Drury stopped after school to work on the blackboard.
> As she reached her hand up on the board from the place where I was
> sitting, I noticed a ring with a skull on it, the facsimile of one my
> mother sometimes wore and the mate to which she had told me was
> lost in the barn. In an instant I had crossed the room and seizing it
> almost frantically took and claimed it as my own. She then told me
> the history. . . and how she had worn it to school that day for sport;
> but as it was no heirloom to her, she was quite willing to exchange
> it…and this is how after sixty years more or less the ring came
> again to its rightful owner."

In 1963, John Rutter Draper of Auburndale donated the mourning rings to the Wayland Historical Society where they are on display from time to time.

N

Native American Arrowheads

Native Americans

If you lived in Sudbury Plantation when it was first settled, you might have met up with the Indian Karto (Cato, Karte) while hiking up Goodman's Hill on the west side of the river. If the hill had an Indian name at the time, settlers were unaware of it, so when Karto took the English name Goodman, it became "Goodman's Hill." A little to the south and west of Goodman's Hill, on Nobscot Hill, lived Tantamous, later called Old Jethro, with about twelve family members. The Indian name for the hill, "Place of the Fallen Rock," describes the many jagged boulders that have fallen from the summit. Old Jethro probably belonged to the Nipmuck tribe and Karto to the Massachusetts Indians.

It appeared that no tribe claimed the area as its own for permanent settlement and that the rich resources of the river valley were shared by a number of different tribes. Wampanoags came from Cape Cod in the south, Massachusetts Indians came from Boston in the east, Pawtuckets came from New Hampshire in the north and Nipmucks came from Connecticut and Worcester to the west. Tribes made seasonal camps along the Sudbury River, Lake Cochituate, and the area's many ponds and streams. The rich diversity of the area offered ample fishing sites, rich soil for planting and open forest with good browsing for game. The combination of meadow, field and forest attracted hundreds of species of birds.

Early records show that relations between the local Indians and the Sudbury settlers were reasonably peaceful thanks to the mutual respect between Karto, Tantamous, and the Sudbury Plantation petitioners. While England claimed the country by right of discovery, there were those who held it by right of ancient hereditary possession. Therefore, claim for land was considered valid after negotiating with the Indians.

The General Court of Massachusetts granted petitioners "five square miles astride the river," but Peter Noyes, Edmund Browne, and Brian Pendleton also purchased it from Karto. Karto sought the advice of Tahattawan who had sold land to Concord settlers in 1635. In exchange for land, Karto requested "five coats, five wastcoats, five shirts, five payre of stokins, five payre of shoes, five hatchets, five houghes, five knives, five pounds of tobacco, and tenne fandome of wampum pege. . . "

In 1649, when the petitioners asked Karto to sell more land, he granted them additional land for £5. It is said that he watched Englishmen scratch broad flowing symbols on the paper. Then, he took the pen in hand and affixed his own signature. It was a carefully-drawn four-legged animal lying on his back with his feet waving in the air. The deed was filed and registered in the Suffolk Registry of Deeds in Boston.

Local Indians taught Sudbury settlers how to weave long nets, or weirs, across the river to catch many fish at a time; to clear forest underbrush to hunt game; and when farming "to watch the rhythms of the seasons." They advised, "When the leaves of the oak tree are the size of a mouse ear, it is time to plant corn."

Indians, in turn, learned to attend church and some of them even converted to Christianity. Karto apparently converted after hearing a sermon given by the Reverend Edmund Browne in the First Parish

Meeting House at the Old Burial Ground. Old Jethro never did convert, but his son Peter, or Young Jethro, became one of the praying Indians who went to live in Natick.

We know from archaeological excavations that have been carried out in town and from the hundreds of stone artifacts that have turned up on various properties, that a variety of people had lived in the region for thousands of years before even Karto and Tantamous. Between Dudley Pond and Lake Cochituate, a cemetery and a stone-lined crematory three to four thousand years old were unearthed in 1959 during excavation for a housing development. (see Simpson Estate/Mansion Inn)

On the north side of town, near Sherman Bridge Road, Archaic Period People camped along Glacial Lake Sudbury and left behind artifacts and stone flakes that are 8,000 years old. Prehistoric people also camped along the river, near the landfill, and left behind evidence of occupation 6-8,000 years ago.

Today, we walk many of the same footpaths traveled by Jethro, Goodman, Tantamous and earlier peoples who trekked through town on hunting and fishing expeditions. Some of their paths are paved over today, but many are not. Others appear as vague tracks or even mounds in the grass of our own back yards.

Old Green Store/Kirkside

Odd Fellows Lodge

On the south side of the Trinitarian Congregational Church on Cochituate Road stands the old Odd Fellows Lodge, a lovely old historic building belonging to the church. The building, originally constructed in 1855, served as the town's high school before it was purchased by members of Wayland's Odd Fellows.

But who are the Odd Fellows? Sources record a number of different reasons for the name, but one history explains: "In seventeenth century England, it was odd to find people organized for the purpose of giving aid to those in need and/or for the benefit of all mankind. Those who belonged to such an organization were called Odd Fellows. Odd Fellows–known as the "Three Link Fraternity"–stands for Friendship, Love and Truth.

It is not surprising that such men resided in Wayland. The Odd Fellows had organized in 1894 and wanted a lodge of their own. When the town sought to replace its first high school with a new Center School, the Odd Fellows of Wayland offered to buy the building for $200. There was only one catch–the town fathers wanted to place the new Center School between two large oak trees on Cochituate Road. To do so meant that the Odd Fellows had to have the old school moved a little bit north. Undaunted, they agreed. The move placed their new headquarters at its present location closer to the Trinitarian Congregational Church.

John Bryant, a member of the Wayland Odd Fellows remembers when the group met to organize a baseball team that drew members from Wayland, Cochituate and surrounding towns. For this farming community, the lodge provided a place for men to meet and socialize. Members have met in Wellesley since the Odd Fellows Lodge was sold in 1964. The 1897 Center School that stood beside the Odd Fellows Lodge was torn down in 1978 and the site was converted to a park.

Old Green Store/Kirkside

It is difficult today to imagine the elegant residence next to the First Parish Church at 221 Boston Post Road as having started out as a simple two-story combination store-residence-public meeting hall in 1815.

When the town needed a hall to hold public meetings in 1815, after it was decided that the fifth meetinghouse would be used only for religious purposes, town fathers contracted with Luther Gleason Sr. and Jonathan Fiske Heard to dismantle the fourth meetinghouse, built in 1726, and rebuild next to the fifth meetinghouse. (see Fifth Meetinghouse)

On June 5, 1815, Town Meeting voted: "Messrs. Gleason & Heard offers in consideration of the Old Meeting house, excepting the Pews, to furnish the town of East Sudbury with a Hall finished to the acceptance of the town committee for the time of thirty-five years the town to improve said Hall at all times when requested by the Selectmen of the town of East Sudbury for the purposes of transacting town business, for a singing school and for the choice of Militia officers for May inspection and any other Public Town Business free of expense to the town or any Individual."

The result was a two-story hip-roof five-bay Federal style building with a dry goods store and living quarters on the ground floor and a meeting room with a separate entrance on the second floor. Although the fourth meetinghouse had never been painted, Gleason's and Heard's new building was painted green. It would not be confused with the Old Red Store near the railroad station owned by Newell Heard. The 20 x 40-foot meeting room on the second floor had high ceilings with coved molding all around. Two fireplaces on inside walls provided the first heated public meeting space. In addition to town functions, the room was a popular place to hold dances and rehearse the First Parish choir. The floor had been built on arches which gave it "spring" for dancing. When the Reverend Edmund Sears wrote "It Came Upon a Midnight Clear" in 1849, choir members rehearsed in the meeting room.

For the next twenty-five years town meetings were held upstairs in what would be called the "Old Green Store." The town built its first town hall in 1841–the white-columned Greek Revival building at 21 Cochituate Road which many old timers still call Collins Market. Slowly the Old Green store became a dilapidated, run down tenement that spoiled the appearance of town center. In 1888, Heard sold the Old Green Store to Willard Austin Bullard and a year later sold him the Pequod Inn. Horace Heard was one of the center's largest property owners. Bullard was the son of Joseph and Harriet Loker Bullard who lived on land that is now part of Sandy Burr Country Club. Willard Austin Bullard (1837-1912) was president of the First National Bank of Cambridge (later the Harvard Trust Company) and lived in Cambridge. He purchased the Old Green Store as a country residence, remodeled it and christened it "Kirkside"–beside the church. By then, three elm trees graced the outside lawn and a dozen of their cousins surrounded the church–planted some years earlier by Deacon James Draper. The Bullards remodeled the exterior in the Colonial Revival style adding porticos and dormers and rearranging the downstairs spaces. They papered the great sweep of upstairs walls in rare mural wallpaper from Zuber of France. The wallpaper, called "Les Zones Terrestres" (the terrestrial zones) depicted scenes from around the world. It has been enjoyed by occupants ever since the Bullards installed it and remains intact. The Bullards also papered the downstairs dining room in another rare French wallpaper manufactured by Joseph Dufour, a rival of Zuber. It is titled "Le Bresil"and depicts birds and tropical vegetation. This wallpaper is also still intact. After his death in 1912 the family maintained Kirkside as their permanent residence.

Mr. and Mrs. William C. Loring purchased Kirkside in 1920 and shifted the driveway from the east side of the house to the west. They took great pride in the beauty and antiquity of the house. Mildred Loring, a nationally-known antique dealer, converted the upstairs meeting room into a sales room for antiques. Henry Ford visited Mrs. Loring's showroom when he was building the Wayside Inn and fell in love with the great forty-foot sweep of the meeting room. He was so impressed with it that he had it duplicated, sans wallpaper, upstairs in the Wayside Inn. Mr. Loring, a portrait painter, taught at the Rhode Island School of Design and built an art studio for himself behind Kirkside. He painted a portrait in his dining room of Mary Adams Heard, a life-long resident of Pelham Island who was active in the community and the First Parish Church. The portrait is at the Rhode Island School of Design.

The Lorings sold Kirkside in 1937 to sisters Helene L. Hobbs and Mildred H. Emerson. Hobbs, an antique dealer, worked with the Emersons for fifteen years making further improvements to the house. They bought pumpkin pine from a house in Vermont to panel their den, built a porch from hand-hewn timbers from an old barn in Maine and installed all white steel kitchen cabinets with stainless tops. Antiques filled every room, silk and velvet draperies covered the dining and upstairs meeting room windows, and an oversized 17 x 35 foot Oriental rug covered the floor in the meeting room. Mrs. Emerson also added Irish Waterford crystal lamp sconces in the meeting room.

The Emersons sold Kirkside in 1950 to the Vinsonhalers. Mrs. Vinsonhaler was a southern lady who loved gardening and laid out vegetable and flower gardens behind the house. On the south side she harvested raspberries which she sold for thirty-five cents a basket each year at a Weston grocery store. The Vinsonhalers were sociable people who loved to entertain in the large meeting room. They often hired a small orchestra, rolled up the Oriental rug they had purchased from the Emersons and danced to candlelight from the crystal lamps. While taking loving care of Kirkside, the Vinsonhalers raised two daughters in the house.

The Vinsonhalers sold Kirkside in the early 1970s to the Chase family who sold it to Leonard and Virginia Hagger in 1975. The Haggers, parents of the present homeowners, fell in love with Kirkside and bought it even though their two grown sons no longer lived at home. In 1985 Chris Hagger, the younger son, was married in the First Parish Church next door to Kirkside. Chris and his wife Joan inherited the house in 1989. "This Old House," of Public Broadcasting Service (PBS) fame, selected Kirkside for the main project of their thirteenth season in 1991. Millions of viewers watched the restoration go forward on television, but none enjoyed it more than those who live in Wayland.

1771 Pequod House

Jonathan M. Parmenter

Jonathan Maynard Parmenter was a typical Yankee farmer, cattle dealer, good citizen, and the greatest benefactor the town ever had. As a native son, born in 1831 when Andrew Jackson was president, he was a familiar sight in town for generations, riding in his old buggy or driving a herd of cows along dirt roads. When he died on January 11, 1921, there was much regret that this short, wiry, soft-spoken man, liked and respected by all, was gone. After all, there had been Parmenters in the plain white farmhouse on the corner of Concord and Bow roads as long as a man could remember. However, there was nothing remarkable about J.M. Parmenter until the neighbors learned that his will had been filed for probate listing the value of his estate at $1,500,000.

Parmenter's wealth and legacies amazed the town when they became known. A week after his death when his neighbors learned that he had been a millionaire, the burning question was, "How did he get it? The answer invariably was, "Don't know, but not from cows, you can bet!" That was only partly true, because certainly cows explained the start of his fortune.

Jonathan and his brother Henry Dana were descendants of John Parmenter, Sr., a deacon of the Sudbury church and one of the early selectmen. Their farm had descended from father to son for eight generations, with no deed recorded. As young men, the bachelor brothers began to operate as partners in the cattle and dairy business. Cattle dealing was not merely a way to make a living but was the major enthusiasm of their lives. In 1880, the brothers owned 160 acres of farmland with a larger-than-usual amount of river meadow. The 1883 Wayland Valuation List indicates they had the largest herd of dairy cattle with sixty-seven head. As soon as the Massachusetts Central Railroad began operating, milk could be shipped from here to Boston via rail. By 1885, Wayland's reported milk production had more than doubled that of 1880.

As the Parmenter herd grew and Wayland pasturage proved insufficient, the brothers purchased many acres of grazing land in Troy, New Hampshire. In spring, they bought up cattle around the Wayland area and drove them to Troy to graze for the summer on "good grass near clear springs and cool mountains." All along the route, when the rolling, drifting curtains of brown dust was sighted, farmers quit their plows, wives left churns and wash tubs and the children swarmed from every direction to watch the herd plod by. The Framingham gazette of May 19, 1876, noted that:

> "The annual migration of cattle from this region to South
> New Hampshire came off this week. Maynard Parmenter
> was up and on his way with 80 head this morning."

In the fall, the same cattle, grown plump from months of grazing on New Hampshire pasturage, returned over the same route. The Parmenters occasionally sold some of their cattle on the way home, either as beef cattle or milkers. They did not mind the prolonged bargaining and, indeed, would have felt cheated without the dickering, particularly when it concerned cows.

Even after the cattle business became a success, nothing about the Parmenters suggested that they were any wealthier than their neighbors. The family home lacked a good many modern conveniences. They were not misers but merely lived according to the traditional way of a New England farmer. This meant rising at five, going to bed at nine, and tending strictly to business in the hours between.

Through the years, only one man knew the extent and growth of the Parmenter wealth. He was summer resident Willard A. Bullard, president of the First National Bank of Cambridge located in Central Square across the Charles River from the Brighton stockyards. The Parmenter brothers would sell their cattle at the stockyards, cross the Charles River to deposit the day's receipts in the First National Bank, which in 1904 became the Harvard Trust Company, and then visit with their friend Willard Bullard.

In the mid 1880s, a few New England cotton mills were moving to the South. When the Wellington-Sears Co. of Boston planned to launch some mills in that region, Bullard proposed to the Parmenters that they put some of their savings into the venture. The brothers took plenty of time to weigh the risks and ponder the wisdom of this "flyer in the market." Perhaps because Wellington was a friend of banker Bullard, whom they trusted, and also because they had known Sears for many years in neighboring Weston, they followed Bullard's advice and put $10,000 of their money into the southern mill project.

Earnings soon piled up as the mills prospered. With Bullard's guidance, the Parmenters reinvested in more stocks, bonds, real estate and mortgages. The brothers did not change as their wealth accumulated and no one in town suspected they were wealthy. Although both men wore fine clothes on special occasions, they never thought to dress up when they went to deposit money in the bank. The story is told of how Jonathan entered Harvard Trust in his badly worn work clothes with cow manure on his shoes, sat down on a bench, opened a paper bag and started to eat his sandwiches. The startled teller ran to report this to banker Bullard who took one look and said, "Oh, that's Jonathan Parmenter. Why, he *owns* the bank!"

When Henry died in 1907, Jonathan was sole heir of his brother's estate. Jonathan made a gift of the parsonage at the First Parish Church in his brother's memory–a modest and appropriate tribute from a brother who was pretty well fixed and had no family to provide for. Jonathan showed no outward signs of wealth–his office remained under his hat, his transportation a dusty buggy and ambling horse.

Since Parmenter had grown to depend on the advice of his close friend Willard Bullard, after Bullard's death, he naturally turned to his successor, Walter F. Earle. With Earle's prudent advice and Jonathan's native shrewdness, Parmenter became a millionaire. During the last ten years of his life, Parmenter began to worry about what to do with all his money. Earle's concern with public welfare influenced Parmenter in disposing of his fortune for the benefit of Wayland and humanity in general. Together, they drew up a will that fulfilled Jonathan's wishes.

In 1921, when Jonathan Maynard Parmenter died, the Harvard Trust Company became executor and trustee of his estate. Before making any public legacies, Parmenter took care of family members. Nine cousins were willed $25,000 each, some receiving land or real estate in addition, with lesser amounts for their children. Bequests were also made to Wayland men and women who, because of friendship or loyal service, had a claim on his affections. As proof of lasting gratitude to his first financial adviser, Jonathan left $25,000 to the widow of Willard Bullard.

Parmenter left $7,000 to the First Parish Church, the income to be used for church expenses; $5,000 for upkeep of the Parmenter family cemetery, and for the care of other cemeteries as well; and

$10,000 to be used in the same way by the library. He allotted, and later increased, bequests for the assistance of needy students, preferably residents of Wayland to Radcliffe and Harvard colleges. In memory of his mother and sister, he left two $5,000 scholarships, to Radcliffe College, and to Harvard College, he left $200,000 in securities which were to be held in trust and the income used for scholarships.

A Parmenter bequest of $225,000 was to be held and expended by the Harvard Trust Company for the installation of a water supply system for part of Wayland. (see Water Works) Also made was a bequest of $200,000 with which the same trustees should establish a hospital in Wayland or its vicinity. The bank became totally involved with installation of the water supply system, which took little more than a year to construct and was completed within the amount specified in Parmenter's will. The system began operation in 1928 and the bank turned over to the town a $17,500 balance for future use.

Jonathan Parmenter's wishes to build a local hospital proved more difficult. At the time, there was no clear need for a hospital. The town was small and residents were receiving good care in hospitals in nearby cities and towns. In addition, economic conditions made it an increasingly doubtful venture. Hospital experts advised against building a hospital with the funds available even though the original $200,000 continued to grow. In the 1950s, the idea of a community health center developed and that appealed to many people. Rather than build a hospital, it was decided to distribute $90,000 among five hospitals in adjoining communities and build a health center instead of a hospital in Wayland. An agreement was reached, presented to the Probate Court, and approved. Suitable land was acquired at 266 Cochituate Road in 1953, and an attractive $165,000 brick building opened in 1954. There was even enough money left to produce sufficient income to pay the operating expenses of the center. In spite of the expense of building and operating the center, and the added $90,000 given outside hospitals, the market value of the investment remaining at the end of 1959 was $811,650.

Since that time, Parmenter Health Center has provided a range of clinics and community education programs as well as visiting nurse services. The enactment of Medicare and Medicaid in the mid 1960s reduced the need for care through clinics and Parmenter became primarily a home care agency. The Center's ongoing commitment to the community is demonstrated through contracts with Boards of Health, operation of a Pantry Program for Wayland, establishment of Wayside Hospice and most recently development of a new Adult Day Health Program and a residential hospice. Today, Parmenter's primary source of income is reimbursement by Medicare and private insurers. Their mission is to provide care regardless of ability to pay. Insurance often does not cover the full cost of health care. Although it is expected that the Center will continue to operate at a loss, plans are being made to make up differences through annual fund-raising events and to grow the current $600,000 endowment to $5 million over the next several years.

Harvard Trust Company reported in 1960 that thirteen hundred Harvard students had received scholarship aid and forty-six Radcliffe women had received help from the Parmenter scholarship fund. The Parmenters $200,000 bequest in securities for scholarships for Harvard students, known as the Henry D. Parmenter and Jonathan M. Parmenter Scholarship Fund, is currently held in trust at Fleet Bank (soon-to-be Bank America) and in May 2004 the value of the fund was $2,010,448.60. It is managed by the Cambridge Community Foundation. One hundred percent of the net income, or the estimated annual income, is distributed twice per year in June and December. In May 2004 the distribution was $37,398.37. The Foundation does not handle scholarship awards, which are done by Harvard.

Since "it is the internal policy and practice of Harvard University not to release any information regarding our donors or the funds they have established to a third part," it is not possible to update any of the information regarding how many scholarships have been awarded since 1960, nor is it possible to establish the current value of Parmenter's $10,000 bequest to Radcliffe.

When told how fast his fortune was growing before he died, Jonathan Parmenter told his banker with a chuckle, "Won't the people of Wayland be surprised when they find out?" They were and some still are!

❏❏❏

Pequod House

Imagine an old four-horse yellow stage coach pulling up in front of the Pequod House, a famous tavern in the center of town where the Public Safety Building now stands. As a relic of stage-coaching days, the Pequod House was one of the favorite inns on the route from Sudbury to Stony Brook in Weston. The arrival of a coach bringing mail, passengers and supplies was the big event of the day as townsfolk gathered to greet it. This landmark occupied one of the most prominent sites in a town which was named Sudbury when the inn was built by Elijah Bent in 1771 and continued to provide refreshment to travelers after the name of the town changed to East Sudbury in 1780. It was still the principal gathering place for the discussion of politics, religion, crops and livestock in 1835 after the town was renamed Wayland. Eventually, the hostelry was called the Wayland Inn. For many years an old sign, reading "Pequod House," hung from the limb of a large tree in front of the building. By 1928 when the Wayland Inn was razed, the sign had become idle, worthless and somewhat unsightly.

The original Pequod House was two stories high and had a lean-to at the back. A third story was added in 1825. A three-sided verandah was a prominent feature of the building. The inn had about thirty rooms. The original part of the building had a barroom with a large open fireplace. Beside the fireplace was always a large pile of oversized logs to aid in warming the wayfarer who stopped at the inn. The atmosphere was homelike and comfortable.

Extending down the north side of the inn was a long open ended drive-through barn where farmers and market men sheltered their wagons when putting up at the inn overnight. Side stalls held the teams of horses out of the way. To swell the wheels and tighten the tires farmers drove their wagons through Mill Brook which ran alongside the inn. The powder wagon from the Acton powder mill made regular trips to Wayland and occasionally parked at the inn for the night, fully laden with explosives. It is said that the tavern guests and everybody in the neighborhood rested uneasily until the powder wagon was safely on its way in the morning.

112

The town watering trough and pump were located in front of the inn on Cochituate Road. Across the street where the Mellen Law Office now stands, the town pound held stray livestock until retrieved by their owners. Across the Boston Post Road was the Old Green Store and First Parish Church. Because there was no heat in the church and parishioners were required to attend both a morning and afternoon session, men left at noon and hurried across the road to warm up and renew the live coals in their foot warmers.

In the earliest days, the "cup that cheers" was served openly at the inn. As time went on and the town became "dry," the inn continued to do a good business. Folks say it was always possible to procure the desired kinds of beverages at the inn.

A little more than a hundred years after the Pequod House was built, the first train came through town on the Massachusetts Central Railroad. Inevitably, even though horses were still the main mode of transportation, the local community around the inn slowly changed. Horace Heard, who in 1880 was one of the town's fifteen top taxpayers, listed his occupation as a farmer. Yet, he is listed as one of the largest real estate owners in town. From 1828-1880 he owned the Old Green Store across the Boston Post Road and was listed as owner of the inn in 1850. Heard sold the Old Green Store to Willard A. Bullard in 1888 who remodeled it into a handsome residence. (see Old Green Store/Kirkside)

The inn had a series of owners until 1920 when it was purchased by trustees Edmund H. Sears, Walter B. Henderson and J. Sidney Stone with financial aid from Edwin F. Greene, Charles A. Phipps, Wallace S. Draper, and Francis Shaw. An elaborate deed of trust was executed with the above-named men as trustees. Money was raised to pay the taxes, cover repairs, and clear the mortgage. The deed stipulated that the land would ultimately go to the town as a site for a new town hall.

After considering use of the inn as a teacher's lodge or a community house, it became apparent that it had outlived its usefulness and the trustees decided to have the structure torn down. The trustees offered the land and the parcel behind it, donated by Edmund Sears as a permanent gift to the town, to be used for park purposes until a town hall could be built. The town accepted the land from the trustees in 1927.

Demolition of the inn revealed that all of the timbers in the structure were rough-hewn with ax and adz. Some of the floor boards were twenty-eight inches wide and cut out with old-fashioned up and down saws. All spikes and nails were hand-forged. Much of the brick used in the chimneys, fireplaces and foundations, had been brought over from England in trading ships as ballast. The bricks were purchased by Henry Ford and used in the Wayside Inn in Sudbury. The fine old doors, rare paneling, and odd bits of original wood found their way into the hands of few local homeowners. When the large post in the dining room was ripped out by workmen, a secret compartment with shelves cut into the post was discovered. After the old timbers and ancient clapboards were carted away, the site was leveled. During World War II, an enclosure was built around the site and people were encouraged to leave metal or rubber scrap to be recycled for the war effort. Nearly seven tons were salvaged in this way.

113

Town meeting eventually voted funds to build a municipal building on the site which was ready for occupancy in September 1957. Twenty-one years later, only police and fire departments remained in the building after municipal operations moved to the vacated 1935 High School at the southwest corner of the intersection of Boston Post and Cochituate roads. (see Public Safety) The police and fire departments remain at the old location, but with a greatly expanded facility.

Perambulation

Perambulation is the process by which government officials check the location and condition of those markers that identify and designate the boundaries of cities and towns. Perhaps the earliest perambulation was made by John Goodenow and recorded in 1640. (Colony Records, Vol. IV, p. 53.)

"The committee appointed to lay out the Watertown and Sudbury boundary report that the line drawn by John Oliver three years previous called the old line shall be the line between the two towns and forever stand. This line, beginning at Concord south bound, ran through a great pine swamp, a small piece of meadow to upland, and then to an angle betwixt two hills. After the line left the aforesaid angle on its southerly course, it had these remarkable places therein: One rock called Grout's head, and a stake by the cartway leading from Sudbury to Watertown, and so to a pine hill being short of a pond about eighty-eight rods, at which pine hill Sudbury bounds ends."

Many handwritten reports of perambulations from the 1780s through to the 1850s have been preserved in their original form and are archived at the Wayland Historical Society. Some include neat line-drawn maps indicating a line from, "the fallen hemlock tree, thirteen rods to the standing white oak." By the 1830s, however, selectmen no longer used trees as boundary markers but referred instead to "stone" monuments.

Wayland's boundaries with its five neighbors are marked by fifty-seven granite monuments of varying sizes–from four inches by four inches to twenty-four inches by twenty- four inches. One is eight inches by sixteen inches. All of the monuments have either a W for Wayland or ES for East Sudbury, carved on one side and the first letter of the neighboring town on the other. The S seemed to cause a lot of grief to the stone cutters, and was occasionally carved backwards. One huge stone, very rough in shape, lies at the point where Wayland, Natick and Weston meet, off Mainstone Road and resembles something from Mayan or Aztec regions. Some stones are under water during the spring floods, and many lie in swampy areas. Snow plows have broken several stones over the years. When the sand hill on Route 20 was partially removed in the 1950s for sand and gravel, several stones were temporarily "lost." One of the replacements lies in the play area of the Longfellow outdoor swimming pool! On the bluff behind Longfellow is one of the most handsome monuments, unusually large and beautifully cut and finished. It marks a corner of that peculiar piece of Sudbury that juts into Wayland like a hernia. Blame farmer Wheeler who didn't want to live in East Sudbury. (see Separate Towns)

114

In the 1970 Town Report the following perambulation was reported: "In accordance with the state law the selectmen made their quinquennial perambulation of the town bounds. Some of the markers are missing on the Wayland-Sudbury line and on the Natick-Wayland line. The others are mostly in place, although a few of them are leaning at a severe angle which is to be expected after nearly 70 years in marshy land. A five-year program with the bordering communities will be undertaken to take care of the deficiencies."

Perambulation continues to be carried out every five years by two of the selectmen of the town or by two substitutes designated by them in writing. In Wayland, two town surveyors meet with selectmen, or their designates, from towns that share a common boundary: Sudbury, Framingham, Natick, Weston, or Lincoln. Not every town boundary is done at one time, usually one boundary at a time. Numerals are painted on the side of the monument indicating the year of the survey. Some Wayland markers still show as many as five dates.

The Wayland Surveying Department visited all monuments in 2000 and recorded their condition and photographed all of them, including some very difficult markers in the Sudbury River. They would be happy to show visitors their record.

❏❏❏

Public Safety

In the early years, local residents took responsibility for public safety. When a fire broke out, every available hand showed up, grabbed a bucket, and helped douse the fire. Their efforts probably did some good, but few establishments were saved in this way. The real problems arose when the village of Cochituate moved from farming to shoe manufacturing in the mid nineteenth century and huge wooden factories began to dominate the village. Without running water volunteers could do little to protect multistoried factories, stores, and homes during a fire. With the advent of the first waterworks installed in Cochituate in 1878, two volunteer fire departments were formed and a fire house built at Main and Maple streets. At the time, a system of privately-organized volunteer fire departments had evolved around the country and Cochituate obviously followed that pattern. After hoses, hooks and ladders, and man-drawn carts had been purchased, the James M. Bent Hose Company and the Charles H. Boodey Hook and Ladder Company were organized. A year later, the two companies celebrated their first anniversary with a parade and a competition of "speed trials." With the hose carriage pulled by a team of men, the Charles H. Boodey Hook and Ladder Co. No. 1 ran a quarter of a mile, spliced ladders, and put a man on a roof in two minutes and ten seconds. The James M. Bent Hose Company No. 1 ran a quarter of a mile, laid 150 feet of hose, and put a stream of water on a roof in one minute and fifty seconds.

The firemen's ball was a popular social event and fund-raiser held during Thanksgiving and Christmas in the 1880s and 1890s to help support the various activities. The 1878 firehouse built on the east side of Main Street was moved in 1882 to the south side of Harrison Street.

The north and central part of town waited another thirty years for an alternative to the "bucket brigade" to fight fires. In 1908 they purchased a truck designated to dispense firefighting chemicals. Up until that time, town meeting had only discussed fire protection for this part of town because there was no public water supply.

When Jonathan Maynard Parmenter died in 1921 leaving $225,000 to build a water system for the north and central parts of town, genuine firefighting equipment could be purchased and a viable but still volunteer fire department established. (see Water Works) Twenty years later, the department was still run by a volunteer crew of thirty-five call men who received eighty-three cents an hour for answering alarms. Alarms were called in on phones that had to be cranked to reach an operator. Operators generally knew the whereabouts of volunteer firemen.

The old Cochituate firehouse on Harrison Street was demolished in 1953 after the town built a new brick firehouse on the northeast corner of Main and East Plain streets, where it remains today. Three years later, town meeting approved funds to build a municipal building on the north side of town on land acquired for this purpose some thirty years earlier. (see Pequod House) Located on the northeast corner at the intersection of the Boston Post and Cochituate roads, it was designed to house Wayland's town offices, the police department and the center's division of the fire department (Station One). In 1957, this new town building was ready for occupancy and town meeting voted to demolish the 1878 town hall.

The first full-time professional firefighters joined the Wayland force in 1956: two at the Cochituate Station and two at the Wayland station located at the back of the 1878 town hall. Twenty-three years later, the force numbered twenty-five full-time firemen, the department owned a rescue ambulance, and the town had been wired for fire alarm boxes.

In 1974, a town-approved municipal planning committee recommended that municipal operations with the exception of the fire and police departments, be relocated to the recently vacated 1935 High School at the southwest corner of the intersection of the Boston Post and Cochituate roads. The relocation would give the fire and police departments breathing room in the old town hall building and create much-needed space for various town offices, including the school department, in the renovated high school building.

In earlier times, town officials and local committees, rather than police, dealt with petty thievery and cheating. Town records reveal that in 1651 stocks–wooden frames that held a person's head and hands in place while they stood for public viewing and ridicule in front of the meetinghouse–were used for punishment. Records reveal that in 1773 the town chose a committee "to consider and report what is proper to be done in order to suppress that set of men in this town, who make it their business to trade with and cheat strangers." The committee later submitted the names of those who "go about the country and cheat honest men by purchasing horses, cattle and other effects, by telling fair stories, and promising short pay, should be published in several newspapers, that the Public may be cautioned against trading with or trusting them on any account." The Town Clerk then sent the names to several printers in Boston "to be printed for the benefit of the public."

All through the nineteenth century, town officials dealt with drunkenness. Taverns had sprung up

116

all over town and citizens needed protection from unruly drunks. In the north side of town, drunks were placed in a "lock-up" in the basement of the town hall. In Cochituate, which became a magnet for immigrants looking for work, workers seeking relaxation, and transients looking for adventure or a place to settle, town officials had to build a "lock up" on the south side of Harrison Street to accommodate them overnight. The overseers of the poor took responsibility for their care. (see Almshouse/Poor Farm)

Eventually, a Police Chief had to be employed to enforce law and order. From 1917 to 1952, Chief Ernest Damon was the only full-time policeman in town. An influx of new residents caused the town's population to double in the decade of the fifties and the number of police employees increased to eleven full-timers. By 1988, the number of full-time police employees numbered twenty-five.

By 2004, the police department employed twenty-one male and one female full-time sworn officers, one part-time officer, and one female detective. Seven male and one female civilian dispatchers handle both police and fire department calls and one full-time female administrator assists the police chief, along with one female part-time intern. There are twenty members of the Wayland Police Auxiliary, a volunteer organization of individuals with an interest in law enforcement. There are several women in this group. The department has had other females in the past, and future hiring will come from the Civil Service list which includes both male and female applicants.

Today, the Police and Fire Departments, along with a Joint Communications Center, remain at the old site, but in a new 26,000 square foot building. The $7,600,000 Public Safety Building was dedicated on August 7, 2003. It features a state-of-the-art training room and Emergency Operations center that is also used as a community room for meetings of town government and local organizations.

2

Tower Hill Depot 1915

Beaver Hole Meadow - A meadow in the southwest part of Wayland once inhabited by beaver. In colonial times, the right to catch beaver was sold to individuals by public authority. By the end of the eighteenth century few beaver remained in the river meadows.

Bee Hive - A building located on the corner of Winter and Willard streets in Cochituate until 1891. The Bent Shoe Company used the Bee Hive to house shoe workers' families. In June 1885 the *Natick Bulletin* reported: "The tenement house known as the 'Bee Hive' has five families with thirty children. There are eighteen children in the two families that occupy the lower floor." Whether the house was occupied by factory workers or children, the image of a bee hive applied. The Bent shoe factory, located on the southwest corner of Main Street and Commonwealth Road, was in full swing in the village. French-Canadian factory workers swarmed in and out of the building on a daily basis. When it became vacant, Bent Bros. moved it to their new and by then only shoe shop in the Lyon shoe building. Noble Griffin later purchased this factory on the west side of Main Street beside the Cochituate School, as well as the Bee Hive.

Bentville and Lokerville - Up to the mid 1840s, the name "Cochituate" was not used but instead the area was referred to as "the south side of town." It consisted of two clusters of houses and several public buildings. Bentville was the area centered on the present corner of Main Street and Commonwealth Road, running north to the intersection with Plain Street. It was lined with dwellings, shoe shops, and stores. It was named for the family that was taking the lead in developing the shoe industry. Lokerville was another cluster of buildings located a half-mile to the east at the junction of East Plain Street and Commonwealth Road. It was named for Loker families who lived in that area. Both "villes" later became known as Cochituate, although the Lokerville section alone maintained its name until the twentieth century.

Happy Hollow - A neighborhood on Old Connecticut Path near Stonebridge Road. It is still referred to as Happy Hollow. It was supposedly named for the "happy" patrons of the "Moulton Tavern" which was located in the area about the middle of the eighteenth century. The original proprietor, Caleb Moulton, was succeeded by his son who served as a captain in the Revolutionary War.

Jericho - A small village with seven homes that straddled Wayland and Weston in the northeast of town. It was a triangular-shaped area of meadow, swamp and woodland near Draper Road. Dr. Jesse Wheaton, a Tory, lived until 1777 in the Weston section. The house is still standing.

Pine Brook - A small stream that originally skirted a part of Pine Plain on the easterly side. It was crossed by a small bridge, near the south cemetery, running around the lower part of Sandy Burr Country Club Golf Course, before joining Mill Brook. Mill Brook extends from Claypit Hill Road to Plain Road at the site of the old Cakebread Mill, to its junction with Pine Brook, from where they flow together into the Sudbury River.

Pine Plain - The pine lands east of Wayland Center in the vicinity of the James Sumner Draper house that still stands at 110 Plain Road. It is mentioned in the records and probably took its name from the growth of pine forest found there.

Pock Pasture - A pasture area northerly of Pine Plain (vicinity of Plain Road) which derived its name from the smallpox hospital formerly located there. There was also a smallpox hospital on Pelham Island. The treatment in the two hospitals is alleged to have been different. Most of the patients died in one of the hospitals, and most recovered in the other. The records do not indicate which hospital succeeded or why they did but patients in the Pelham Island hospital were said to have been inoculated. During the mid 1700s inoculation with a live smallpox virus became popular in Britain and in Boston because it saved many lives. However some patients died as a result of immunization and the practice lost favor. Two local victims were buried just east of the Route 20 Bridge and their gravestones remained into the twentieth century.

Pod Meadow - An extensive area of the river flood plain in the southwest corner of Wayland, south of Stonebridge Road on the Framingham line. The river here forms the boundary between Wayland and Framingham at Saxonville and is owned by the Metropolitan District Commission for use as a "blow-off" drainage area for the two aqueducts that cross the river in this area. Major Framingham water supply well fields lie immediately adjacent. The river's main flood plain starts here and extends more than twenty miles north to Billerica. The entire flood plain was purchased in 1961 by the U. S. Department of the Interior, Bureau of Sport Fisheries and Wildlife, as part of the Great Meadows National Wildlife Refuge.

Timber Neck - A piece of land on the northern edge of the Sandy Burr Country Club south of Mill Brook. It was the home site of the Reverend Edmund Browne, first minister of the Sudbury settlement, and included seventy acres of land. Reverend Browne's home served as an early garrison during King Philip's War when Sudbury was still a frontier town.

Tower Hill - A small hill on Plain Road in the easterly part of Wayland near the railroad station of that name. In October 1881 the first trains from Boston to Hudson passed Tower Hill on their way through Wayland. The hill took its name from the wooden tower, or lookout, which was erected by Richard Fuller, Esq (brother of Margaret Fuller) who purchased a small farm there in the mid 1800s.

R

Wayland Center Railroad Depot

Railroads

The sound of a train whistle through Wayland Center has not been heard since 1980. The track on the right of way under the electric towers is still there next to the Library parking lot. The Depot itself, now transformed into a gift shop, suggests the importance that trains once had as transportation for people and goods coming and going.

Wayland Center had been relatively prosperous in the early years of the nineteenth century when it was on a through stage line to the west. In the late 1860s a group of men, led by James S. Draper, believed that a railroad was needed to stimulate Wayland Center's lagging economy. They joined a group who petitioned the Massachusetts legislature for permission to build a railroad from Mill Village in South Sudbury to Stony Brook in Weston. This Wayland and Sudbury Branch Railroad never gained ground.

The plan for a railroad from Boston to Northampton through the central part of Massachusetts was more successful. The Massachusetts Central Railroad received its charter from the Massachusetts legislature on May 10, 1869. In the charter, towns along its route were authorized to subscribe for stock up to five percent of their assessed valuation. A strong vote of 103-2 in favor of subscription at a Wayland special town meeting resulted in permission to borrow up to $32,500. However, the Massachusetts Central had difficulty in raising enough capital and was slow in acquiring the rights-of-way. Four years later, Wayland had not yet paid its money and a proposal to invest the town's money in another railroad from Cochituate to Hopkinton was put before the voters.

An attempt to get a railroad to Cochituate was in response to Cochituate's shoe factory owners. Again, the town was authorized to borrow for that purpose. A real struggle ensued within the town about the railroad stock subscriptions: some wanted to rescind the votes, others did not. It became an issue and in February of 1874 the town voted against buying the note issues of the Massachusetts Central Railroad.

Nothing much was done to advance the construction of the Massachusetts Central until 1878 when a new board of directors and slate of officers were elected, among whom was Wayland's James Sumner Draper as treasurer. In October 1880, the first rails were laid from South Sudbury to both the east and west. The track progressed at the rate of a quarter of a mile per day. On October 1, 1881 a grand opening of twenty-eight miles of track from Boston to Hudson was held. Six hundred passengers traveled the route, including legislators, state officials, and businessmen. Groups cheered the train at decorated railroad stations along the route. The Tower Hill flag stop shelter, near James S. Draper's home, was elaborately decorated for the occasion. Wayland's railroad station, completed in September, was the scene of a celebration. It was hoped that eventually summer residents, visitors, and commuters would use the route to town. Initially, there were four round trips a day from Wayland to Boston. A horse-drawn coach line was started from Cochituate to Wayland Center to make connections with the Massachusetts Central. A special Saturday excursion with a round trip fare of $1.00 from Cochituate to Boston introduced Cochituate residents to the railroad.

In addition to passenger service, the new railroad line meant that Wayland Center farmers could ship farm products such as milk and in return have feed delivered. It was a long time before the anticipated arrival of industry in the north end of town would match the growth in Cochituate.

A financial crisis at the Massachusetts Central Railroad in the spring of 1883 caused the suspension of all operations after nineteen months. While the property was turned over to trustees of the mortgage bonds, the railroad was shut down for twenty-nine months until September 28, 1885. Reorganized as the Central Massachusetts Railroad, it resumed operations with the financial backing of the Boston and Lowell Railroad running seven round trips from Wayland to Boston.

By 1887, the line had been extended to Northampton, Massachusetts, 104 miles from Boston. That same year, a turntable west of the Wayland Depot and south of the track was completed to enable engines to turn around, and an engine house was built to store engines overnight. A water tank was also built near the turntable, but north of the track, to provide Mill Pond water for the steam locomotives. The establishment of this railroad terminal enabled five daily round trip passenger trains to begin and end their runs in Wayland. In addition, six other round trip passenger trains ran through Wayland between Boston and such points as Northampton, Ware and Hudson.

During 1889, a meeting was held in Cochituate to try to persuade the Central Massachusetts Railroad to build a branch to Cochituate. The Bent shoe factory even promised to take the company teams off the roads and use the railroad exclusively. This was never done, perhaps because the Bent firm's financial reverses made this railroad extension an even more risky proposition.

In a complicated series of leases and takeovers, the Central Massachusetts came under the control of the Boston and Maine Railroad. The completion of a bridge spanning the Hudson River at Poughkeepsie, New York, in 1890 resulted in the creation of a competitive all-rail link to New England from the south. A through overnight train was established between Boston and Washington, D.C. via the Central Massachusetts branch. After departing from Boston at 5:45 P.M., the first stop was at South Sudbury and arrival in Washington, D.C. was at 11:20 A.M. the following day.

There was a fatal accident at Wayland Center in October of 1905 when a freight train heading west from Boston backed onto a sidetrack for the Clinton to Boston passenger train to pass. The crew of the freight train neglected to close the switch and the passenger train collided with the freight. The engineer and a baby on the passenger train were killed. Approximately fifty passengers riding in the coach were badly hurt.

There was an upswing in traffic on the Central Massachusetts branch generated by World War I. By 1916, there were twenty-two passenger trains plus six to eight freight trains a day through Wayland. Then came automobiles, trucks and the Great Depression. In 1932, the last Boston to Northampton passenger train ran through Wayland. Through-freights disappeared forever, leaving only local freight trains.

By the spring of 1956, the last regular steam-powered trains on the entire B&M system were three early morning and evening passenger runs from Clinton (through Wayland) to Boston and return. On May

126

5, 1956, the steam era came to an end on the Boston and Maine. Budd self-propelled railcars were introduced to the line in the late 1950's in an effort to retain what little passenger business remained, but even that measure only delayed the eventual curtailment of all commuter service.

Cutbacks continued. The number of round trips was reduced to two daily except Saturday and Sunday. On January 15, 1965, service was cut back to South Sudbury. In mid-1971 it was announced that the final run would be July 30, 1971. Meetings were held, ad-hoc committees were formed, and pressure was brought to bear on the various State Representatives of the communities involved. At the last minute the MBTA's Advisory Board announced that service would continue until further notice. Credit for the stay of execution belonged to a small but dedicated group of Wayland residents who devoted many hours to spearheading the "save the train" movement. Without knowing, they expressed the sentiments of their fellow citizens of just a century before who had argued convincingly to bring the railroad to Wayland.

On November 26, 1971, a single Budd car arrived in South Sudbury at 7:13 P.M. It coupled up to another Budd train and together they deadheaded back to Boston. Ninety years of passenger service on the Central Massachusetts had come to an end.

A daily freight train continued to use the tracks through Wayland on its way to South Sudbury, Hudson and Berlin. Watertown Dairy was the last freight customer in Wayland, receiving boxcar loads of feed on the freight house track next to the Library. As the condition of the track deteriorated, the freight train ran less frequently. In August 1980, the last freight train slowly passed through town, almost 99 years after the first train had run through Wayland.

Recreation

The American passion for organized outdoor competitive sports has been visible in Wayland for nearly a century and a half. The Live Oak Baseball Club, formed in Cochituate in 1867, first played the Natick Eagles at City Pastures which was located south of Commonwealth Road (Route 30) just west of the intersection of Main Street and Commonwealth Road (Routes 27 and 30). Home teams played at City Pastures for sixteen years before moving to the "New Baseball Ground,"a field behind the Lyon's Shoe Factory on Main Street–now Griffin Ballfield. Games continued there between the Wayland Meadow Hens and Cochituate Shop Ends, the lasters at Bent's factory and the lasters at Bryant's factory, and between the boarding houses of the Lovejoys and American House. Cochituate teams also played against the Waltham Watch Factory team and a Harvard College team. Two Cochituate selectmen, Dr. Charles H. Boodey at 230 lbs. and William Hammond at 210 lbs., played on a team called the Fat Man's Nine. During the years before World War II, Wayland Center fielded a baseball team called the Wayland Grays that played similar teams from Lincoln and Weston.

When Noble Griffin, a successful shoe manufacturer, purchased the Lyon factory on Main Street in 1892, and later the Lyon house at the corner of Main and West Plain streets, he kept the field behind the building for ball games. A dozen years later he had the factory demolished but left standing an ell that

127

had been attached to the building. The ell, long referred to as the "Bee Hive," (see Quaint Names) had housed local shoe workers and remained standing until 1912 when it is believed to have been moved to Bradford Street and today it is an apartment house. An Olympic size hockey rink was built on the land that fronts on Main Street. It was owned by the Cochituate Hockey Club, a non town-sponsored club, which held skating competitions there from 1936-39. Players, mostly from Cochituate, belonged to the Amateur Boston Olympics, an organization equivalent to the present American Hockey League. Games at the rink drew large crowds. A bright red-flashing light recorded goals and during intermission music from 78 rpm records filled the air. Old time Cochituate residents remember watching these weekend competitions.

Griffin donated his ball field to the town in 1912 after which it was managed by the Playground Association which had been established sometime prior to 1910. After World War II, Griffin Field was home to the VFW's football team and the Cochituate Girls Softball Team–contending state champions in the 1950s. Today, the four-acre "Griffin Ballfield" remains Noble Griffin's legacy.

In 1920, Arthur Williams purchased business properties on the east side of Main Street to create a child's playground in honor of his mother Hannah Williams. Arthur had prospered in the shoe business, first in Cochituate, and later in Holliston. He was one of thirteen Williams children–five of the boys lived and did business in Cochituate. The Hannah Williams property was privately owned and managed by local trustees until the town bought it in 1966. Volunteers raised money and built an elaborate wooden gym on the grounds in 1987 and 1988. The park has become a popular family gathering place at all times of the day and year. Wayland's Park and Recreation Department maintains the park's grounds and the safety of its equipment but volunteers continue to raise money to replace equipment.

Since the earliest days of settlement, residents have been generous with donations of time and money to the town. The Playground Association began a movement to set aside play areas for children in the early 1900s. They enlisted the help of Edmund Sears, who served as a selectman and was active on the committee to build the 1910 Cochituate School. Sears and Edwin Farnham Greene, a wealthy Boston businessman who was the Treasurer and Chief Executive Officer of Pacific Mills purchased thirty-three acres of land behind the Odd Fellows Hall and Trinitarian Congregational Church for use as a public park and playground. (Greene had built a stately Georgian brick mansion in 1911 on two hundred and nineteen acres of land overlooking a bend in the Sudbury River–currently the home of Traditions.) The town transferred a portion of the thirty-three acre park and playground in the early 1930s to build a new High School. Transfer required approval by the Massachusetts Legislature. Most of the original parkland remains today–the John Bucyk Field–which includes a fine baseball diamond, an excellent soccer field and a child's playground. There is also a soccer field and a child's play area on Alpine Road.

Unorganized sports have been popular in town since skaters first came from Boston around the turn of the century to glide around Lake Cochituate and the town's many ponds–ladies wearing long dresses and men in nifty wool suits. Local residents still rush out to skate in winter when thick ice forms on the town's lakes and ponds. Only the Mill Pond, however, is maintained today by the town with snow being cleared in winter and night lighting provided. In summer, locals and many visitors, cool off at beaches on

Dudley Pond and Lake Cochituate. Baldwin Pond, no longer used for recreation, was once the "official" town beach in Wayland Center where children were given swimming lessons. The beach was under the control of the American Red Cross. A dock and float, complete with diving board, were maintained, and a small boat was available for emergencies. Golf enthusiasts play at two fine golf courses in town, Sandy Burr Country Club on Cochituate Road and the Wayland Country Club on Old Sudbury Road.

Many summer camps around Dudley Pond and Lake Cochituate were owned by nonresidents, some as far away as Boston. Day-trippers could take the Route 9 trolley to "Sunnyside" at Natick and transfer to another trolley that took them to Cochituate.

Today the town maintains a sizeable beach at Lake Cochituate with lifeguard supervision. Children take swimming lessons directed by the town's Park and Recreation Department. The town maintains a boat launch just south of the town's beach and the state maintains one at Lake Cochituate State Park off Commonwealth Road (Route 30). Until the 1960s, boats could be rented on Heard's Pond. Boating remains popular on Lake Cochituate and Dudley Pond as well as all along the Sudbury River. Heard's Pond, which is too shallow and polluted for swimming has good fishing and boating. Canoeing is enjoying a tremendous revival–attested to by the many canoes that ply the Sudbury River in all but the coldest months of the year.

Red Scare

On the night of June 8, 1954, the Wayland School Committee convened a public hearing to determine whether Anne P. Hale Jr., a second-grade teacher in the Wayland Center School, should be dismissed because of her membership in the Communist Party between 1938 and 1950. The first session attracted an audience estimated to be between 750 and 1,000 in size. Subsequent sessions filled seven more June evenings before ending on June 25. The Committee then reviewed the evidence produced during the hearing, prepared a report of its conclusions and fired Miss Hale.

Just as the hearing was getting underway, afternoon network television was carrying live broadcasts of the U. S. Senate hearings initiated by Senator McCarthy's allegation that Communists had infiltrated the U. S. Army. The evening television news each day was filled with coverage of the Senate proceedings. The public perception of a "Red Menace" had reached its zenith just when Miss Hale's hearing began.

A half-century later, it is difficult to appreciate the climate of public opinion that made the School Committee's actions necessary. In the 1950s, to be suspected of being a Communist (a "Red") or a Communist sympathizer (a "pinko") was a very serious matter. Events leading up to that era's anti-Communist furor started with activities of the U.S. House Un-American Activities Committee ("HUAC") in 1947. The HUAC was at the time chaired by J. Parnell Thomas, a Republican bent on portraying the Truman administration as soft on Communism. Truman responded by insisting upon loyalty oaths for all Federal employees and promising that any government employee found to be a Communist would be discharged. In 1949, the Massachusetts Legislature added to the public's perception of a "Red Menace" by passing a law making it illegal for the Commonwealth or any political subdivision thereof to employ a Communist, and requiring that all public employees sign a loyalty oath.

In 1950, the U. S. joined several other UN member nations to repulse North Korea's invasion of South Korea. The Korean War had ended just a few months before the School Committee learned of Miss Hale's membership in the Communist Party. Thus, images of the killings of American soldiers by a Communist nation's army – an army advised and supplied by USSR and China, both major Communist powers – were still fresh in the minds of Wayland residents. And throughout the early 1950s, Senator Joseph McCarthy was basking in the publicity generated by his zealous investigations of alleged Communist infiltrations into federal governmental departments.

Sometime in the early months of 1954, The Massachusetts Commission on Communism found the name of Anne P. Hale Jr. among the members of a Cambridge cell of the Communist Party and notified the Wayland School Committee of its discovery. The school committee summoned Miss Hale to appear at its meeting of April 23. At that meeting, Miss Hale readily acknowledged that she had been a member of the Communist Party between 1938 and 1950 but stated that she had not since been involved with the Party.

The committee subsequently notified Miss Hale in writing that it was probable that her dismissal would be warranted for one or more reasons. The listed charges included conduct unbecoming a teacher because she failed to truthfully inform the committee at its April 23 meeting about the nature and extent of her involvement with the party, and unfitness to teach because her statements about her knowledge of the Party's purposes and activities demonstrated a lack of "perception, understanding and judgment necessary in one who is to be entrusted with the responsibility for teaching the children of the Town." The committee suspended Miss Hale and informed her that under Massachusetts law she was entitled to a hearing before it voted on her dismissal. Miss Hale requested that the hearing be conducted in public and the committee granted her request.

Who was this person that the school committee charged with conduct unbecoming a teacher and with being unfit to teach? A pariah who needed an affiliation with a radical organization to shore up self-esteem? An uneducated person lacking the sophistication to fathom the implications of the Communist agenda? A member of a family so new to the United States that it had not yet fully assimilated American values? Hardly. Miss Hale could trace her heritage back to colonial America. Her father had been a delegate to a Massachusetts Constitutional Convention early in the century. As to her education and intellectual qualifications, Miss Hale was a Radcliffe graduate and had taught in prestigious private schools in New York and Massachusetts before joining the Wayland faculty in 1948. With respect to her social standing in Wayland, the forty-six- year-old Miss Hale resided alone in a home that she owned on Plain Road, was a popular teacher with her pupils and their parents, was a member of the League of Women Voters, was a registered voter in the town between 1952 and 1955, and was a member of First Parish Church in Wayland.

Prior to the hearing, Miss Hale wrote several letters to parents of her present and past second-grade pupils and to her Wayland neighbors. She made no apology for her prior affiliation with the Communist Party but instead said that her membership in the party and in several other organizations was motivated by her desire to contribute to the improvement of public schools, to the end of racial and religious discrimination, to the improvement in wages and working and living conditions of workers, and to the defense of civil liberties, such as freedom of speech, press and assembly.

The public hearing began on the evening of June 8 and continued through a total of eight sessions ending on the night of June 25. Town counsel Roger Stokey presented the School Committee's case, the thrust of which was aimed at Miss Hale's contention that she had not heard anyone connected with the Communist Party advocate the violent overthrow of the government. Mr. Stokey called witnesses and introduced evidence intended to demonstrate that either Miss Hale must have known the Communist Party's agenda and therefore had lied about her knowledge when explaining her involvement to the school committee, or that she lacked the "perception, understanding and judgment" to discern the implications of the party's agenda and therefore was unfit to teach. Mr. Stokey's widow remembers that her husband privately debated whether to serve as legal counsel for the School Committee because, in his view, the Hale matter was being distorted by anti-Communist hysteria. After reflecting on the situation and notwithstanding his reservations, he decided that by conducting the hearing as town counsel, he could ensure evenhanded treatment for Miss Hale. Witnesses recalling the hearings describe them as orderly, fair, and so lacking in drama that attendance declined significantly after the first several nights.

In the end, school committee members Maguire and Newton voted to dismiss Miss Hale and Chairman Waldron voted against dismissal. Waldron later explained that although he did not find the charges against Miss Hale proven by the facts developed during the hearing, he would have voted for her dismissal based on her refusal to answer many of the questions put to her if such refusal had been included at the outset as a basis for dismissal.

Life became difficult for Miss Hale following her dismissal. Acquaintances became wary about acknowledging that they knew her. She found it difficult to find employment. She was fired from a menial job at Angell Memorial Animal Hospital when her Communist history was discovered. Her brother was fired from his position as a lawyer in a Federal agency when the agency learned of his sister's prior affiliation with the Communist Party.

Miss Hale died in 1968. Her obituary in *The Wayland-Weston Town Crier* notes that "The publicity and notoriety forced Miss Hale to leave Wayland, but she maintained her home on Plain Road. During the past five years, she was at different times a teacher and director of Governor's Center School for Children with Learning Disabilities in Providence, RI, commuting to Wayland on weekends. Miss Hale died at the Waltham Hospital on October 2, after an illness of several months. Before her illness, she had accepted a position in the Wellesley Public Schools, as a teacher of dyslexic children. In the words of a friend, 'It was her vindication.'"

More information about the 1950s "red scare" in Wayland, and about the proceedings that resulted in Miss Hale's dismissal, can be found in the files of the Wayland Historical Society.

❑❑❑

Revolutionary War

What was Sudbury like in 1775? East Sudbury did not exist as a separate town and Wayland was sixty years in the future. Separate meetinghouses had been constructed: one in Sudbury Center and the other, the fourth to be built, on the east side at the corner of Pelham Island and Cochituate roads. There was very little disagreement, however, about grievances against the English king and Parliament. The well-known confrontation at the Old North Bridge attracts tourists to Concord. But Sudbury shared a common concern with several provincial towns as they tried to overthrow the old government and establish a new one. Sudbury was the most populous town in Middlesex County with 2,160 people, extensive territory, and for a time, close to the fight. The town, expected to supply its quota of men and supplies, did not fail its patriotic duty. As protests were repeatedly presented to the English king against oppressive taxation, denial of rights, and of representation, Sudbury's delegates were in the forefront for the continental cause. After the passage of the Stamp Act in 1765, the people of Sudbury chose a committee to prepare and present instructions to Peter Noyes, Representative to the General Court, stating their very strong opinions against that act. Record after record shows that people were patriotic and forthright in declaring their opposition to the Stamp Act. William Baldwin, who lived near the Old Town Bridge, was the only accused Tory in town.

In 1770, people expressed their agreement with the merchants of Boston "to stop the importation of British goods, and engaged for themselves and all within their influence, to countenance and encourage the same." As tension mounted, on Nov. 14, 1774, "it was voted that the town recommend to the several companies of militias to meet for the choice of officers of their respective companies, as recommended by the Provincial Congress." The east side and west side companies held separate meetings to choose their officers. In addition to establishing a militia, the town took measures to form companies of minute men. These, as the name implies, were to hold themselves in readiness to act at a minute's warning. The officers received no commissions, but held their positions by vote of the men. Two such companies were formed, one on each side of the river. There was also a horse troop, or cavalry, composed of men from both precincts. Additionally, there was an alarm company composed of men exempt from military service. The muster rolls of six companies–three hundred and forty-eight men–have been preserved and indicate that nearly one-sixth of the population responded to the call. On the day of the Concord and Lexington conflict, members of the alarm company and troop were mingled with other companies of the town. The number in actual service there was three hundred and two.

Among town papers, a bill to one of the minute companies for ammunition supplied by the town indicates the troops were well equipped for service before April 19, 1775. Each man had, for the most part, received about a pound of powder and two pounds of balls at a cost of one pound, one shilling. A considerable quantity of patriot supplies had been deposited at Concord. On March 29, 1775, a report came that the British were about to proceed to that place. To safeguard these supplies, some were moved

132

to Sudbury–fifty barrels of beef, one hundred of flour, twenty casks of rice, fifteen hogsheads of molasses, ten hogsheads of rum, and five hundred candles, fifteen thousand canteens, fifteen thousand iron pots. Spades, pickaxes, bill-hooks, axes, hatchets, crows, wheelbarrow, and several other articles were divided among the towns–one-third to remain in Concord; one-third to Sudbury, one-third to Stow, and one thousand iron pots to Worcester.

Early on the morning of April 19, the East Sudbury troops gathered on the common in front of the meetinghouse at the corner of Pelham Island and Cochituate roads. One eyewitness described the scene: "The incessant crashing of the bell and the rolling of drums accompanied the hoarse shouts of Sgt. Robert Cutting and Sgt. Nathaniel Reeves as they called the rolls. Before the church, twenty-one horses and riders under Captain Isaac Loker stood waiting quietly. Soon all was ready and 136 men swung into a column, shouldered their flintlocks and started up the road to Concord." These men, marching on the east side of the river through Lincoln, were commanded by Capt. Joseph Smith. It is believed they attacked the retreating British at Merriam's Corner as well as on Hardy's Hill. The west side force under Capt. John Nixon arrived at Concord too late to aid in repelling the Redcoats at the Old North Bridge.

The militia and minutemen were far from being composed of rabble and irresponsible hotheads as some have claimed. An examination of the muster roll lists men of the most prominent and respected citizens of Sudbury. For example, eighty-year-old Deacon Josiah Haynes, who fought with strength and tenacity at both Concord and Lexington until he was killed by a musket ball at Lexington, was a leader in the west side church.

At the Battle of Bunker Hill on June 17, 1775, Sudbury soldiers again played a valiant part. The Sudbury detachment was among reinforcements that had to make a perilous ascent to join the forces from other towns already on the heights. In two assaults, the British were mowed down and had to retreat. In the third assault, with Continental ammunition exhausted, the Sudbury regiment fought a rearguard action in hand-to-hand combat and was the last to leave the field when their "retreat" was ordered. Joshua Haynes, Jr. was killed in the battle and General Nixon and Nathaniel Maynard were wounded.

In 1776, the town "voted to pay each of the minute men one shilling and sixpence for training one half day in a week, four hours to be esteemed a half day, after they were enlisted and until called into actual service or dismissed; and the Captains three shillings and Lieutenants two shillings and sixpence and the ensign two shillings." As the war dragged on summertime soldiers deserted Washington's armies and towns and colonies failed to supply quotas of men and supplies. Sudbury, however, continued to contribute more than its share. When Sudbury was required to supply nine tons of hay for the army at Cambridge, only three other towns in the colony were assessed this quantity.

As encouragement for men to enlist in the cause, money was voted by the town to pay each enlisted man, and to buy shirts, shoes and stockings for those who would fulfill the town's quota. Records show that an amount of "thirty-nine pounds, fifteen shillings and ten pence" was appropriated for Uriah Moore's wife on May 17, 1779. Often the men or families were paid in produce or cattle.

133

During the Revolutionary War soldiers were paid in paper money issued by the newly formed Congress. Because they preferred using coins made of reliable metal, paper money quickly depreciated and led to the expression "Not worth a Continental." The value of currency greatly concerned town fathers who met and fixed prices on Indian corn, wheat, rye, butter, cheese and other commodities. Those who violated set pricing were warned–"the good people of the town should withhold all trade and intercourse from them."

When the long struggle for independence ended, Sudbury soldiers returned to their families as citizens of the nation they had fought to create.

<hr>

❏❏❏

Rosebud Gardens/Ten Acres

In the mid nineteen thirties, a bankruptcy sale was held at Rosebud Gardens, a nightclub located on the Boston Post Road east of Wayland Center, now the site of Temple Shir Tikva. The owner of Rosebud Gardens had allegedly siphoned funds from the nightclub to support his semi-pro baseball team whose home field was down the hill in back of the nightclub.

The father of longtime resident John Seiler, came to the sale to buy kitchen equipment for his catering and restaurant company. He ended up buying the entire nightclub operation, which was renamed Ten Acres, although the property was considerably larger than that. The nightclub building was Italianate in style, two stories high with a four-sided pitched roof. The interior was reminiscent of a Neapolitan streetscape. The oval dance floor, surrounded by a short stucco wall, was slightly below the dining level. The booths nestled under red tile roofs. John Seiler, a ten-year-old at the time, remembers this intimate setting as very seductive with richly gowned women and well-dressed men dancing to swing orchestra music. Vaughn Monroe, of "Racing with the Moon" fame, made his national debut in this setting, complete with coast-to-coast radio broadcast.

The baseball diamond down the slope behind the building was made into an outing pavilion that included a clambake area, a banquet hall, swimming pool and, across a brook, a shaded picnic area. In the summer, a week-day children's camp, run by a Weston athletic coach, took place. The onset of World War II, and the attendant gas rationing, shut down the nightclub. The outing pavilion was converted to house a large number of turkeys being raised to help support the Seiler catering company's war-related food service contracts. One of young Seiler's summer jobs at the time was to tend the stubborn birds who liked to huddle together in a corner and, if not prevented, suffocate each other. He purchased lunch at a sandwich shop located where Luigi's now stands. Next door to the sandwich shop he purchased gasoline for the mowers used to cut the high grass on the outing grounds.

Seiler did not reopen Ten Acres after World War II. The outing area was sold to the Newton YMCA which established Camp Chickami there. The owners of a fashionable society orchestra purchased the nightclub, invested in major renovations and additions, and changed the name to Robin Hood's Ten Acres. Their investment did not produce a successful nightclub, however, and it too was sold. The

Wayland House restaurant followed in the 1970's but it closed before long. The building was vacant at the time the newly formed Temple Shir Tikva purchased it in 1980. The original restaurant building was renovated, later enlarged, and finally demolished. Today, a handsome new temple occupies the site. (see Houses of Worship)

Bent Shoe Factory about 1860

Separate Towns

After the first meeting house was built on the west side of the river in 1723, houses sprang up around it and new roads appeared. The population of Sudbury's west side continued to grow over the years and by 1771 it exceeded the east side by an appreciable amount. That year, a proposal was made at Town Meeting "to see if the Town will enlarge or rebuild the West Meeting House." It was an unusual proposal given the circumstances of the time. Only a year before, the Boston Massacre had set the stage for war and Sudbury had braced itself to support the Continental cause. (William Baldwin who lived near the Old Town Bridge was the only alleged Tory in town.) Talk of war probably brought more inhabitants out to meetings and caused crowding in the west side meetinghouse. The proposal, however, did not set well with east siders who already paid higher taxes as a result of their greater wealth and more highly developed land–even though their land area and population were smaller. At the time, the cost of enlarging the west side meeting house, in addition to the town's commitment to the Revolutionary War effort, appeared too costly even to some residents on the west side of the river.

During the fall of 1774, war was on everyone's mind. The Provincial Congress depended upon Sudbury to train militia and store supplies. Sudbury was the largest town in Middlesex County, and the first line of defense. Slowly, townsmen gained guns and ammunition and helped stock meetinghouses and the government storehouses that had been built on the northerly part of Sand Hill, east of Old County Road. Throughout town, families hid extra stores of food and ammunition in their homes and barns. Minutemen began military drills in town barns under the darkness of night, secretly preparing for war. (see Revolutionary War)

On the night of April 19, 1775, Dr. Abel Prescott Jr. of Concord, galloped to the Sudbury home of Thomas Plympton, a member of the Provincial Congress, and announced that the Regulars were coming. Sudbury sounded its call to arms. By sunrise, 302 Sudbury men had assembled on both commons, prepared to march to Concord. After the historic battles at Lexington and Concord, Sudbury men continued to serve the cause. Three Sudbury regiments fought at Bunker Hill on June 17, 1775 after the battle at Concord.

In spite of the war, Sudbury town meetings and business in general continued to go forward. So too, did debate about enlarging the second meeting house on the west side of the river. Arguments became so heated between east and west siders that frustrated east siders eventually decided to form a separate town and call it East Sudbury.

In 1778, John Tilton, a relative newcomer to town, presented the proposal at town meeting. The town appointed a committee to come up with a line of division, but when no one could agree on one, town meeting began to debate again the wisdom of the original idea. At last, a proposal was made to divide the two sides of town by the Sudbury River, with two exceptions: Pelham's Island would be included in East Sudbury, and the Wheeler farm and the training field would be included in Sudbury. (Wheeler wanted his children to continue in school on the west side.) The proposal must have shocked east siders who had expected some more equal division of land. The river did not divide the territory in half. Two-thirds of the land lay on the west side of the river and one-third on the east. The question of whether more land could be added to the east side to achieve a more equitable division, resulted in a negative vote. East siders had no choice but to take their case to the General Court.

A committee appointed by the Court met with selectmen and heard from a number of west side citizens who had begun to oppose the separation. Various proposals were considered and additional town meetings were scheduled, but the river division seemed to be the most popular solution.

East siders realized that if they wanted to establish a separate town they were going to have to settle for less land. They submitted a petition to the General Court, and on April 10, 1780, the bill taken up in the House–Chapter 34 of Province Laws 1769-1778–became Wayland's charter as the separate town of "East Sudbury." Historian Helen Emery notes that this is of special importance in the history of Wayland as it was East Sudbury's declaration of independence.

East Sudbury's boundary lines, as spelled out in the house bill, took into account Pelham's Island and Caleb Wheeler's farm and the training field adjoining it. The fifty acres of Wheeler's farm caused a permanent and definite jog in the boundary line between Sudbury and East Sudbury. When Matthias Mossman surveyed the two towns for the Commonwealth in 1795, he recorded 18,030 acres, including waterways and roads, in Sudbury, and 8,123 acres in East Sudbury. The boundaries have remained pretty much the same since then, but modern surveys register 9,800 acres in Wayland or 15.28 square miles.

In addition to the town's boundary lines, the bill to partition covered other concerns: joint maintenance of Old Town Bridge and causeway, town's arms and ammunition to be divided according to the proportion of men able to bear arms in the two towns, donations for the poor, funds for schools, and all lands and monies in the treasury.

For the most part, the town's division, which had been slowly evolving since discussions first started in 1707 to build a west side meeting house, formally ended when East Sudbury held its first town meeting on April 24, 1780. (see Meetinghouses)

Shoe Industry

Cochituate began its colonial history as farmland, as did the bulk of the area west of Boston. Natick, however, was designated a "praying village,"where the clergy settled to convert Native Americans to Christianity. At first, Cochituate was not part of a particular settlement, its land having been granted to private owners as part of colonial politics and investment. As towns began to form, the settlers knew they must join a town–either Sudbury to the north or Natick to the south. Not wanting to join a town inhabited largely by Indians, they chose Sudbury. (see Separate Towns and Land Grants)

It is thus that Cochituate is now part of Wayland and not Natick. In the nineteenth century, however, Natick was a much closer kindred spirit, since both were in the midst of the industrial revolution boom. The industry was shoemaking. Beginning in the 1840s, shoe factories sprang up in Cochituate, Natick, Saxonville, and many surrounding villages. A pioneer in this business was James Madison Bent, who is generally credited with turning Cochituate from a quiet farming community to a bustling industrial and political center.

Shoemaking by hand was common in all communities in the 1700s. Some small shops were established where the work was done by hand. The craft of items like shoes and clothing was largely an individual affair during colonial times. These crafts coexisted with farming, and had little economic impact above meeting the basic needs of the people in the area.

The shoe shop established in the 1830s in Cochituate by William Bent and his brother James Madison Bent grew rapidly over the next fifty years and expanded from their small shop into a prominent shoe manufacturing company with many employees and rapid community development.

The growth of this industry is a microcosm of the wider industrial revolution in the United States. It is a story of workers, owners, tenements, unions, immigrants, social life, schools, churches, political power, and–ultimately–how the groundwork was laid for the population growth and the geopolitical framework which now exist in Wayland, Cochituate, and surrounding towns.

The industrial revolution did not turn solely on the invention of the steam engine and other such devices. The invention of complex machines was just taking hold at that time; their source of power could be water or human or animal. The important distinguishing feature of these machines from their predecessors is that they performed operations repetitively, accurately, and quickly, thus allowing an efficient operation to develop which was more than the simple assemblage of a set of independent craftsmen. Thus, the idea of a "factory" was born, with all it implies.

Another important addition to the landscape was the development of the rail system in the mid 1800s. Before the early 1800s, fast transport of bulk materials and finished goods was simply not possible. The railroad, however provided the capability of moving raw materials from one area to another and building things started to become economically feasible.

As the Bent family expanded its business, complex machines combined with steam power and rail transportation for raw materials and finished goods became available to them. They were among the first to grasp this technology and began building shoe factories, rather than simple shoe shops. By 1860 their factory was steam-powered and they were importing workers from the surrounding area, many of them immigrants from Europe, Nova Scotia, and Quebec.

The Bent factory occupied a large site on the corner of what is now Commonwealth Road and Main Street where Starbuck's coffee shop is now located. Low-level workers lived in tenement halls near the center, or in private homes in Natick or Saxonville. Owners, managers, and higher-level workers dwelled in more spacious quarters, also near the center, some in houses that were considered opulent in their day. Many of these houses are still standing, and are in good order, and form the core of the historic appearance of Cochituate.

James Madison Bent became a prominent leader in the region. His house stood where Cochituate

141

Motors is now, and was heralded for its splendor. Bent also owned property on Dudley Pond, where his family could spend the summer. One did not travel far to the country hideaway in those times. Accounts from the period tell of families escaping to local ponds or hillsides to escape the "dusty city" of Cochituate.

While Bent was the largest shoe manufacturer in the area, other factories were also established, and did well in their time. Names such as Lyon, Dean, Griffin, and Williams can be found in the histories and photos of their factories appear from the 1880s. These factories were largely clustered around Cochituate Center. Meanwhile, other towns like Natick, also experienced a boom, and by the 1860s sported larger shoe industries than Cochituate. Due to specialization of products, these firms did not completely overlap in their markets, and coexisted until the industry fell away in general. Cochituate specialized in a shoe style called the "brogan" for men and boys.

The shoe industry brought Cochituate out of a largely agrarian way of life. At the time, this was considered a boon, since farming was a hard existence. With population and wealth shifting to the growing south side of town, political power shifted to that side as well. By the late 1800s, most of the major town offices were filled by south side residents. Major changes were made to the infrastructure–at least on the south side–such as the construction of a water system, electric street lighting, and the addition of schools to serve a growing population. Becoming politically as well as financially prominent, James Madison Bent presided over the renaming of the village in 1846 to "Cochituate," at the dedication of Boston's new water source: the newly named Lake Cochituate itself. The ceremony was attended by the mayor of Boston, Josiah Quincy, and by former president John Quincy Adams. Having previously had informal names like Bentville or South Wayland, there was considerable pride in this new name, and a new post office was even established with a Cochituate postmark. The growing population and power in Cochituate had the effect of increasing the tax burden on North Wayland as well. Still mostly agrarian, the north side of town did not benefit from the industrial base as much as those in the newly urbanized area and this led to frictions which culminated in a petition for separation in 1881. While this petition failed to garner the needed votes, it stimulated town officials to favor North Wayland somewhat more than before by holding more public meetings in Wayland Center.

There were subsequent, weaker attempts to split into two towns as well, or to join Cochituate to Natick. In the 1890s, there was some talk in Natick about annexing Cochituate so that Natick might then become a city. The people of Cochituate apparently still did not like this idea, this time not because of Indians but because of taxes. Although attempts at separation finally died down, the political situation remained tense for a number of years as more and larger municipal projects, such as schools and town halls were considered.

In the meantime, the shoe industry prospered. However, the village failed to get railroad service. The Cochituate Crossing railroad spur of the Boston and Albany Railroad had been established in 1874 as a freight stop across the lake on the border of Natick and Framingham but Cochituate never had its own railroad service. From what can be gathered, however, times were still good for owners and workers alike. Although the forty-hour week had not yet been developed, it seems that the Cochituate factory owners, and others in the area, were more benevolent than many in other parts of the country, and tried to keep workers happy to get a good product, rather than work them to death.

Perhaps the best known of the perquisites were the baseball teams. Factories closed early on Saturday, and employees played against other factory employees, informally organized neighborhood teams, and college teams such as Harvard's. The Cochituate Ball Field was created for these games; it was originally part of the Lyon shoe company property. The teams grew to fair prominence in the region, sporting such names as the Wayland Meadow Hens (North Wayland team), Cochituate Shop Ends, Natick Eagles, and Natick Mystics. The Bent company also granted half-day holidays every few months to attend local fairs and celebrations, often arranging transportation to these activities. Although these benefits seem to be precursors to modern labor practices, we do not really know the motivation behind them. The Bents and other factory owners retained most of their companies' wealth and enjoyed most of its leisure time as well. Although it appears they had the better interests of the workers in mind, it does not seem to have been sufficient, and the Cochituate companies were caught up in the labor unrest which swept the country in the late nineteenth century. Striking increased in frequency in the industry in general in the 1880s and 1890s, resulting in the formation of unions for specific kinds of workers. As a result, the owners provided the workers incrementally better conditions. The workers' success portended the day when large national unions would gain significant power.

The factory owners, while relatively wealthy from a local point of view, were not in the same league as the Rockefellers and other well-known families. They tended to stay local, building homes for their families in the Cochituate Center area, and cottages on Dudley Pond and Reeves Hill. Remaining close to the factory was important; although they had more free time than the workers, running the business was still a day-to-day affair, and competition was always just around the corner. These were times of great technological advances, and one could not be caught napping.

Finally, however, technology, population growth, and advances in transportation made the shoe industry in Cochituate uneconomical. Larger, more efficient factories were being built in the south and west, and the railroads were able to transport finished goods inexpensively to wherever they were needed. The Bent company was sold to Dean, and eventually it also failed and the factory was torn down in 1916.

The Bent/Dean factory was the last to leave Cochituate. Some factories were still in operation in Natick and Marlborough, but the consolidation of the shoe industry was rapidly advancing, and soon only a few large factories remained in New England.

James Madison Bent died in 1888. His grave can be found in Lakeview Cemetery. Obituaries hailed him as a visionary and pioneer of industrialization. His sons carried on the business, hampered by lagging economic conditions. The factory was sold, and the family members went to other locations and occupations.

The shoe industry left important imprints on the town. First, several structures of historical importance still exist in Cochituate, including the Griffin house (Waterman Funeral Home), the Methodist Church, and several homes along Commonwealth Road, Main Street, and side streets of the Cochituate

143

Center environs. These buildings were not only living quarters, but were also used as shops, sometimes called "ten footers," for shoe piece work, complementing the factory work. The physical character of Cochituate was cast by the 1870s, and photos from that time show much of the same village style that we see today.

Another imprint is in the general flavor of the neighborhood, somewhat more village- oriented than the area around Wayland Center, which became a residential community directly from farmland. Cochituate's growth was also greatly affected by that of Natick and Framingham, which also show their industrial periods very clearly. Interestingly, however, since Wayland Center and Cochituate Village have always been one and the same town, the farming industry has helped to stem much of the business tide that has overtaken adjacent parts of Natick and Framingham and thus has helped the town retain some of its history and identity.

The history of Cochituate illustrates how decisions made hundreds of years ago shape the environment of the present. From the time of settlement to the establishment of factories to the modern world of residential and retail development, our past remains with us. The factory era was an important time of setting roots for the town. It would do us all well to learn more about this era and to preserve what we can of what remains of it.

_____ ❏❏❏ _____

Simpson Estate/Mansion Inn

Could Michael H. Simpson have known that the mansion he was building in 1880 on the corner of West Plain Street and Old Connecticut Path was on the site of an ancient cremation cemetery? Probably not.

Simpson, a widower, was seventy-two years old when he married his second wife Evangeline Marrs in 1882. Twenty-seven-year-old Evangeline had lived with her family in a home adjacent to Simpson's property to the east on Old Connecticut Path (about in the middle of today's Hawthorne Road.) The couple's new home was close to Simpson's place of business, the Saxonville Mills and Roxbury Carpet Company which he owned and managed. Before the age of twenty-five, Michael H. Simpson, Charles H. Coffin, and George Otis, son of Harrison Gray Otis of Boston, had formed a partnership and opened a trading business at # 38 India Wharf. By the early 1830s, the partners had purchased a ship, taken cargo to Calcutta and then began to import horns, hides, and wool from Buenos Aires. When a ship filled with dirty, raw burry wool arrived from South America, Simpson set about finding a way to turn a profit on what appeared to be useless cargo. Eventually, he designed and patented a machine that would remove the burrs from the wool and turn it into flexible fiber. With yet another partner, Nathaniel Frances, Simpson set up shop in the Saxonville Mill and Carpet Company building in 1858 and developed a highly successful business producing woolen fabrics. The mill had been in operation since 1822.

Although Simpson, his first wife Elizabeth Davis Kilham, and their five children, had always lived in Boston, the widower chose to live in Cochituate after his marriage to Evangeline Marrs. The mansion was built on a knoll that rose some fifty feet above Dudley Pond at the intersection of West Plain Street and Old Connecticut Path. Locally referred to as the "Castle," it cost an estimated $150,000 to build. Thirty men spent most of 1882 completing the house, stable, servant's quarters, and windmill. The windmill pumped water from Dudley Pond in 1811, but Simpson also financed water mains that brought water from Cochituate's Rice Reservoir down West Plain Street to his mansion, enabling households along the route to have access to running water. The mansion's main driveway led up to a covered entrance, entered from a point on Old Connecticut Path close to West Plain Street. Remnants of the gate to the south driveway remain today at the entrance to Castlegate Road off West Plain Street. An "H" and "Y" carved into the two gateposts are rumored to represent Harvard and Yale, the schools Simpson's two sons attended. The north gate, which was located on Old Connecticut Path opposite J. P. Richardson's, is no longer evident. The grounds of Simpson's mansion were extensively landscaped and the public was encouraged to enjoy the property. It is said that Mrs. Simpson could be seen riding along a bridle path adorned by four stone-carved lions. Simpson died in 1884, two years after moving into his new home. His wife Evangeline later married a retired Episcopal bishop, the Rt. Reverend Whipple. The couple held prayer meetings in the house until Whipple died and Evangeline moved to Minnesota.

After the Simpson mansion was sold it became a popular and often lawless establishment serving food and providing entertainment. It is reputed that liquor was served at the inn during this time and local residents reported hearing gunshots one night in the 1920s.

Later, it was called "Mansion Inn" and became an elegant dining/dancing establishment patronized by Bostonians as well as suburbanites. The new owners built a large one-story room on the southwest side of the inn for dancing on "spring" floors made by special arched supports in the flooring. This great ballroom became a public dance hall with an imposing plaster statue of Venus in the center surrounded by tables covered with white cloths. And while one waited to be served, interesting reading filled the back cover of the menu . . ."to those impelled by a discriminating desire to meet under a soft and pleasant glow of inspiring light, and surroundings of enchanting gaiety to partake of choice cuisine and gratifying delectables where melodious strains of music lend an atmosphere to retire and abandon one's care. We bid you welcome." How could one resist?

John Bryant, who was born and raised in the area, remembers watching wrestling matches held in the garden behind Mansion Inn. The four stone-carved lions that had once marked Evangeline's riding trails had been moved to encircle a large grassy arena in the shape of an amphitheater. Wrestlers used the grounds for a training camp and on weekends people came from great distances to watch men work out. Today, one of the lions can be seen on the grounds of the Grout-Heard House, another at 2 Hayward Road on the corner of Rich Valley and Hayward roads, a third in Weston on the lawn of a home at 655 Boston Post Road next to the Baptist Church, and the whereabouts of the fourth lion is unknown.

On March 24, 1956, nearly three-quarters of a century after Simpson had built the mansion for his new bride, it was ravaged by fire. The mahogany interior went up in flames and destroyed the much admired plaster Venus statue in the dining room. Ironically, members of the Cochituate Fire Department had just returned from funeral services for retired chief Theodore Harrington. They were still wearing their uniforms and riding a fire truck when the call came to go to Mansion Inn. Wayland had a "call" fire department at the time. A month after the fire, a permanent fire department was established.

Unfortunately, four feet of snow covered the ground the day of the fire and much of the house was inaccessible to the firefighters. After the fire subsided, all that remained were the front and side walls on the first floor which were built of stone, and a partial wood-framed second story. The rest was ash.

Was that the end of the Mansion Inn story? No. There was more to come. Three years after the fire, the property was sold and construction of fourteen new houses began. In the process of reducing a portion of the knoll by eight feet to level the land for houses and provide better vision for automobiles at the intersection, a bull dozer operator unearthed charcoal and a variety of stones that had clearly been shaped into axes, adzes, and gouges. Word got around and before long neighborhood children and a few adults began to collect whatever they could find. When amateur archaeologists from surrounding towns examined the site, they were astounded at the amount of material that had been uncovered. Children had discovered that the most "finds" were located where the soil was black, i.e., charcoal. Eventually, the developer halted work on the area and the police placed a round-the-clock guard on the site until professional archaeologists arrived. Unfortunately, much of the important data had already been lost before representatives from the R. S. Peabody Foundation of Andover could collect scientific data. The soil had been turned over so many times it was impossible to reconstruct an actual picture. Hundreds of stone axes, adzes, gouges, pestles, and a soapstone bowl, had been unearthed. Professional archaeologists determined that the site was probably a three-to-four-thousand year old cemetery site dotted with pits that contained debris that had been burned elsewhere and placed in the pits, and one stone-lined crematory. Professional archaeologist Dena Ferran Dincause of Harvard University, who analyzed data from the site said, "A period of from one to three centuries of use is considered reasonable for the cemetery; the longer span is favored."

Dincause's finding were published in Papers of the Peabody Museum of Archaeology and Ethnology, Harvard, University, Vol. 59, No. 1, by the Peabody Museum, Cambridge, MA, in 1968, "Cremation Cemeteries in Eastern Massachusetts." She concluded, "The available evidence from Mansion Inn supports at best a partial and uneven understanding of the site. A cemetery was located on the western, riverward, slope of a knoll. In an area at least forty by fifty feet in extent, there was an intensive concentration of burial pits. To the south, separate from the pits, was a stone-lined crematory. One cannot even guess how much more there may have been."

Many artifacts from the site are housed at Harvard's Peabody Museum of Archaeology in Cambridge, the Peabody Museum in Andover, and the Massachusetts Archaeological Society's Robbins Museum in Middleboro. Some of the artifacts unearthed by local children in the 1950s have been donated to the Wayland Historical Society where local residents can view and even hold stones, axes, and pestles created by native peoples thousands of years ago.

Slavery

Very little is known about slaves in Massachusetts before 1700 due to poor record keeping, a lack of wills, and newspapers to advertise slave sales or announce rewards for capturing runaways. Many of Sudbury's settlers, along with the rest of New England's colonists, were simply too busy clearing fields and raising livestock, dividing land and preparing for Indian attacks to have the leisure time to write letters or journals. Thus far, only one record has been found of individual slaves or slave owners living in Sudbury before 1700. But that does not mean there were no slaves here. Slaves may have been part of Sudbury households as early as 1653 which is implied by the difference of opinion at town meeting regarding the division of a new land grant. Most town freemen wanted the land to be divided equally, but a small number had a different suggestion: "The lands shall be divided by the inhabitants according to their several estates and family and counting the family to be the husband, wife, children and such servants as men have that they have either bought or brought up . . ."

Why would this method of land division be proposed if no one in the town had an indentured servant or slave they had paid for?

The earliest mention of a slave in Sudbury is in the will of Thomas Read who died in 1701 and left a Negro woman named Frank to his wife, Arabella. Arabella's will, dated 1716, also refers to Frank, but in a very different way. Mrs. Read grants Frank her freedom, all of the widow's moveable estate, and makes Frank executrix of her will. Whether or not Frank really inherited this estate is not indicated in existing records. However, in 1742 town meeting appropriated money to pay the Read's son, Isaac, for Nursing of and Provision of Frank Negro in the year 1740. The same town meeting also voted to compensate Dr. Ebenezer Roby for Frank's medical care. If Frank was in possession of any goods of value, she could have paid for her own care. It is reasonable to assume, therefore, that the two "Franks" are one and the same. At Thomas Read's death in 1701, Frank was a woman, and no longer a girl. By the 1740s, she would have been an elderly woman in need of care

Samuel Parris of witchcraft fame was another early slaveholder who left in his will an "Indian" girl named Violate, worth thirty pounds. There has been speculation that she was the daughter of his slave Tituba whom he brought from Barbados. Parris always referred to this West Indian as "Indian." (see Witchcraft)

There is some evidence that New England slaves were treated differently than those in the South. The Puritans did not pass laws denying or limiting a slave's right to learn. In fact, learning was encouraged through the Puritan belief that everyone should have a personal knowledge of the Bible. Slaves in Sudbury most often slept in their master's house and were considered in many respects part of the family. It was usual for slaves to eat at the same table as the rest of the family. Although slaves in Massachusetts could own property, few of them did. Yet, it was not against the law. In certain cases, a slave could earn wages when he worked for someone other than his master–with, of course, the consent of his master. That simple phrase "with the consent of his master" pretty much sums up what defined the life of a slave in Sudbury or in the rest of Massachusetts.

Unlike in the South, where slaves were forbidden to marry, Puritan slaves were encouraged to marry. Sex without marriage was a big no-no in Puritan New England whether slave or free and marriage gave sanction to sexual intimacy. Although slaves assumed no surnames or titles upon marriage, the name of their master was often used to record the marriage. In 1762, when Cuff and Hagar married, they were given the last name Noyes since both were then servants of Col. Noyes. Slave couples could be sold or willed to new masters, as happened to the slaves of Rev. John Swift of Framingham after he died in 1745.

Not all slaves remained together after marriage. Dinah, slave of Josiah Richardson of Sudbury, married Caesar, servant of Mrs. Love Flint of Lincoln in 1761. They each stayed with their respective masters. Children of slaves could be sold, as happened in Sudbury in 1764. Phebe, a slave of Josiah Richardson, was sold to the widow Balch of Framingham for 1 pound six shillings eight pence. Phebe was, "A Negro female child of about two years old." Her mother, presumably also Josiah Richardson's slave, was not sold. Parental duties lay not with the slave mother and father but with the master.

Israel Loring, who served as Sudbury's minister for sixty-six years, from 1706 to 1772, left letters, journals and sermons covering almost the entire century in Sudbury before slavery was declared illegal. His writings provided the greatest amount of information on slavery in Sudbury. He wrote that African Americans, whether slave or free, could be admitted to church membership. They took part in prayer, singing, and took communion.

Although Rev. Loring left no slaves at the time of his death, he was a slave owner during his lifetime. In his *History of Sudbury,* Hudson specifically cites Rev. Loring's love and esteem for his slave Simeon, also known as Simeon Harry. Simeon was born in Rev. Loring's home in 1734 and, for unrecorded reasons, was given his freedom twenty-one years later. A short time after that, he took ill and died. Rev. Loring wrote, "He was greatly beloved by the family and his death has drowned us in tears." A few days later, Rev. Loring wrote, "In the evening we committed the remains of Simeon to the dark and silent grave. A great number of the congregation attended the funeral." On May 13, 1775, Rev. Loring wrote, "My wife before Simeon died took to her bed being overcome and worn out through labor of body and distress of mind about Simeon."

Loring also wrote on the day Simeon died, "The Lord sanctify this death to us all particularly to the mother of the deceased." And three days later, "Died Susanna Harry sister to our hired woman servant Hannah. . . The loss of her son and now her sister. . . " It then became clear that Hannah, another of Loring's servants, was Simeon's mother. Earlier references to Hannah in the Reverend Loring's diaries call her "his Negro maid servant" indicating that she was a slave. Perhaps Hannah gained her freedom in 1742. That year the Reverend Loring recorded that his study caught fire, and "through the great goodness of God and endeavors of my servant maid Hannah and Mrs. Haiden it was extinguished and the house preserved."

148

There are no existing emancipation papers, if there ever were any, for Simeon and Hannah. Only one such paper has been discovered for a Sudbury slave, and that was for Nero Benson who belonged to the Reverend Swift of Framingham. Nero was known for his musical talent and in 1725 was a trumpeter in Capt. Isaac Clark's militia troop. He had married Dido Dingo in 1721, a female slave of the Reverend Swift. When Swift died in 1745, Dido and a daughter [presumably belonging to her and Nero] were left to Swift's family in Framingham, and Nero, with whom Dido had been married for almost twenty-five years, was willed to Dr. Ebenezer Roby of Sudbury, the Swift's son-in-law. By 1747, it is recorded that Nero belonged to a man named Samuel Wood who granted him his freedom. It was recorded in the only discovered Emancipation Paper that pertains to Sudbury. "The said Nero Benson is absolutely a free man and fully set at liberty from all slavery whatsoever by or under me."

Emancipation meant the former slave owner would pay for the support of a former slave if he or she ever became a town charge. In the same document, Samuel Wood paid the town of Sudbury a bond of £100 "to indemnify and save the town harmless from all and any charges toward the support and maintenance of a Negro man named Nero Benson." One last entry from the Reverend Loring on July 4, 1757: "This day attended the funeral of Nero Benson who died at the schoolhouse July 3rd Lord's Day. A Negro man admitted into the Church Nov. 9, 1746. Left behind him a widow, apparently also free, and three children." Nero's wife Dido is mentioned years later in Sudbury town meeting and poor records asking the town for support.

In 1754, each town in the Bay Colony appointed assessors to report on the number of slaves in their town. Sudbury reported nine males and five females. No names of slaves or slave owners are included. A 1749 tax list for Sudbury still survives in the Town Clerk's Office which lists the number of slaves at seventeen. The twelve slave owners in Sudbury in 1771 were taxed for one slave each, a deceiving number since any slaves less than fourteen or more than forty-five years of age were not included. While we might know the actual slave population, it appears the usual number was one per family. While the Reverend Swift, as mentioned earlier, owned as many as five slaves at his death, David Baldwin of Sudbury topped that figure with six slaves when he died in 1770 [only a year before the census of 1771]. Baldwin left the Negro boy Juba to his son William and the girl Candace to his son Samuel. He left the Negro girl Violet to his daughter Abigail, Nancy to daughter Elizabeth, Cloe to daughter Lydia and Nell to daughter Mary.

Noyes family genealogy written in 1904 claims that Col. John Noyes (1715-1785). . . "owned much real estate and a considerable number of slaves." Existing information shows that Col. Noyes sold a slave named Cato to Jonas Noyes in 1767.

In addition to wills, there remain property deeds for slaves and receipts of payment. There was the sale of Frank Benson to Josiah Richardson in 1745. The seller was the Reverend John Swift of Acton who inherited Frank when his father, the Framingham minister, died. A 1779 Receipt for Payment is to Ezekiel Howe who paid 200 pounds for a Negro girl. In the diary of Experience Wight Richardson, Josiah Sr.'s wife. Dec. 9, 1776: "This day my servant Dinah had her freedom."

Other sources of hard evidence for slave populations are census records. The first federal census in 1790 reported Massachusetts as having no slaves. However, earlier census records indicate that there had been slaves and slave owners in Sudbury. The 1771 Provincial Census stated that 911 residents of the Bay Colony owned 1169 "servants for life" [i.e. slaves], including "Indian, Negroes, mulatto, from [ages] fourteen to forty-five." Twelve slave owners on that list lived in Sudbury. We have their names and the number of slaves they owned, which was needed for tax purposes. The names of the slaves were not given.

Although it is impossible to assess the degree of anti slavery sentiment in Sudbury, Samuel Wood's action to grant freedom to Nero Benson and Mrs. Richardson's diary entry regarding her slave Dinah seem to indicate that some people in Sudbury must have been opposed to human bondage. Interestingly enough, Mrs. Richardson made a diary entry in 1777: "O now that I live alone I may converse with God more than ever the last of my family is gone now Dinah is gone." It sounds like Mrs. Richardson would have liked Dinah to stay in spite of being free, but Dinah chose not to.

Lydia Maria Child, a devoted abolitionist and one of Wayland's most famous residents condemned slavery. She once wrote: "While we bestow our earnest disapprobation on the system of slavery, let us not flatter ourselves that we are in reality any better than our brethren of the South. Thanks to our soil and climate, and the early exertions of the Quakers, the form of slavery does not exist among us; but the very spirit of the hateful and mischievous thing is here in all its strength."

--□□□--

Special Prosecutor

Archibald Cox had been a familiar figure in Wayland long before he made national headlines and the nightly news in October 1973. A tall, handsome man who wore a characteristic bow tie, Cox had lived in Wayland for almost thirty years before that fateful night he was fired from his job by order of President Richard Nixon.

Cox, Special Watergate Prosecutor, had subpoenaed President Nixon for his audio tapes which the president refused to release. After two appeals of the subpoenas were turned down, the president offered to give the Senate and Cox written summaries of what was on the tapes. Cox turned down the deal and things got ugly. The president ordered Attorney General Elliot Richardson to fire his former professor. Richardson refused and instead resigned. The President ordered Assistant Attorney General William Ruckelshaus to do the firing and when he refused, Ruckelshaus was dismissed. Finally, the president ordered Robert Bork, Solicitor General, to do the firing, which he did. The event became known as the "Saturday Night Massacre."

Archibald Cox, born in 1912 in Plainfield, New Jersey, entered St. Paul's School in New Hampshire, an Episcopal boys school outside of Concord, at the age of fourteen. In the fall of 1930 he entered Harvard University, and four years later Harvard Law School, from which he graduated on June 9, 1937. Three days after graduation he married Phyllis Ames, a Smith graduate whose family owned a farm on Glezen Lane. The Ames family had been linked to Harvard Law School for generations. Phyllis's grandfather, James Barr Ames, had been the dean of the Law School in the 1890s and her father, Richard Ames served as administrative secretary at the law school for sixteen years . Her maternal grandfather, Nathan Abbott, founded Stanford Law School. Archibald's father, a Harvard graduate, practiced law in New York while Archie was growing up and Archibald's great-grandfather, William Maxwell Evarts, defended President Andrew Johnson during impeachment proceedings in 1868.

Before Archie finished his last Law School exam, he was called to Professor Felix Frankfurter's office at the Law School. The Professor offered to recommend Archie to clerk for Judge Learned Hand on the U.S. Court of Appeals in New York for a year. Judge Hand, a legend in the legal world, is often mentioned in the same breath as Oliver Wendell Homes. The couple packed up and moved to New York City. When the year was up, they returned to Boston and Archie entered private practice with the firm of Ropes and Gray. Charles Wyzanski, a brilliant labor relations attorney and one of the firm's partners, chose Archie to work on his cases. In 1941, when Wyzanski was called to Washington as Vice Chairman of the National Defense Mediation Board, Archie was asked to serve as one of his assistants. Archie and Phyllis moved to Washington. Five months later the board was disbanded. Within weeks, Archie was asked to join the Solicitor General's Office at the United States Justice Department–a chance to represent the United States in the nation's highest court. Two years later, Secretary of Labor, Frances Perkins called Mr. Cox and asked if he would be interested in serving as Associate Solicitor in the Labor Department. This would be Archie's fourth job in less than two years. The family rented a house in rural Maryland.

When the war ended, Cox returned to the firm of Ropes and Gray and the family moved to Wayland. Phyllis' father had died and her mother, remarried, had moved to California. The couple was offered the Ames' family home on Glezen Lane, a reasonably easy commute to Boston. In the fall of 1945, Archie accepted a teaching position at Harvard Law School and began a new commute–to Cambridge. The Cox's raised two daughters, Phyllis and Sally, and a son, Archie Jr. in Wayland and summered at the Ames' family farm in Maine.

Phyllis Cox was an experienced and avid horsewoman who lent her time, skill and wisdom to Wayland's young riding enthusiasts. For many years she led the Wayland 4-H Club and worked endless hours as mentor and coach at local riding rings. Mrs. Cox taught young riders technique and proper horse care and often visited them at home to monitor their progress.

Wayland residents who had worked with Archie knew his deep respect for public service and reverence for the law. It was no surprise that Cox would defend his values nationally and face down Richard Nixon. A pioneer in labor law, Cox shared his expertise from 1954-59 as a member of the town's Personnel Board. He served on the Board of Assessors from 1951-54 and as a selectman from 1959-1960. Cox also served as President of the Wayland United Nations Association and the Wayland Chapter of the Red Cross. In 1961, Archie took a four-year leave from Harvard to serve as Solicitor General in the Kennedy administration. During that time, he often appeared before the Supreme Court pursuing legal remedies to injustice. Among the cases was Baker vs. Carr, which set standards for reapportionment;

Heart vs. Atlanta, which broke ground on public accommodations for all; South Carolina vs. Katzenbach, which upheld the Voting Rights Act; and Buckley vs. Valeo which reformed campaign financing.

For many years professor Cox was Carl M. Loeb University Professor Emeritus at Harvard University having retired from full time teaching in 1986. After his Harvard retirement he taught full-time at Boston University and remained a visiting Professor of Law until 1996. He worked with Common Cause, an advocacy group that lobbies for campaign finance reform and ethics laws and joined the legal team that defended the constitutionality of the 1974 campaign finance laws. Former president Bill Clinton in 2001 awarded Cox the Presidential Citizens Medal for exemplary service, an award, ironically, established by Nixon in 1969.

Archibald and Phyllis retired to the Ames family farm in Maine where the family had spent many summers. Professor Cox died in Maine on May 29, 2004 at the age of 92.

❑❑❑

Sudbury River

The Sudbury River wends its way from Cedar Swamp in Westborough through Framingham, Wayland, and Concord where it merges with the Assabet to become the famed Concord River. Such historic fame does not attach to the Sudbury, which may be the slowest river in the nation! As the often threadlike river traverses the length of Wayland, south to north, so too its languor has influenced Wayland's evolution from its agricultural beginnings to the residential town it has become.

What do Wayland's early nineteenth century farmers and twentieth century developers have in common? The frustration caused by periodic spring and fall floods, not just beneficial spring freshets but gently spreading waters that fill the wide river marshes and may even creep across roads to wind around the town center itself, much to the delight of the media. An almost flat gradient throughout the river's thirteen mile course from Stone's Bridge to Concord's Egg Rock and its confluence there with the faster flowing Assabet is said to result in reverse flow on occasion. Struggling farmers who lost their marsh hay to flood waters blamed the downstream Fordway Bar and dam in Billerica for causing the river to back up. Developers blamed flood plain zoning and wetland's law for preventing filling for new development.

The river in flood was an early impetus toward the eventual political separation of East Sudbury from Sudbury. In the days when rivers generally provided the power for mills and industrial centers, the same lack of gradient that creates flooding meant that this long stretch of the Sudbury River was not useful for commercial developments–except, of course, to accept discharges from upstream industries that still contaminate its sediments and fish.

In the 1970s, Wayland citizens, anxious to preserve the agricultural character of the town, negotiated to buy some large tracts of undeveloped farmland along the river. The state viewed the river as the nexus that made these wetland and upland parcels together significant for conservation and passive recreation. Substantial state and federal funds were awarded to partially reimburse the town for the purchases.

Throughout Wayland's history, naturalists and hunters have recognized the Sudbury River and its water-retaining marshes as valuable habitat for wildlife, particularly migratory birds. This recognition has led to continuing acquisition of river wetlands by the Federal government to form part of the Great Meadows National Wildlife Refuge. This ownership, beginning in the 1950s has protected many of the values that resulted in the Sudbury, along with the Assabet and Concord Rivers, being designated as Wild and Scenic Rivers in 1999. As a result, a stewardship council of town, state and federal representatives was formed, whose goal is to protect multiple river assets–scenic, historic, literary, recreational and wildlife. Because a prerequisite for wild and scenic designation is that river flow be unobstructed by impoundments, only that part of the Sudbury below the Saxonville dam in Framingham was eligible.

Thus, as a function of gradient loss, what flow the river maintains in Wayland beyond the halfway point, depends largely upon how much comes over or through a complex of upstream dams in Framingham where two branches of the river converge. Until the mid 1980s, these dams were operated by the state's Metropolitan District Commission (MDC) which by law was required to release water to the river below the Framingham dams but only by a minuscule amount–an amount sufficient to fill two side-by-side fire hoses. Wayland became alarmed when the MDC proposed augmenting the Boston metropolitan area water supply from Quabbin Reservoir by reactivating the Sudbury Reservoir in Southborough, which had been rarely used since the 1940s. The loss of the Sudbury Reservoir's high-quality water would be a great loss to our sluggish river. In addition, recharge of the aquifer that supplies Wayland's well water would be threatened. The "Sudbury River diversion" proposal was but one alternative plan to meet projected urban demand. The MDC's grandiose plans, however, were eventually abandoned in favor of conservation, leak repair, and the like, thanks to the concerted efforts of people opposed to diverting rivers out-of-basin, and thanks to the Massachusetts Water Resources Authority (MWRA) management of the urban water system. Now, legislation requires release of a reasonable flow at the Framingham dam and the MWRA will consider use of the Sudbury Reservoir for water supply only in an emergency.

Sudbury Valley Trustees

The Sudbury Valley Trustees, Inc. is a local conservation organization, founded in 1953 by seven Wayland residents to acquire and preserve open spaces in the Sudbury River watershed, to protect its wildlife and native plants, to promote outdoor recreation, and to educate the public in the values of conservation. Current figures show over 3,000 individuals, families, and corporations are members. The Trustees own over 2,000 acres of open space in thirteen valley communities and oversee 500 acres of conservation restrictions. This vital organization has been instrumental in the preservation of thousands of acres of land by local, regional, and federal public agencies.

Over the years, the Trustees have promoted the passage of legislation to protect wetlands and mark flood plain boundaries, to establish conservation commissions, to protect aquifers, and to designate areas of critical environmental concern, scenic roads, and river ways. Many of its members now serve as members of the public agencies set up to promote the preservation of natural spaces in the Sudbury River Valley.

The Trustees manage over twenty parcels of land in Wayland, ranging in size from one-half acre to eighty-four acres in size. The largest and most frequently used tracts in Wayland are Hamlen Woods on Rice Road, Upper Millbrook on Concord Road, and Green Ways near the intersection of Old Connecticut Path and Cochituate Road. All of these areas offer a variety of walking trails and examples of every type of natural area from bare bedrock to deep coniferous forest to sphagnum bogs. Many SVT tracts lie next to land managed by the Wayland Conservation Commission.

There are dozens of SVT reservations in other towns in the Sudbury River Valley, shown on maps available from the Trustees. These include extraordinary areas like Round Hill, Brues Woods, the Memorial Forest, and the Gray Reservation in Sudbury.

❑❑❑

Surveyors of Lumber & Measurers of Wood and Bark

Public servants given responsibility as surveyors of lumber and measurers of wood and bark were important in the seventeenth century, especially to the settlers of Sudbury Plantation who had a great deal of lumber and a need for saw mills.

There was little chance early settlers would be filling their need for sawmills on the almost flat and lazy waters of the Sudbury River. But they wasted no time finding a suitable swift-moving brook to serve their purposes. Hop Brook, rising in Marlborough, flows into the town at its southwesterly corner, winding easterly until it emptied into the Sudbury River near the Route 20 bridge.

In 1677, Peter King, Thomas Read, John Goodenow, John Smith and Joseph Freeman were granted the right to build a saw mill on Hop Brook upstream from the grist mill run by Thomas and Peter Noyes in South Sudbury–today's Mill Village. The saw mill owners were granted "twenty-tons of timber of the common lands for building the mill, earth for their dam, and they were to make a small dam or sufficient causage so as to keep the waters out of the swamp lands there . . .." Further, the sawmill owners were made responsible for taking over the Noyes' gristmill should it ever become abandoned. It was recorded that visitors to the mill heard the saw as it dragged up and down through the log saying, "Shall I go or shall I not."

In 1799, Samuel Freeman, Esq. published the first edition of "The Town Officer: Laws of the Commonwealth of Massachusetts and Forms for use by Towns, Parishes, and Plantations and how to keep accounts." Isaac Damon Jr. wrote on the fly leaf of the Wayland library copy: "Esto studiosus et lege legem." (Be studious and read the law.)

It was an important civic duty to guarantee a prospective buyer that he or she was getting his or her money's worth at the sawmill. Officials acted only when the surveyor "shall have any doubt as to the measure." Freeman elaborates on the "causes for inspection" and describes the fee involved: twelve shillings per one thousand board feet. Of the fee paid, one-half went to "the poor of the town" and the other half to the surveyor. There were penalties for fraud, ten pounds for each offense.

These positions have historical origins that spread over two centuries. Today, Surveyors of Lumber and Measurers of Wood and Bark have similar duties, although fireplace owners will be most interested in the latter. Massachusetts General Law states that Surveyors of Lumber must "assure that if any warfinger or carter shall cart or carry any firewood from any warf or landing place before the same is measured shall forfeit $1 for every load of wood carried off and the money goes to the poor." The law further states that Measurers of Wood and Bark must assure that "for the purpose of ensuring cordwood sold and offered for sale shall be four feet in length. Firewood shall mean and include wood cut to any length of less than four feet and more than eight inches. Cordwood and firewood shall be advertised, offered for sale and sold only in terms of cubic feet or cubic meters."

Again, one person is elected annually at the town meeting by the Town Clerk casting one ballot for each.

1878 Town Hall

Taverns

Local taverns were the centers of a town's social and political life during the seventeenth century. The original Sudbury settlement had many taverns. The first was established in 1653 by Jonathan Parmenter who petitioned the General Court to open an Ordinary on his land along the road leading from the early town center on Old Sudbury Road to the mill on Mill Pond. It was not only a resting place for travelers, but served as the local meeting place where farmers socialized and townsmen met to decide the future of the community. Early taverns were governed by laws including a statute that defined a tavern as "an establishment where alcoholic beverages may be served with or without food." The tavern keepers had to be persons of high character and standing in the town since they were selling liquor. The Parmenter Ordinary survived for more than 100 years but was demolished in the early nineteenth century. Today the property is marked by a 1770s Parmenter house on Bow Road at Concord Road.

Another prominent tavern that no longer stands was Pequod House. Established in 1771 by Elijah Bent and situated where the present Public Safety Building is located, this large edifice was painted yellow on the front and vivid red at the rear. In later years, a third story, a wide front verandah, and a long two-story rear ell were added. A long drive-through barn extended along the north side of the inn to shelter horses and wagons overnight. (see Pequod House) It is reported that General Washington stopped here on his way to take command of the Continental Army in Cambridge in 1775. Rates for tavern fare were set and enforced by the local selectmen and the Clerk of the Market. Thus, Pequod House and other local taverns, charged the going fares of twenty shillings for a "good dinner," twelve shillings for a "common dinner," four shillings for one-night's lodging, and fifteen shillings for horse-keeping on hay, or ten shillings on grass. To stable a pair of oxen cost fifteen shillings a night. In the late eighteenth century, Pequod House was known for its suckling pig dinners and for its sleigh parties. For 150 years it was a gathering place for local townsmen. Travelers came by stage coach in the early and mid-nineteenth century, by train in the late nineteenth century, and by trolley in the early twentieth century.

There remain at least three buildings, now private dwellings, which served as taverns in the eighteenth and nineteenth centuries. The earliest of these is the Hopestill Bent Tavern–still standing–at 252 Old Connecticut Path. It was built in the early 1700s by Thomas Frink, a carpenter from Connecticut, who upon marrying one of the daughters of Peter Noyes, lived for some time in the nearby Noyes-Parris house in which his wife had inherited a part interest. Hopestill Bent, the first tavern keeper or inn holder at this site, was a descendant of early Sudbury and Framingham settlers. The location on the old path to Connecticut made the early tavern an important rest stop for travelers from Boston to Connecticut and New York. It reportedly served as a tavern until about 1780. However, there is no knowledge of succeeding tavern keepers.

Perhaps a competitor was Jacob Reeves who opened his tavern farther east on Old Connecticut Path in 1764. Reeves had come to East Sudbury from Roxbury, purchased a small farm in 1762, and enlarged the modest two-room house, built by Matthew Hasey, to begin his tavern business by 1764.

Within a short time of arriving here, Reeves became active in local politics, becoming one of the first selectmen when East Sudbury separated from Sudbury in 1780. Bits and pieces of historical information provide a taste of life at Reeves Tavern. There is a 1764 account of the Sheriff of Middlesex County stating that a complaint had been filed on behalf of "Jacob Reeves of said Sudbury Inn holder" that ". . . a man and a woman – strolling persons in said house – whom said Reeves vehemently suspects have feloniously taken or stolen away said silver spoon contrary to law . . . "

John Adams' diary mentions stopping at the tavern in 1775 on his way to Connecticut. And lest we wonder what was served at the tavern, a large collection of receipts from the 1780s demonstrates that Reeves purchased gallons and gallons of rum usually by the barrel, and substantial amounts of sugar and molasses. Other receipts for fine salt, rock salt, tea, and coffee are in the collection and many of them note the excise tax on imported products. The proprietor of the tavern following Jacob Reeves' death, in 1794, was his son, Jacob Reeves (1762-1845). Known as "Squire Jack," young Reeves followed in his father's footsteps and served his community as Justice of the Peace, Town Clerk, a church deacon and, for a short time, as representative to the General Court. Today the old tavern retains some of its features including the tavern desk in the front hall, the old kitchen with a side bake oven next to the large fireplace outfitted with a crane for hanging pots over the flame, and a wall on the second floor hung on hinges at the top so that it could be raised to form a dance floor or ball room during the tavern days.

The Luther Moore Tavern opened during the 1770s. It was located at the northern end of town on the corner of Concord and Oxbow roads. For about twenty years, Luther Moore was the proprietor. Two other taverns that did a hearty business but no longer exist, included the Corner Tavern and Loker Tavern. Loker Tavern was located on the present site of the Villa restaurant off Commonwealth Road in Cochituate. The Corner Tavern, which is reported to have opened in about 1765, was run by Nathaniel Reeves on the site of today's Coach Grill on Boston Post Road (Route 20). It was quite a large establishment with not only a large house and barn, but also a harness shop, paint and varnish shop, a blacksmith shop, and a carriage shop–all necessary businesses for stage coach stops. This tavern closed in 1850 and the buildings burned in 1902 or 1903. It is interesting to note that both were on sites that today are occupied by restaurants, carrying out the historical land use.

The tavern business ended in the 1910s and Pequod House was demolished in 1928. At various times, many other taverns operated throughout town. East Sudbury had about a dozen taverns during the time of the Revolution.

Town Halls

The town needed a separate public meeting hall for the first time in 1815 after townspeople decided the fifth meetinghouse was to be used for religious purposes only. Legally, the meetinghouse would remain a municipal building for eighteen more years until separation of church and state in Massachusetts but the town was willing to support separate operations. (see Fifth Meetinghouse)

Town fathers sought various locations before they finally struck a good old Yankee deal. They contracted with two long-time well-respected residents, Luther Gleason Sr. and Jonathan Fiske Heard to dismantle the fourth meetinghouse–then near the corner of Pelham Island and Cochituate roads–and build another structure next door to the fifth meetinghouse on the Boston Post Road. Gleason and Heard agreed to build a store/residence/town hall using materials taken from the old meetinghouse, excepting the pews. The town, having assumed responsibility for "improving the town hall at all times. . ." used the space for town meetings, a singing school and the choice of militia officers. The contract was for a period of thirty-five years. (see Old Green Store/Kirkside)

Messrs. Gleason and Heard took their obligations seriously and made the second floor of what became known as the "Old Green Store," into public space. The Old Green Store, when it was completed, very much resembled the old fourth meetinghouse (1726)–simple and square. Indeed, some of the timbers used to frame it had come from the third meetinghouse (1686) which had been moved from the Old Burial Ground to the town center. The town hall space had two fireplaces built on the inner wall creating the very first heated public hall. An entrance and stairway were made separate from the rest of the house. In January 1816, the first town meeting was held upstairs in the Old Green Store, where meetings would be held for the next twenty-five years.

When Deacon James Draper contracted to build the first town hall in 1841, he offered to donate the land and to accept his fee in $200 annual payments until "the debt becomes extinct." The town promptly accepted his offer. And that was the last time building a town hall in Wayland was easy and without controversy.

The white-columned 1841 town hall at 21 Cochituate Road had a school room and small entry room on the first floor and a public meeting room upstairs. Apparently Draper's finished structure wasn't considered quite perfect, because in agreeing to pay him the $1,700 building costs, town hall committee members deducted six dollars, "on account of the window blinds not being quite so good as we thought they should have been."

Thirty-six years later the Town needed a roomier, more elaborate town hall. The Grout-Heard house site on its small height of land was felt to be the most appropriate spot to locate the tall imposing Gothic structure the town planned. The Heard family agreed to have their house moved to the west side of Old Sudbury Road. There was near universal approval of the building site. Even Lydia Maria Child, Wayland's famous abolitionist, wrote, "I am glad the Grout estate is to be purchased for the town hall, because the situation is central and convenient." But Mrs. Child did not approve of much else: "I suppose the New Hall will be a pretext for increasing the taxes, which are already so heavy as to render Wayland an undesirable residence in that particular," she told one correspondent. The town hall was, she wrote, "no more needed, than a coach needs a fifth wheel." She called the extravagant building "the Wayland Folly . . . dedicated . . . to debt and taxation."

The 1878 town hall contained six town offices and a two-room library on the first floor and on the second floor, a meeting hall which seated 500 and a balcony called an orchestra gallery. The library was in the rear until it moved in 1900 to the new library building. It's removal left space for a fire department in the rear. The four-story tower was used for drying hoses. The building was dedicated on Christmas Eve with a fancy ball and lengthy ceremonies presided over by James Sumner Draper.

Was there controversy eighty years later when the town decided to build the 1957 town building (the building recently demolished to make way for the new Public Safety building)? YES! On first glance one would think not, judging by the glowing account in the August 1958 *Town Crier* when the building was dedicated, having been occupied for a year. It was reported that the building site had been given to the town thirty years earlier and the $340,000 building was largely paid for by prudent appropriations made over a number of years before the building opened. Further, the reporter pointed out that the "handsome Colonial-type structure" had been planned for all future needs. It was "built to meet the needs of the town of 17,000, Wayland's estimated maximum possible population."

One can only speculate on the controversies that preceded this successful opening, by reading the whimsical piece written by Crier editor Donald B. Willard, in his November 10, 1955 column:

"You, too, can build a Town building . . .

". . . you get a site committee. This committee will go out on Sunday mornings and case the whole community. Its members will fall into swamps, get hung up on brambles, be viewed with suspicion by property owners and tend to wrangle among themselves . . ."Having picked a site, you have the committee bring it into town meeting. Interested citizens, who have heretofore never heard of the project, will immediately rise to say the site is no good. It's too hot, too cold, too wet, too dry, too expensive, too near a cocktail lounge, too near a school, too far from transportation, and too near Tierra Del Fuego. In short, it will be pointed out that it is about the worst site possible.

"After the site is finally picked–and this may take from ten to twenty-five years–you appoint a building committee. This committee will waste its time hiring an architect . . ."Then you have the committee bring the building plans into town meeting. That's when you find out what's wrong with the building.

"Wrong type entirely. Should be early/American, not modern. Faces wrong way. Should face the town pump, not the hog reeve's office. Hot top driveway is wrong. Should be brickwork with a design showing the Town seal and maybe a wreath of lucky horse shoes . . . "

There's a sense of deja vu as Wayland went about building its public buildings in this, the twenty-first century.

ꗏ

Town Historians

Throughout the seventeenth century townspeople had struggled to survive–hefting stones from fields, replacing them with crops, fighting a war with Indians and establishing a town government. During the eighteenth century they struggled for identity–to remain one with Sudbury or become an independent East Sudbury? To remain subjects of Britain or be part of a free nation? The town's ministers and town meeting clerks were responsible for record-keeping during the early centuries. Beginning in the mid-nineteenth century townspeople began to reflect upon their past. Sudbury had been divided into two towns–Sudbury on the west side of the river and East Sudbury on the east side, Americans had won the Revolutionary War, and the little Puritan village of the previous two centuries had evolved into a energetic little town.

During the nineteenth century, the Draper name was often associated with town history–Deacon James Draper and his son James Sumner Draper. James Sumner Draper created several valuable maps and wrote a history of the town's service in the Civil War. (see Draper, James Sumner) Other local contributors to the town's history over the years have been: Alfred Sereno Hudson, Alfred Wayland Cutting, Helen Fitch Emery, George K. Lewis and John C. Bryant.

Alfred Sereno Hudson

Alfred Sereno Hudson was born and raised in Sudbury. He was one of three children born to Martin Newton Hudson of Framingham and Maria Mossman Read of Sudbury. The Hudson family is descended from Nathaniel Hudson of Lancaster, born in 1671, who had lived in Billerica and settled in Framingham.

Alfred Sereno Hudson is best known locally for *The History of Sudbury Massachusetts 1638-1889,* published in 1889, and *The Annals of Sudbury, Wayland, and Maynard, Middlesex County, Massachusetts,* published in 1891. Unlike many local historians who voluntarily wrote town histories, Hudson, no longer a resident, was commissioned by the town of Sudbury to write a town history. When Hudson accepted the town's commission, he was acting pastor of the First Congregational Church at Ayer, a position he had held since 1883 and where he lived until his death in 1907.

Hudson was asked to write a general history of the town that would be readable by a wide audience. (There is some debate about whether these two objectives were actually met.) But even critics agree that Hudson's history of the town remains the primary source of Sudbury and Wayland history through 1889. As one critic commented, "its inclusiveness is both its value and its weakness." Hudson's love for the town and its people is evident from the many interviews, conversations and anecdotes with local residents which he recorded.

Hudson attended Wadsworth Academy, graduated in 1864 from Williams College, and spent time in Virginia with the United States Sanitary Commission during the Civil War. In 1867 he graduated from the Theological Seminary at Andover and married Miss Lydia Rutter Draper of Wayland. Prior to going to Ayer, Hudson had assumed pastoral duties at Congregational Churches in Burlington, Easton, and Malden.

The vast amount of historical material Hudson gathered for his books came from original sources–town records, the Stearns Collection, State Archives and interviews and conversations with local inhabitants. James Sumner Draper, supplied Hudson with his map, "First Roads & House-Lots in Sudbury."

Alfred Wayland Cutting

During the last decade of the nineteenth century and well into the twentieth century, Alfred Wayland Cutting was the town's unofficial historian. "Al,"as he was known, was called upon to give and write speeches for important civic and historical events. His great passion for town history is apparent in his many writings. He wrote in an appealing and engaging style and spoke with experience, knowledge, and eloquence.

Alfred Wayland Cutting represented the sixth generation of the Cutting family to live in Wayland. Robert Cutting, the first Cutting to own land in Sudbury (Wayland) built a "lean-to" on Reeves Hill in 1713. Charles Cutting built the old house on the top of the hill in 1816. He also raised his family there, including a son, Charles Alfred (1822-1914) who left home when he was young.

Charles Alfred Cutting returned to Wayland in 1857 after purchasing the Samuel Stone Noyes house and land on the corner of Old Sudbury Road and Glezen Lane for summer use. He also bought the adjacent Moses Brewer house (circa 1700) from William Heard at about the same time. He had married Marcia Roby Drury, the daughter of a Boston merchant on March 24, 1850 in Boston. The Drurys were also prominent residents of Wayland. Marcia Roby Drury Cutting (1831-1917) was a cousin of Warren G. Roby who donated the present Public Library building and land to the town. Charles A. Cutting, Al's father, was engaged in the stationery business in Boston for many years. He also invested in the Massachusetts Central Railroad–later the Boston & Maine. In 1881, Charles and Marcia purchased the cottage of David Lee and Lydia Maria Child on Old Sudbury road and enlarged it in 1885 to accommodate their family. Townspeople said that Charles A. Cutting's great love for Wayland "amounted almost to a passion."

Alfred Wayland Cutting, called "Uncle Al" by neighborhood children, was born in Boston in 1860, the second son in the family and the third child. He had four siblings: Charles Franklin (1851-1914), Mary Elizabeth (1854-1896) who married Edwin B. Buckingham in 1874, Marcia Sophia "Madge" (1861-1931) and William Warren who died in infancy. Al attended Dwight Grammar School and spent three years at English High in Boston where he delivered the valedictory speech on June 30, 1876 in spite of poor health. After graduation he took the "grand tour" of Europe where he took many photographs. Upon his return he became a bank teller in Boston for nineteen years before retiring to the family home on Old Sudbury Road–the renovated Lydia Maria Child homestead.

Al's primary avocation was photography which allowed him to express himself artistically. His camera was always with him recording important, and not-so-important, events, people, and places which otherwise would have been lost in time. He preferred to think of himself as "semi-professional" although his photographs won prizes and were often published in contemporary magazines. When asked how he managed such success without formal training, he said, "by the use of plain common sense or good judgement. . . by a fair amount of manual dexterity. . . and last, and most important: sticking to one lens, one plate, and one printing medium."

But photography was not Al's only means of expression. He wrote as eloquently as he captured images. His interest in local history made him somewhat of an authority on the town. He prepared lectures and published two of his public addresses in pamphlet form: *A Hundred Years of the Old Meeting House,* and *Historical Wayland.* A third publication, *Old Time Wayland,* "depicts the quaint, picturesque and lovable features of the town's life in the olden time."

Today, an extensive and valuable collection of Cutting photographs are housed at the Grout-heard house in Wayland and the Cutting Collection at Historic New England, formerly the Society for the Preservation of New England Antiquities in Boston, which includes almost three thousand images. The Cutting collection includes many photos taken both locally and during his extensive travels.

Cutting died in August 1935 and is buried in North Cemetery in the Cutting family plot.

Helen Fitch Emery

Helen Emery became active in town affairs in the 1960s, about the time her children say she realized Wayland needed a comprehensive town history. Helen, a consummate researcher, enjoyed digging into primary sources at the Massachusetts State House, researching deeds at the Middlesex County Registry of Deeds, and compiling genealogies. Wayland's three and a half centuries of history provided a challenge for Helen's fervent curiosity. A humble and serious researcher, Helen worked behind the scenes to gather every important bit of information available on the town. *The Puritan Village Evolves, a History of Wayland, Massachusetts* published in 1981 states on the dust jacket that it was written between 1975 and 1981, but friends and family know it began at least a decade earlier. Perhaps Sumner Chilton Powell's *Puritan Village, The Formation of a New England Town* published in 1960 was inspirational–Helen's title suggests it may have been a model for her own book. Powell, whose book won a Pulitzer Prize in 1960, focused on the foundation of Sudbury Plantation tracing the genealogical origins and antecedents of four-fifths of Sudbury's first settlers. Emery's book, chronicles the social and economic history of the town from its beginning as a farming community to the development of a shoe manufacturing center and the recent evolution into a modern suburb. She interviewed well-informed citizens, read town reports, newspapers and valuation lists and researched numerous deeds in an effort to present a picture of life in Wayland for three centuries. Helen's painstaking research and her academic training in economics makes her book far from a routine history book.

Born in Manchester, Massachusetts in 1912, Helen grew up in Chestnut Hill and Cohasset. She was educated at the Winsor School in Boston and graduated Phi Beta Kappa from Vassar in 1934. Three years later she received her Masters degree in Economics from Radcliffe College. Helen taught Economics at Katharine Gibbs School in Boston and Smith College in Northampton.

She left work on her doctorate during World War II to take a job at the War Production Board in Washington. One of her major duties was setting production quotas and prices for stoves and refrigerators rationed during the war. In 1943 when Helen's office was moved into the newly opened Pentagon, she met her future husband, George I. Emery, a Boston banker serving as an Army Air Force lieutenant colonel. Two years later they were married and soon returned to the Boston area. The family moved to Wayland in 1946 where the Emerys raised two sons. Helen declined an offer to teach at

Wellesley College, staying at home with her children and volunteering her talents instead. A founding member of the Wayland Historical Commission, she served as its first chairwoman.

With her husband, George, Helen moved to North Hill in Needham, Massachusetts in 1990. After his death, she remained at North Hill where she died at the age of 91 in September 2003.

George K. Lewis

If there is such a thing as a historical baton, Alfred Wayland Cutting reached out over the decades and handed it to George K. Lewis. An unofficial town historian for the past five decades, George is the person everyone turns to for answers. When community groups need a speaker, George generously obliges. When a historic photograph needs explanation, George studies it until he identifies time and place. Like Cutting, George carries a camera, albeit a smaller one, with which he has documented town progress since the 1930s.

George was raised in Wayland and educated in Wayland and Weston Public Schools. He graduated in the class of 1944 from Harvard University, two years after his marriage to Shirley Peakes of Weston. After graduation he enlisted in the United States Navy and served two years overseas as both an enlisted man and officer. George took advantage of the GI bill and enrolled in Harvard for graduate work in 1946. In 1950, while a student, he was offered a teaching position at Boston University in the Department of Geography. He and Shirley built a house in Wayland that year but had to rent it out a year later when George was called by the Navy Reserve to serve in Washington. He worked in the Pentagon as a geographer for two years before returning to BU and Wayland in 1953. That is when Wayland's love affair with George really began.

Soon after the family moved back to their Concord Road home a very friendly and astute neighbor took George under her wing and made him a Friend of the Wayland Public Library and its chairman at the same time. She was intent upon capturing the "young intellectual with the camera" to help sponsor the town's first historical society, officially chartered by the State on May 6, 1954. When the group became organized enough to assign specific responsibilities, George became the Society's photographer. George's camera had been documenting town events for a long time–like the 1938 hurricane when it tore through town–an event he still vividly remembers. A talented geographer, map maker and educator, George had a long-standing interest in the "layering" of the landscape. "I wanted to know how things worked. What can the present landscape tell you about what's happened in the past." He found out by exploring the fields and forests of town and by paddling up and down the Sudbury River.

George and six fellow conservationists met in 1953 to organize a group for the purpose of saving environmentally threatened areas along the Sudbury River and to establish a way to purchase some of the town's fine old farmland before losing it to developers. Christened "Sudbury Valley Trustees," the group contributed money and raised other monies to purchase these lands. Once the group became known, large land owners interested in land preservation began to contribute parcels–often hundreds of acres.

George's commemorative history of SVT, *Sudbury Valley Trustees, 50 years of Conservation,* was published in May 2004 in celebration of SVT's fiftieth anniversary. As featured speaker and only

166

surviving founder of SVT, George was honored on May 22, 2004 for his many years of service to the organization as a "stalwart steward of the land."

George and Shirley raised two daughters and a son in Wayland. George commuted daily to BU at the same time that he served SVT and the town in various capacities. He was a Water Commissioner in 1958, 1960, 1961, a Selectman from 1961-67, on the Historical Commission from 1974-1983 and chairman from 1977-1979, the Historic District Commission from 1970-1995 and chairman from 1989-1995, Growth Policy Committee 1976, the Historic District Study Committee 1988-89, Executive Search Committee 1988-89, and the Records Management Committee from 1993-97.

George was chosen one of the first recipients of a Bay State Historical League's "Local Hero" award in 2004 for lasting impact in activities not limited to local history. He has worked extensively with Sudbury citizens on local maps.

In 1989 George and his late wife Shirley sponsored the George and Shirley Lewis Conservation Award which recognizes the actions and work of a local individual who "toils in our local environmental vineyards, and encourages others to do the same. At a well-attended ceremony at the Grout-Heard House on September 19, 2004, the Wayland community celebrated "George Lewis Day," honoring him for his many years of service to the town.

George continues to serve the town unofficially and to share his vast knowledge through writing and lecturing. His books include: *Growing Up in Wayland,* a memoir, published in 1997; *Images of America, Wayland,* published by Arcadia Publishing in 2000; and *Sudbury Valley Trustees, 50 years of Conservation,* published by the Sudbury Valley Trustees in 2004.

John C. Bryant

The rivalry between the north and south sides of town has ebbed and flowed over the years. The north side of town remained predominately a farming community even into the early twentieth century and Cochituate, the south side of town, developed into a thriving industrial community a quarter of a century earlier. Yet both sides of town had citizens eager to report the town's history. Men like James Madison Bent (1812-1888), one of Cochituate's leading shoe manufacturers, kept the town informed about happenings in south Wayland by writing for the *Framingham Gazette* and using the pen name "Quill."

John Bryant–no nom de plume–is today's unofficial historian for the town's south side. He became a specialist in Cochituate history partly from his great pride in the area and in part because many long-time friends and residents bequeathed to him their most valued photographs and records. Today, he is the person to whom officials go when they want a knowledgeable guest speaker on the history and happenings in Cochituate.

Born in Cochituate, John also has an ancestral "foot" in the north of town. Zachariah Bryant owned a stable in Wayland Center near today's 233 Boston Post Road (Route 20). The land was taken by the town to locate the new highway–the Boston Post Road. John's great-great-great-grandparents moved to Vermont where John's father was born. His great-great-great-grandfather was a veteran of the War of 1812. His own father, Calvin Bryant moved to Massachusetts and in 1910 married Annie Hook, a

Milford woman. Calvin, who had come from a family of accomplished blacksmiths in Vermont, established a welding business in Framingham. He built a home on Lakeshore Drive in 1920–one of the first permanent houses in the neighborhood. John's mother went home to Milford for the birth of John on Sept. 11, 1924. A sister Mildred had died seven years earlier. John attended Wayland schools, graduating from high school in 1942.

When John was nine years old, his father died and his mother was left to support the family. Annie sewed flannel nightgowns for the Works Progress Administration (WPA) for thirteen dollars per week between the mid 1930s and early 1940s. Workspace was provided in the Legion Hall in Cochituate, at the site of Finnerty's Restaurant today. John attended the Cochituate School, a block from the Legion Hall, and remembers waiting for his mother to finish work so they could walk the mile and a half home together. An entrepreneur at a young age, John established a boat rental business on Dudley Pond before he was a teenager. He would retrieve sunken boats in the pond that people didn't bother to recover, fix them up and rent them to fishermen. His business enabled him to buy all his school clothing the year he entered high school and to deposit twenty dollars in a savings account at Farmers Mechanics Bank in Framingham. By the time he graduated from high school he owned six boats. John credits a Bermudian boatman named Archie Harriot for teaching him all he knew about boats. Archie plied the pond regularly in his large boat, "The Mayflower," and became young John's mentor.

Several months after graduation John enlisted in the Army Air Corp and following training, spent two years in China, Burma, and India. Upon discharge in 1946, John was awarded a bronze star medal for meritorious duties above and beyond what was expected of an enlisted man.

John returned to the family home on Lakeshore Drive where he lived until 1950 when he married a local girl, Lorraine Campbell, who lived on the west side of Dudley Pond near the town beach at West Plain Street and Mansion Road. Before getting married, John had already developed a successful construction company and employed some of the finest carpenters in the Metrowest region. He built his first home on the corner of Old Connecticut Path and Hawthorne Road. The couple had three children, Cynthia, Deborah and John Jr. For the next twenty years John remained active in his company. Still, he had time to explore other interests and beginning in 1953 began to apprentice at the Gibbs Funeral home on Commonwealth Road (Route 30). He attended the New England Institute of Funeral Directing and Anatomy in 1965 graduating with highest honors. In 1961, J. S. Waterman Company bought the Gibbs Funeral home and hired strangers to run the business. A lack of personal attention to long-time residents by the new company's employees disturbed John and he left after a year and a half. Seven years later, in 1968, John opened his own funeral establishment to serve town clientele and residents of surrounding towns.

Until the late 1960s, people from the north side of town made funeral arrangements in Waltham and other nearby towns. That changed when Effie Shepard, who lived on Plain Road, had her son's funeral arrangements made by the John Bryant Funeral Home. From then on many others began to make funeral arrangements at Bryant's and by the time Waterman's closed in 1985, John had the lion's share of the business in town. The same kindness and honesty that have made all of John's ventures successful are being maintained today by two of his children who carry on the business.

At the same time John was building and running his funeral business he was also serving the town. In 1950 he was on the Memorial Day Committee; 1957-2000 an Allen Fund Trustee; 1974-1998 the Historic District Commission; 1979 Historical Commission; 1979-1990 Park and Recreation Commission; 1985-86 McManus Planning Committee; 1988-2004 Agent, Board of Health.

John and Lorraine's residence on Pemberton Road is the handsomely renovated home of a former 1840 shoe shop owner. In addition to the Bryant Funeral Home, the family owns three other houses on the property currently occupied by children and grandchildren. An octogenarian this year, John continues to serve the town as a volunteer, competent professional, and a valued friend to many.

□□□

Training Fields

Why would Sudbury need a training field in the seventeenth century and later? Sudbury, as a frontier town, was expected to serve as a bulwark for the entire Massachusetts Bay Colony. Since the General Court had granted Colony lands to Proprietors, towns were ordered to prepare their defenses, build a fort or watch tower, provide officers and ammunition, and supply guards and fighting men when needed. Many colony records show that Sudbury received directions to train troops and maintain garrison houses. Fear and apprehension lingered among the townspeople and relations with the local Indians had been uneasy since the fierce Indian attacks that occurred during the King Philip's War in 1676. (see Haynes Garrison) The Proprietors of the Common and Undivided Land of Sudbury voted on May 25, 1713 to lay out two convenient training fields, one on each side of the Sudbury River. The training field on the east side of the river was laid out in 1714. It was an eight-acre, 114 rod field, a successor to the 1640 training field and was sold in 1804. (see Memorials and Markers)

The Sand Hill Training Field on the west side of the river contained three acres and was laid out by the Proprietors on February 29, 1720. It is on Old County Road one third of a mile from the junction with Boston Post Road (Route 20). It and the government powder house are marked by a rough stone: "1720–Training Field–Sand Hill Plain–[and] Government store house were near by. Erected by the Wayside Inn Chapter of the DAR, 1914." In addition to training minutemen, Sudbury had charge of a government storehouse containing munitions. The town voted in 1771 to erect the powder house at Sand Hill.

In the early 1700s, Sudbury, like other provincial towns, could not escape involvement in the far-off wars waged between England and France. The second war of the period called Queen Anne's War (1702-1713) required men and material to attack Acadia and the Penobscot and Passamaquody Indians. Later, a campaign was organized for the capture of Quebec. Although Sudbury itself did not suffer attack, in was rumored in 1706 that a large force was coming to New England. To prepare, the Colonial government passed a resolution ordering that "such and so many of the soldiers enlisted in the military companies and troops within the respective towns and districts herein after named, shall each of them at (his) own charge be provided with a pair of good serviceable snow shoes, mogginsons (sic) at or before the tenth of November this present year, which they shall keep in good repair and fit for the service."

The treaty at Utrecht in 1713 brought peace for a time. Soon, however, the Indians went on the war-path. An incident in Rutland, MA., where many people from Sudbury had settled, indicates the peril of the times and need for training men to guard the populace. In 1724 , ". . . this day about 12 o'clock five men and a boy [were] making hay in the middle of the town. A number of Indians surrounded them and shot first at the boy which alarmed the men, who ran for their guns, but the Indians shot upon them, and kept them from their guns, and shot down three of the men and wounded another in the arm, who got home, the fifth got home without any damage."

The war between England and France was called King George's War or the Third French War (1744-1749). The alliance formed by the Indians and French meant terror to the English frontier. The French stronghold of Louisburg on Cape Breton was far from Sudbury but many Sudbury men suffered before the French surrendered to the English after a forty-nine-day siege. A series of blockhouses and forts was built to protect defenseless places to the north and west. One blockhouse, No. 4, located at present-day Charlestown, N.H., was commanded by Capt. Phineas Stevens, a Sudbury native. Nearby settlers had fled to the fort which was constantly under attack.

The fourth and last time the English and French fought against each other, a treaty of peace was signed in Paris in 1763. Canada would no longer harbor enemy able to attack the exposed frontier. Locally trained soldiers learned important European military tactics from their part in the war and were better able to cope in battles with the British during the Revolutionary War. (see Revolutionary War)

Prior to the Revolutionary War, each minute man was issued a gun and bayonet, a cartridge box and thirty-six rounds. Guns were to be kept in good repair. In good weather, men drilled on the town's two commons, on the west side at the present-day Sudbury Center, and on the east side at the present-day Wayland Center, as well as on the training fields.

U

Lydia Maria Child house where Harriet Jacobs visited

Underground Railroad

Now and then tales circulate in Wayland about slaves having been hidden in one or another of the town's older homes. Mysterious and seemingly "perfect" hiding places appear under stair wells or in basement niches which help to make the stories believable. As yet, however, no house in Wayland can be documented as part of the Underground Railroad. We can only keep hoping that at some point a written document will emerge from a still undiscovered treasure trove of papers to shed new light on the subject. What we do know conclusively is that some Wayland people were supporters and contributors to the Underground Railroad and the abolitionist cause.

The Underground Railroad was an informal network of people who helped fugitive slaves from the South escape to freedom in the northern states and Canada. It was especially active during the years 1830-1860. Houses in the North, often called "stations," lived in by abolitionists, sheltered fugitives along their perilous journey to freedom whether by foot, wagon, boat or train. Since slavery was legal in the U. S. until the XIII Amendment was ratified in December 1865, abolitionists could be jailed or fined for engaging in illegal activity, and captured slaves would be returned to their masters in the South. The utmost secrecy prevailed. A relatively small number of written materials have thus far surfaced in letters or journals, but most people left no record of their involvement in the Underground Railroad either during or after their participation.

Lydia Maria Child was Wayland's most prominent anti-slavery crusader. Her efforts on behalf of fugitive slaves and the abolitionist cause have justifiably earned her recognition on a national scale. She pursued an intensely personal quest not only for the abolition of slavery, but for racial equality. While the details remain largely untold, Mrs. Child is known to have aided fugitive slaves. Her stays at the Hooper home and the Carpenter farm in New York, both stations on the Underground Railroad, afforded her many opportunities for direct contact with runaway slaves. The passage of the Fugitive Slave Law in 1850, which imposed stricter penalties for Northerners who were implicated in the workings of the Underground Railroad, roused her to even greater passions. "So help me God, I will bury every friendship on earth, rather than shake hands with a man that has assisted in restoring a fugitive slave *[to bondage,]*" she declared in a letter. When Thomas Sims, an escaped slave was returned to slavery under the new law, Mrs. Child wrote numerous appeals to individuals to raise money to buy his freedom. A U. S. marshal who had helped return Sims to slavery felt guilty and bought his freedom anonymously. It is unclear what Child's role was, but she knew of the marshal's plans. (see Child, Lydia Maria)

In 1861, Mrs. Child edited *Incidents in the Life of a Slave Girl,* written by Harriet Jacobs, a woman who had escaped to freedom via the Underground Railroad. While the book primarily detailed Harriet's life in slavery, her escape was every bit as harrowing, though largely untold. The book was published under the pseudonym, Linda Brent, and the names of her masters were changed, to hide her real identity. Harriet Jacobs was a visitor at the Child home on Old Sudbury Road, one of a small number of guests that were entertained there.

Another way to support the Underground Railroad was to make monetary contributions to an organization that provided clothing and food to fugitive slaves as they made their way to a safe destination. The Boston Vigilance Committee was one such association, formed in direct response to the new Fugitive Slave Act of 1850. *The Account Book of Francis Jackson, Treasurer of the Vigilance Committee*, has survived and contains some Wayland names: Lydia Maria Child's friend and fellow abolitionist, Rev. Edmund Sears and the Unitarian Society, Jonas Scott, Methodist minister in Cochituate, and Martha B. Wight and the Juvenile Association. While the specific names represent their larger organizations and leave unnamed the other contributors, it is obvious that support for the Underground Railroad and its rescue work involved a number of Wayland people. Of course, we still do not know what further assistance they may have given and whether they personally sheltered runaway slaves in their homes.

The need for the Underground Railroad increased as the slave power in the federal government became more entrenched. As early as the mid 1830s, Wayland citizens attempted to put pressure on Congress to abolish slavery and thereby eliminate the need for a secret escape network. Their protests most often took the form of petitions submitted through Congressman John Quincy Adams, a relentless supporter of the anti-slavery cause. Rev. Lavius Hyde, minister of the Evangelical Trinitarian Church in Wayland from 1835-1841, spearheaded the effort in Town. Rev. Hyde, an early advocate of abolition, had been dismissed as minister of the Congregational Church in Salisbury, Connecticut in 1822 for denouncing slavery, well before the Underground Railroad's heyday. As minister in Wayland, he organized a number of women parishioners, who otherwise had no voice in government, to offer petitions to the House of Representatives to end the slave trade, prohibit the extension of slavery into Arkansas and Texas, and declare the District of Columbia a free area. To this day, Rev. Hyde remains an unsung hero in Wayland's efforts to abolish slavery and eliminate the need for the Underground Railroad. One can only guess how many more townsmen/women have been overlooked. There is still considerable research to be done before the full story is known about the extent of Wayland's contributions to the Underground Railroad and to abolition.

V

Beatrice Herford Hayward

Vokes Theater

For almost a century, Wayland has had its very own theater for the performing arts. In the beginning, attendance was by private invitation only. Today, one can purchase a ticket and enjoy quality theater in a setting that has changed very little over the past one hundred years. The theater at 97 Boston Post Road and the old Hayward homestead at 101 Boston Post Road, still stand on their original sites.

Beatrice Herford Hayward was born in England in 1868 but spent time in Boston when her father was minister of the Arlington Street church. She and her six siblings spent nine summers in Wayland after the family purchased the Deacon James Draper house, which still stands on the corner of Plain and Draper Roads.

Beatrice returned to England when she was still a young woman. An actress at heart, she loved to perform original monologues for friends and family. Before long she was entertaining at formal teas and house parties at country estates outside of London. When she was twenty-seven years old, Beatrice gave a recital in London which brought rave reviews. She became an overnight success and went on to perform throughout England and in America. On her return to England in 1897, Beatrice met up with an old friend from Wayland, Sidney Hayward. They were soon married and returned to America to live on Hayward's estate. Sidney Hayward is remembered for his fast horse and carriage rides around town and as the town's first automobile owner. In 1903 Sidney drove his new auto eight to ten miles per hour around town. The great clouds of dust left behind shocked townspeople.

Over the next fifty-five years, Beatrice pursued her passion for the theater at home. She designed a miniature model of a real theater which she gave to her carpenter friends, Everett Small and James Linnehan, to use in the building of her personal theater. After the theater was completed in 1904, Beatrice named it "Vokes Theater" after Rosina Vokes, a turn-of-the-century comedienne whom Mrs. Hayward admired. It had a small stage and only enough room backstage for one person, who had to operate both the curtains and the lights. Actors exited the building and ran around the back to go from stage right to stage left. The theater had seats for ninety people, a balcony, box seats on either side of the stage for special guests, and two dressing rooms roughly the size of telephone booths. No detail was overlooked in the design and decoration of the theater. Beatrice fashioned red plush rails that she stuffed with excelsior saved from the wedding presents of her friend Marian Bennett Robbins. She traced the fancy French wallpaper in her house and used the tracings to create the balcony balusters. She also decorated the top of the stage with gilded bows and knots that she'd made out of putty.

A host of local residents made contributions to the theater. Samuel Mead of Weston, architect of the Wayland library and the Edmund F. Greene mansion, gave the shield with the festoons for the proscenium. Mrs. James Coolidge contributed valances from an old Salem mansion. Mr. Gannon, who painted at The Boston Theater, and according to Beatrice, mixed paints in chamber pots, painted the curtain and Beatrice painted the 'tormentor.' In London, Beatrice purchased the little gilded lion that is seated so regally on a shelf at the foot of the stairs to the balcony.

177

When the theater opened in 1904 with a minstrel show and vaudeville act there were doormen waiting to take tickets. Young ushers, wearing white pants with red stripes along the side and red coats with epaulets, showed people to their seats. For fifteen years local talent performed at least one play a year in the theater. Dances and parties were also held there. Mrs. Hayward continued to give witty and entertaining monologues for years at different meetings of Wayland organizations like the First Parish Women's Club.

In 1937, a small group of amateur players asked and received permission of Mrs. Hayward to use her little theater for their productions. By then the building had been long neglected and players had to work hard to get things back into shape. Once repairs were made, they began to schedule performances. To accommodate props or large casts, they pitched tents beside the building during productions. But when cold weather came, they had to abandon their unheated building and suspend performances until the weather warmed.

In 1939, the Vokes Players put on a play called "The Cakebread Mill," in celebration of the town's 300th anniversary. Many locals appeared, including Allen Morgan, Bill Ryder and George Lewis.

During World War II, when most production companies folded for lack of audience and operating funds, the Vokes Players managed to stay afloat. The group then held their monthly meetings in the vestry of the First Parish Church and sometimes held performances in town hall.

In 1946, Beatrice Hayward gifted the theater property to the Vokes organization which incorporated and took title the following year. Since then, the Vokes organization has remodeled and added to the little building, always respectful of Mrs. Hayward's original creation. Today, the Vokes organization auditions players for each production.

When Mrs. Hayward died in 1952, at the age of 94, the company created a permanent memorial for their generous mentor by hanging a portrait photograph in the box she had reserved for herself. Since her death, that box has been roped off during opening night performances.

$\mathcal{W}$

Rice Reservoir Gatehouse

179

Water Works

Thirty years before Wayland had a public water supply, Bostonians were drinking the clear pure waters of Lake Cochituate. Until 1848, a hollowed-out log system brought water from Jamaica Pond to the residents of Boston. However, the water tasted like "rotten eels" and residents demanded a new source. City officials tested various well sites in the city but the ground water proved unsanitary. At last they found three sources which had the quality and quantity needed and set up a "scientific experiment" to test the waters–Mystic Lake and Spot Pond in Winchester and Lake Cochituate in Wayland. They hitched a team of horses to a wagon that held three clean whiskey barrels and drove to each site filling one barrel from each. Officials set up the barrels in Boston Common, put advertisements in Boston newspapers and invited the public to the Common to vote for their choice for drinking water. Votes were made on a piece of paper put in a cigar box at the site. On this scientific basis, Lake Cochituate was chosen as Boston's public water supply.

The Boston Water Board purchased land and water rights from Wayland on Long Pond twenty-two miles west of Boston. Boston's mayor, Josiah Quincy, Jr., however, believed residents would not accept water taken from some unknown "pond" far from the city. So, he suggested that the name be changed from Long Pond to "Lake Cochituate," the Indian name for the area. The Mayor rationalized that Boston residents would then associate wilderness and purity with their water.

An elaborate ground-breaking ceremony was held in 1846 at the site of the proposed gatehouse, where the aqueduct began its run into the newly created Chestnut Hill reservoir which is still visible in Brookline. Final distribution was where the west wing of the State House now stands. An elevated reservoir, built of granite, held water that was distributed throughout the downtown area. It was demolished when the Back Bay was filled in. A brick aqueduct was built from Lake Cochituate to Frog Pond on Boston Common. It was nine feet in diameter, set in trenches dug by horse-drawn shovels. The gatehouse can still be seen on the east bank of Lake Cochituate near the Lakeview Cemetery. Dignitaries from Boston came to speak and lunch on the edge of the pond. Among them were former President of the United States John Quincy Adams and members of the Boston City Council. Construction started immediately and Bostonians waited only two years for clean clear water to flow through "Cochituate Aqueduct."

As Boston's population increased, the demand for water increased and the city sought additional sources not far from Lake Cochituate. In 1872 the Sudbury River Act was passed, authorizing the diversion of the Sudbury River at a point in Framingham about three-quarters of a mile southwest of Framingham Center. By 1888, the Sudbury Aqueducts and three reservoirs in Framingham had been completed and water had begun to flow to Chestnut Hill in Boston. No sooner were these in operation, when more water was needed and the Ashland and Hopkinton Reservoirs were constructed on the south branch of the Sudbury River. By 1894, the State Board of Health had identified additional water sources for the City of Boston that included the South Branch of the Nashua River and eventually the Ware and

181

Swift rivers. After the Metropolitan Water Act was passed in 1895, cities and towns within a ten mile radius of the State House could join the Water District. The MDC's Weston Aqueduct, built in 1900, and the Hultman Aqueduct, built in 1940, both of which pass through Wayland, channel water to eligible communities along the way. Wayland, however, has never been a participant.

By the end of the nineteenth century, there were ten factories (some very large) in Cochituate. Town meeting agreed that it was time to build a water system, both for residents, and to protect the many wooden factories in the village. Unfortunately, the poor clay-like soils of Cochituate prevented the use of wells and a reservoir/aqueduct system had to be designed. A committee of five Cochituate men was chosen to oversee construction of a water system. A shallow dam was built at the southern end of the Rice Road reservoir and a gate house constructed. The original six acres of pond doubled in size when the dam was finished. A pump was procured from the City of Boston and installed to pump water through portions of Cochituate Village. The gate house, now on private property is an architectural gem constructed of pink, gray and black granite. The first pipes were laid starting at the intersection of Lake (Route 30) and Plain streets in Cochituate on September 26, 1878. Four and one-half miles of cast-iron pipe were laid to twenty-nine hydrant locations.

The reservoir was small and the streams that supplied it meager. When a fire occurred in the village–about a mile from the reservoir–a church bell rang and someone on a bicycle or horse had to ride very fast to the reservoir to open a big gate. Instead of water going directly to town, it went through a water hammer, a device that created water pressure.

Water mains were later added northward on Main Street and westward to the home of Michael H. Simpson on the corner of Dudley Pond. The additional water pipes, financed by Simpson, brought the public water supply to households on what is now West Plain Street. The water, however was often unpalatable due to the woodsy setting of the pond. Organic matter that settled on the bottom of the pond turned the water muddy. Even after the system was flushed, the water was not considered good for drinking or cooking. As a result, families took to drinking milk instead. But the fire department never complained. Brown water put out fires just as well as colorless water.

At the same time, the central and northern sections of town, which consisted of medium to large size farms, obtained water from their own wells. By 1902, however, the population of Wayland center had increased and town meeting began to debate development of a water system for the rest of the town. There were three options: extend the Cochituate water system, pump water from driven wells, or tie into the Metropolitan District Commission. In 1921, before a decision had been made, Jonathan Maynard Parmenter died and left $225,000 to build a water supply for central and northern Wayland.

Construction began in 1926 and two years later water was being pumped from wells near Baldwin's Pond to a .5 million gallon steel riveted tank on Reeves Hill, the highest spot in town. Three years after the Baldwin Pond fields were opened, Cochituate Village was tied into the system because the Rice Road Reservoir was no longer able to meet the needs of the village.

From 1948 to 1972, the town experienced rapid population growth and new wells had to be added. Today, eight gravel-packed ground wells (averaging fifty feet in depth) are located throughout the town from the Campbell Road well in the north to the Meadowview Road well in the south. Happy Hollow wells #1 and #2 are located near the Wayland High School stadium parking area. Baldwin Pond wells #1, 2, and #3 are located at the Water Department's Operation Center off Old Sudbury Road. Chamberlain well is off Moore Road near the Sedge Meadow Conservation Area. In 1958, a second 2 million gallon concrete tank was added at Reeves Hill bringing total water storage to 2.5 million gallons. All the wells contribute to the system that is pumping water to Reeves Hill. The water is pumped from the town's wells into the main pipes that run under all the streets—eighty-five miles of water mains—and individual homes are served by a blend of wells. If more water is pumped than customers use, the excess flows into the storage tanks on Reeves Hill. If customers use more than is being pumped, water flows from the tanks to make up the difference. The wells work on the level of water in the tanks. To meet customer demand, wells are programmed to come on as the water level drops in the tanks.

Since 1997, the entire system has been monitored and controlled by a sophisticated electronic system called, SCADA, or Supervisory Control and Data Acquisition. Information is relayed to the Baldwin Pond Station via a GPS antenna on the top of the larger tank on Reeves Hill. All wells can be monitored at all times. During summer when demand for water is high, it is drawn from six wells. The rest of the year—spring, fall and winter—when demand is low, two or three wells are sufficient to serve the town.

Wayland's water consistently passes monthly tests run by the state. One hundred and eighty different substances are tested for—some monitored weekly and others on a quarterly basis. The Department operates under standards enacted by the U. S. Congress as the Safe Drinking Water Act in 1974 and were amended in 1986 and 1996. In January 1999, the Water Department began to treat the water supply. Prior to this there was no water treatment. Potassium hydroxide (KOH) is added for corrosion control. This process raises the pH and extends the life of the distribution system piping and household plumbing. In February 2000, the Department began adding sodium fluoride to help protect children's teeth. In June 2001, the Department began adding chlorine because of a detection of bacteria in the distribution system. Because town water has always had a high iron and manganese level, the inside of water pipes have become coated with the minerals. Removing these minerals is complex and costly, but the Water Department is exploring solutions to the problem.

During the nineteenth century, water rates were based on the number of household fixtures and the number of animals owned—so much per faucet and so much per horse or cow. Today water is charged according to registered use on each home's water meter. In 2004, town water cost $ 9 per 100 cubic feet for 6000 cubic feet and over. Residents average about ninety-five gallons of water per person per day. Periodic droughts have caused water shortages over the years but residents, when asked, have been willing to conserve water and there has never been a total lack of it.

The Water Department maintains a comprehensive website and includes everything from the history of the Water Department to the specific chemicals added to our water. A section on "Frequently asked questions," informs consumers of the effects on home plumbing from various additives.

It is clear that three quarters of a century after the original water system was installed, residents are still being served with clean clear water—one of the town's greatest assets.

Wayland, the name

In 1835 the town of East Sudbury voted to adopt the name "Wayland." Alfred S. Hudson drew from town records of that year some of the other names suggested: Clarence, Penrose, Fayette, Waybridge, Wadsworth, Elba, Waterville, Auburn, Keene, and Lagrange.

In her book, *The Puritan Village Evolves,* Helen Emery states, "Suffice it to say that no extant town record explains or even gives a clue to the reasons for the choice of the name. When in 1957 this writer undertook extensive research into the adoption of the name Wayland, no contemporary (1835) comment or explanation could be found."

However, Judge Edward Mellen was a friend of the Reverend Francis Wayland, president of Brown University. In 1835, when East Sudbury proposed changing its name, it is suspected that Judge Mellen, who had long admired his friend, may have proposed the name "Wayland." Twelve years later, Dr. Wayland donated $500 to help establish a public library in town–perhaps because he had been previously honored. (see Mellen Law Office)

Witchcraft

Although witchcraft was never practiced in our town, one family that was involved with it in Salem Village came to reside here at the end of the seventeenth century. Samuel Parris was the minister of Salem Village, now Danvers, where, in his household and parish, the Salem Witchcraft episode began. Later, in 1716, he became one of Sudbury's (Wayland) schoolmasters. Classes were held from December to March in his home, the Noyes-Parris house, the town's oldest remaining dwelling.

The Reverend Parris had taken a circuitous route to teaching. He was born in London in 1653, the youngest son of a prosperous merchant. At the age of twenty, while studying at Harvard College, his father died leaving him a small landholding in Barbados. Samuel left school and went to the island to take over his father's business, which he ran until 1680. He then returned to Boston with his family and two slaves, Tituba and John Indian. Samuel became a merchant for a while, engaged in maritime trade. Gradually, however, he devoted more of his energy to the ministry. He served briefly in Stow, and in 1688, the family, now with three children and two slaves, moved to Salem Village.

In January 1692 Parris' nine-year old daughter Betty began feeling sharp pinches on her body when no one was near her. Soon her cousin, Abigail, also experienced painful pinches. Both girls began having "fits" and "seizures" and began seeing "specters" in their rooms. A local physician was consulted who thought that the girls might be "under an evil hand." It soon appeared the two girls with some neighboring friends had been gossiping with the female slave, Tituba, about fortune telling, sorcery, conjuring and the appearance of specters, all popular topics in seventeenth-century New England. The Salem witchcraft frenzy had begun.

The girls and their companions took full advantage of their notoriety and began a variety of wildly deviant behavior. Members of Parris' congregation who believed in witchcraft felt that the girls' bizarre conduct stemmed from the presence nearby of a witch or witches. It did not take the afflicted girls long to identify the witches involved. Witches were nearly universally seen as women so it was no surprise that three women were the first accused: the slave Tituba and two older village women known for their erratic behavior. During the following weeks more women and a child were accused, shackled, and thrown into prison. Soon women from nearby towns were accused and finally several men, including prominent members of Parris' church and a former minister.

Through all of these proceedings, Parris himself played an active role, not only from the pulpit but also as a court clerk and occasional inquisitor at the trials. By mid-June 1692, executions by hanging began on Gallows Hill in Salem and continued through the summer until nineteen people had been hanged and one pressed to death under planks and large stones.

A number of political and theological developments in the summer and fall of 1692 slowed down and eventually stopped the arrests, trials, and executions. Over the following months the accusers and other participants, including colonial officials, began a series of public apologies, retroactive amnesties, and, finally, financial restitution to the victims or their families. Parris and his family remained in Salem Village for four years after the last trial. He was effectively removed from his ministry by a factious congregation, many of whose members had disliked him from the start. Parris fought to keep his house and land and to be paid his salary. His first wife Elizabeth died in 1696 and was buried in Salem Village.

In the fall of 1697, perhaps while preaching in Stow, Parris met and married Dorothy Noyes of Sudbury. Noyes was the daughter of Peter Noyes who had built the first part of what we now call the Noyes-Parris house in 1690. Peter Noyes' father (also Peter) was an original settler of Sudbury Plantation. Dorothy and her sisters spent the 1690s contesting their father's will, including the house.

The Parrises moved first to Newton and then on to Watertown where they bought a farm and Samuel taught school. Three children were born to this second marriage. The family then moved to Lincoln, Dunstable, and finally to Sudbury (Wayland), in 1712 after Dorothy had been awarded the family house.

From 1712, until his death in 1720, Parris lived in the Noyes-Parris house (now a private residence at 196 Old Connecticut Path), farming, running a dry goods shop and teaching school. Upon his death, Israel Loring, town minister wrote: "February 27. On Saturday night died the Reverend Mr. Samuel Parris . . . He was formerly Pastor of the Church of Christ in Salem Village, but by reason of the difficulties occasioned by the breaking out of Witchcraft . . . he removed from thence, and at last came and dwelt at Sudbury. Going to see him in the time of his sickness and not long before his death, he expressed himself in words of the Psalmist, 'Look upon my affliction and pain and forgive all my sins.'"

Although no one was ever accused of witchcraft in Wayland, Samuel Parris serves as a link between this town and one of the most extraordinary events in American history. One wonders what lessons he might have brought from the witchcraft trials to Sudbury children.

185

Xanthium strumarium/Cockleburs

Xanthium strumarium, or Cocklebur

Probably everyone has arrived home from a hike at one time or another with prickly little fruits clinging to a piece of clothing. Or a dog or cat has arrived home with burs tangled in its fur. It could be Cockleburs or Burdock. Both plants have burs that hitchhike on clothing. The field by the parking lot at Lower Snake Brook off French Road in Cochituate is filled with Burdock in fall and several fields at Greenways have plants. Cockleburs, native to North American came to the Sudbury River Valley long before the Indians. The sandy well-drained soils of the region are very much to their liking. After setting deep roots, the light green to straw-colored stems grow two feet high and bear large heart-shaped leaves and tiny football-shaped hairy burs. Burdock, a native of Europe, is believed to have hitchhiked all the way to America with the Spanish. They are well established throughout North America, especially in the East and mid West. Burdock, grows up to ten feet high, has smaller leaves than Cockleburs and rounded burs rather than elongated ones. Burdock burs cluster at the top of the plant stem whereas Cockleburs are attached where leaves join the plant stem. Cockleburs are a short-day plant–meaning at least one leaf of the plant needs fifteen hours of darkness to produce flowers. A protein leaf pigment that controls the release of florigen from the leaves is formed during the hours of darkness and is essential for the release of florigen for the flowering process. If interrupted by even a flash of light no flowers form. Thus, the plants bloom during the fall months when the days are shorter and the nights longer. Except under streetlights!

While Native Americans used the leaves of Cockleburs to counteract hydrophobia, they probably knew better than to collect seedlings. The Weed Science Society of America states, "Only the seedling stage is poisonous when the seeds contain hydroquinone, which is distributed into the seedling during germination. The seeds rarely cause poisoning because, enclosed in the burs, they are not eaten normally."

Today, Cockleburs and Burdock interest us because they are the origin of the fastener known as Velcro®. Although it is not certain from which of the hitchhiking plants the invention originated, they behave the same so it could have been either one. More than fifty years ago, a Swiss naturalist named Georges de Mestral, returned from a walk with his dog. Both of them were covered with little burs. Out of curiosity, de Mestral removed a bur and put it under a microscope. He discovered numerous small hooks on the bur that enabled it to cling to the weave of his wool pants and sweater. And to the fur of his dog. He thought about how tightly the little hooks gripped cloth and wondered if he could invent a rival to the zipper. It took a long time for anyone to take Mestral's idea seriously. But in 1955 a textile plant in France finally created a "hook and loop" fastener. By trial and error they discovered that nylon sewn under infrared light formed tough hooks. And that was the most difficult part. Imitating soft fabric was the easy part. De Mestral called his invention "Velcro" combing two words, velour and crochet. Today, it is a registered trademark of Velcro Industries's products, but there are many other similar fasteners with different brand names. Old-timers remember playing a game of darts with the feisty little burs. Draw a round target on a brightly colored felt board and use Cockleburs or burdock as arrows. Or, stick them together to create various animals shapes.

Yucca filamentosa

Yucca filamentosa

There is no proof that this remarkable plant had made its way north before Native Americans came to fish and hunt in the Sudbury River Valley, but it may have. Yucca filamentosa is native to southeastern regions of North America–there are more than forty species throughout the United States and Mexico–but it became well established in the north a very long time ago. The Yucca was worthy of being carried around by Native Americans because many parts of the plant are useful: medicine was obtained from the leaves, stalks, and roots of more than thirty varieties; weaving fibers from the plant's stems; soap from the roots; juice from the fruits; and food from the leaves, flowers, fruits, and seedpods. Yucca filamentosa is quite happy in the many dry, sandy and rocky habitats of the northeast. Plants are often seen growing in full sun in open fields, at the edge of woodlands, or along road shoulders. In Wayland, Yucca plants grow in the North Cemetery in the center section by the Drury and Smith family plots and in the back next to the Parker grave. Many northerners associate Yucca with the desert southwest and believe the plants they see at the side of the road are desert species planted by amateurs or discarded by disgruntled homeowners. They may have been. But they may just be growing wild.

Yucca filamentosa has sharply pointed leaves with curly threads along edges that grow to two and one-half feet long and one inch wide. Leaves remain green all year long. The flower stalk often reaches a height of twelve feet and bears a loose open arrangement of white or yellow-green bell-like flowers that hang down. Yucca's unique method of pollination is quite remarkable and sets it apart from other flowering plants. Without the presence of a tiny white moth, the Pronuba, the plant cannot reproduce. In the process of laying her eggs in the ovary of the Yucca (the seed capsule), the moth causes pollen to come in contact with the pistil (female seed-bearing organ of the flower), thus fertilizing the plant. Fortunately Yucca plants produce enough seeds to feed the moth larvae and to ensure their own future. Yucca plants could not survive however, if not for the little moth.

Baskets woven from the leaves of Yucca filamentosa were collected in the early 1700s in North Carolina. Bundles of long fiber cells can be pulled out of the leaf blade like strands of thread for weaving and rope making. The greatest number of products made from Yucca plants, however, come from Southwestern varieties. In the Southwest, basket makers remove the Yucca's tough fibers from the pulpy tissue of immature leaves to make twine. Split Yucca leaves are also used to weave baskets and mats. The Hopi use extremely finely divided Yucca fibre for the weft of their coiled baskets, while the stems serve for the body of the coil. The Papago Indians of the Southwest are prolific basket makers. Women bleach Yucca leaves in the sun to use for the white coils in their baskets or dye the leaves using the root of the plant to create designs in red. The greenish-yellow designs are made from unbleached leaves.

Yucca leaves can be dried and boiled in water and drunk as a tea to relieve arthritis and related ailments such as bursitis and gout. The root of the plant is a valuable source of soap and is popular with natives of the Southwest. It was also used to stop minor bleeding from cuts, inflamation and skin irritations. Yucca roots contain saponin, which is poisonous to insects and other small creatures but not to humans unless injected into the blood stream. The flowers of many Yucca varieties are edible and used raw in salads or cooked.

Today, the Yucca is a popular dietary supplement promoted to ease the pain of arthritis, help treat high cholesterol, high blood pressure, and migraine headaches. It is available in liquids, gels, or creams to apply topically as needed. (**Warning:** consult your doctor before self-medicating.)

If live Yucca is not to your liking, owning a beautifully woven Native American Papogo basket would be a good alternative. Papago baskets are still being made and are available in museum shops throughout the country.

Howard Russell

Zea Mays or Flint/Indian Corn

Indian corn has been grown in Wayland since Cakebread opened his mill at Mill Pond in 1643. During the nineteenth century farmers began to fertilize their fields–there was plenty of barnyard manure around–they started to compete with one another for yield per acre. In 1855 Indian corn grew on 312 acres of town land. It had to be dried and ground into meal. Farmers like Parmenter, Flint, Damon, Heard and Gleason owned land that yielded 30-40 bushels of corn per acre in 1882. Hodijah B. Braman's farmland, however, yielded 80 bushels per acre that year. Total yield then was 9,360 bushels. By 1875, it had dropped to 3,348 bushels but some acreage had been replaced with green corn and popcorn.

While there are no large farms in Wayland raising Indian corn today, the farm manager at Mainstone Farm at the corner of Old Connecticut Path and Rice Road still raises cattle corn. He and his family sometimes raise enough sweet corn to sell at a stand on the corner of Rice Road and Old Connecticut Path. The farm manager also raises a crop of cattle corn on Cow Common on Old Sudbury Road, alternating it with a crop of hay. The corn crop enriches the soil for increased hay production. Some farms west of Wayland, in Bolton and Berlin, raise small quantities of the brightly colored Indian Corn which suburbanites and city-dwellers use for household decoration in fall. Although it feels and looks like plastic, it is the same brightly-colored Zea mays that was uncovered so many years ago in a basket in Wellfleet.

As the Pilgrims skirted the coast of Cape Cod late in the fall of 1620 looking for a good harbor, men on the Mayflower prepared to release a large shallop stowed in the ship's quarters. The shallop, capable of holding sixteen men, had been brought from England for the express purpose of navigating shallow or unfamiliar waters. Unfortunately, it had been badly battered during the Atlantic crossing and would need to be repaired before being used. Anxious to go ashore, a group of men left the boat to explore on foot. Climbing a sandy hill in present-day Wellfleet, they found an open area. In the middle was a section of hand prints as if the sand had been patted down in place. The men dug down into the sand and discovered huge baskets filled with corn cobs covered with bright red, blue, maroon and white kernels. Hungry, and in need of nourishment, they took one of the baskets with them intending to repay the owners some time in the future, and returned to the ship. The Indian grain helped stave off starvation that first winter and later supplied the Pilgrims with a crop that would sustain them for many years to come. They eventually met and repaid the Indians whose corn they had taken.

Zea mays, or Indian corn has large tough kernels that cannot be digested if eaten from the cob. The natives of New England ground their corn and showed the English how to do the same. Because the brightly colored kernels are filled with starch they served as a staple food, the way bread had done for centuries in other parts of the world. Indian corn was New England's staple grain after the establishment of Plymouth Colony. It grows successfully farther north than other kinds of corn because cold soil does not significantly inhibit its germination. By the nineteenth century nearly every town in Massachusetts had grown it. Sudbury settlers probably obtained corn from Watertown settlers before settling in the Sudbury

RiverValley. And they were undoubtedly given additional sacks by Karto and Tantamous, the Indians who lived here. (see Native Americans)

Throughout the Americas, the Indians have legends about the coming of corn. Roger Williams said the Indians told him how, in the beginning, corn was brought to their ancestors "a graine of corne in one Eare, and an Indian or French Beane in another from the great God *Kantantowit's* field in the Southwest, from whence come all their Corne and Beanes."

Nineteenth century herbalist Edward Lewis Sturtevant reported: ". . . culture of corn was general in the New World at the time of the discovery; that it reigned from Brazil to Canada, from Chile to California; that it was grown extensively in fields and that it produced many varieties–always an indication of antiquity of culture. It furnished food in its grain, and, from its stalks, sugar to the Peruvians, honey to the Mexicans and a kind of wine or beer to all the natives of the tropics."

Native Americans had many uses for their valuable corn harvest in addition to storing it for winter food. Dried cobs served to fuel the fire and husks were cut into strips and used for weaving. The Iroquois people make corn-husk baskets by coiling and sewing the husks or by braiding them into strips which are sewn together. Twined, watertight bottles, salt dishes, and mats are also made of corn husks. In addition, they make very clever doormats, woven so that the husk ends protrude from one side and create a stiff pile to wipe muddy feet. Many New England Indians made corn husk dolls for their children and for the tourist trade.

By the end of the eighteenth century, the varieties of corn in America had become so diffused that corn kernels became palatable and tasty enough to be eaten from the cob. Slowly varieties of Sweet Corn began to appear. Sweet Corn is mentioned in early nineteenth century journals. In 1881, sixteen varieties were listed for sale in one New England seed catalog.

American farmers continue to raise quantities of Zea mays to be ground for animal feed. In addition, Zea mays products are exported all over the world: Maize, Indian corn, Corn, Maize grain, Hominy feed, Maize-and-cob meal, Maize cobs, Maize gluten feed, Maize gluten meal, and Maize-germ oil cake.

The increased value of land in town caused farmers to sell their farmland for housing development and commercial farms no longer exist. However local food markets buy Massachusetts grown sweet corn, farmer's markets sell locally grown corn and a few roadside stands in town still sell it.

Fall in New England means boiled corn on the cob for dinner. And people wait anxiously each year, often as early as July, to taste the latest variety of "sweet" or "sugar" corn.

Zoning

Zoning is an important legal tool by which cities and towns control the use of land within their borders. Zoning has become a "hot" political issue in Wayland. Until the 1920's, Wayland–with its two town centers–just grew like topsy, following a pattern of growth guided by the wishes of landowners. Most early

New England town centers grew up around a meetinghouse, tavern, country store, school and town green surrounded by houses. The center at the north end of Wayland represented this more or less typical pattern of growth. Cochituate Village, on the other hand, had grown rapidly during the nineteenth century and by 1880 the population had reached 1,161.

By 1926 Wayland had grown in all directions and random development was no longer working. The town needed to plan for its future growth as a whole. Howard Russell, who had come to town in the 1920s, was a critic of unregulated growth and stepped forward to champion the cause for town zoning. Russell had been dismayed by the uncontrolled development that had wreaked havoc on the land around Dudley Pond, Riverview, and elsewhere. He objected to the bars and the gangsters who hung out in the area which gave the town a bad name. He had a vision for the town: ". . . the town's life can be preserved along with the growth and improvement that will take place and everyone who lives or works here will gain in the process."

Wayland's annual town meeting voted to establish a Planning Board in 1933 with a five-person committee charged with preparing an official town map, designating streets, and delineating the established uses for which all of Wayland's 15.2 square miles of land could be used, especially for businesses and industries. Howard Russell chairman of the new Zoning Committee, was the guiding hand for this new venture in town government. Many future political leaders in Wayland cut their teeth on the Planning Board. Allen Benjamin, Bill Bertelsen, Fred Perry, Hugh Morton, and Bob Charnock were "pioneer" planners.

Within a year, the map had been completed. The following year, the Wayland Zoning Committee set forth a plan that zoned the entire town "residential," except for small business districts in Wayland Center and Cochituate Village. The 1934 Report, appended to the proposed Zoning bylaw, noted that "[zoning] is a means of securing order and good arrangement within the town." Examples of some of the proposed objectives were: (1) To protect the town and the home owners in it from speculative land development schemes. Such developments often result in cutting up desirable building land into lots too small to build a house and garage on, and leave no land for garden and lawn . . . (5) To protect our townspeople who own or operate roadside stands from the competition of hucksters who purchase produce elsewhere for resale."

One proposal to zone much of the Boston Post Road "business" greatly upset residents living along the road who feared their homes would become worthless if commercial business dominated both sides of the road. Ned Bennett, a lawyer who lived opposite one of the "drinking" establishments, complained that patrons left at night shouting and roaring their car engines. The Zoning Committee understood the problem and zoned the road "residential" but allowed existing businesses to remain zoned as "business." Thereafter, to change property from residential to business required a special permit from the Planning Board.

Later the Planning Board established a set of rules governing the erection of houses and the laying out of new streets. The entire town was zoned for 10,000 square foot lots in 1934. However, other categories were added in 1939 including 15,000 and 20,000 square feet. In 1953, all three residential zoning categories were doubled to lot sizes of 20,000, 30,000, and 40,000 square feet and a fourth category of 60,000 square feet was added for areas known as Claypit and Tower hills. A special board, later called the Zoning Board of Appeals, was set up to adjudicate complaints from owners and developers who found circumstances that warranted a possible variance.

Town planning continued under Russell's stewardship after World War II when people began to flock to the suburbs. In the town report of 1946, Russell was quoted as saying, "what the townspeople can do is to try to guide this growth so as to retain the village atmosphere and the charm of the ponds, river, woods, farms and natural features, while fitting into the environment the new neighbors who hope to join us."

Another long-time member of the planning board, Allan R. Finlay, became concerned about the development of large estates coming onto the market. Of particular interest was Francis Shaw's 720 acre estate (now Woodridge) offered for sale in 1942 by his heirs. Local residents and the planning board learned about plans to develop the property from a national architectural magazine. An article on the estate's subdivision described the creation of a complete community including a movie theater, stores, and house lots that would be a mere 10,000 square feet in size. Fearing that such development would ruin the town's rural atmosphere, Finlay gathered a group of like-thinking residents, including Nathaniel Hamlen, who, with family members, owned Mainstone Farm on the other side of the hill from the Shaw estate, and formed the Wayland Real Estate Company. The group acquired all but one piece of Shaw's estate which had already been sold.

The original Woodridge proposal included an area east of Cochituate Road where a gentler topography facilitated construction and was laid out in large lots at higher prices. Land west of Cochituate road, known as Happy Hollow, with a more irregular terrain was divided into smaller lots of more modest prices. Soon, lots there were selling like "hot cakes," and became the first homes of Wayland's early "boomers."

The success of the Woodridge project set an example for future development of large parcels of land in town. The influx of new residents caused the town's population to double in the decade of the 1950s. Homes went up on newly subdivided land, on long-established roads, and wherever zoning laws permitted building. Daymon Farms in the Cochituate section of town was developed in 1953, and land in the northern portion of town in the Claypit and Tower hills sections was developed in the late 1950s and early 1960s.

In 1954, however, when a housing sub-division was proposed for seventy-three acres of land in the center of town on the present Raytheon site, the Planning Board began to rethink the "residential" zoning status of that parcel of land. They came up with a new category, "Limited Commercial," that might bring needed tax money to the town without overburdening schools and other services. After town meeting had approved the zoning change, the selectmen and the Planning Board began negotiations with the Raytheon Company to build a plant on the site. Raytheon bought the property in the early 1950s, but because of government contract accounting rules, it was discovered early on that the company would be much better off leasing the site. So the land was sold to a Chicago firm which leased it back to Raytheon. Raytheon retained ownership of the tiny piece of land containing the Grout-Heard House and donated the house to the newly organized Wayland Historical Society which moved it back to town center in 1962. Raytheon remained a generous friend and neighbor until the plant closed in 1996.

In 1962, residential land on the corner of Rice and Commonwealth roads was submitted for re-zoning to "Limited Commercial." Town meeting approved the zoning change and, after numerous restrictions were placed on Dow Chemical Company, the sale was approved. Thirty years later, Dow had vacated the property and it was again up for sale. A large building was proposed for the site but in 1998 some concerned citizens united and convinced town meeting to purchase the site for conservation and recreational use and to demolish the commercial building. Today, the building is gone and the area is open to the public.

Another in the sequence of zoning changes guiding residential growth was the establishment in the 1970s of a form of clustered development, tailor-made for the expansion of housing on open land along Rice Road. At "Mainstone" builders were permitted to cluster attached housing units while preserving large amounts of open space to be owned by the town or by Sudbury Valley Trustees. These dwellings, limited to two bedrooms, became a popular purchase for older families and individuals, many already residents of Wayland. Other cluster development has occurred on other prime parcels of land in order to preserve significant amounts of open space. The most recent development has been the former Paine Estate which preserved approximately 130 acres while developing only about twenty-six acres with cluster single-family housing and senior housing and a municipal land bank parcel.

Now, at the seventieth anniversary of Wayland's Zoning By-laws, the wisdom of these statutes is evidenced by the wide variety of residential landscapes that still retain a semblance of rural atmosphere. Commercial and industrial businesses occupy less space than in many surrounding towns, yet still add a utilitarian aspect of busyness (and business) to the town. In addition, twenty-seven percent, or 2,700 acres, is permanently protected open space, including large portions of the Sudbury River corridor.

Relevant Historical Events

1630 Watertown established as a town

1635 ". . a plantation at Musketaquid" hereafter to be called Concord

1638 Settlement of Sudbury Plantation

1639 Sudbury called a town

1639 Construction Cakebread's Mill

1638-40 Individual Land Grants (Cochituate)

1640 Estimated 5,700 people in American Colonies

1642-43 Construction Old Town Bridge/Cart Bridge

1643 First Meetinghouse at Old Burial Ground

1650 Estimated 40,000 people in American Colonies

1653 Second Meetinghouse

1651 Indian Plantation at "Naticke" granted 200 acres

1660 Bounds of Indian plantation at "Natick" established

1660 ". . . name of the said plantation shall be called 'Marlborow'"

1674 Construction of first bridge at Stone's Bridge

1675-76 King Philip's War

1689-97 First French and Indian War

1691 Mass. Bay and Plymouth Colonies become a Province

1692 Salem Witch Trials held

1700 Framingham established as a town

1713 Weston established as a town

1721 Certain farms annexed to Sudbury (Cochituate)

1723 First Meetinghouse on west side of river

1726 Fourth Meetinghouse on east side of river

1743 Construction of Sherman Bridge

1754 Lincoln established as a town

1770 Boston Massacre

1771 Construction of Pequod House

1773 Boston Tea Party

1775 American Revolution begins in Lexington & Concord

1775 Construction of first Pelham Island Bridge

1775-76 General Knox's journey from Fort Ticonderoga to Boston

1780 Part of Sudbury established as East Sudbury

1780 Adoption of the State Constitution

1815 Dedication of Fifth Meetinghouse (First Parish Church)

1820 Construction of Route 20 Bridge

1833 Separation Church and State in Massachusetts

1835 Name of the town East Sudbury shall be Wayland

1840 Beginning of shoe industry in Cochituate

1841 Construction of first town hall (Collins Mkt.)

1850 Establishment of state's first free public library in Wayland

1846 Lake Cochituate water flows to Boston

1848 Construction of four-arch Old Town Bridge

1850 Wayland's first free public library opened

1855 Construction of first high school

1857-58 Stone's Bridge replaced

1885 First horse car line (Cochituate)

1878 Victorian Town Hall built in center

1896 Ground breaking for Center School

1897 Center School Grammar/High School opens

1899 Electric trolley extended from Cochituate to Wayland Center

1926 First Planning Board

1942 Village Bugle first published

1945 Jeep first published

1953 Construction of Cochituate Fire Station

1953 Founding Sudbury Valley Trustees

1954 First dial phones in town

1960 Construction of new high school

1972 Construction of new Jr. High School/Middle School

1990 Wayland's present library building opened

1999 Sudbury Rivers designated Wild and Scenic

Bibliography

Benes, Peter and Phillip D. Zimmerman. *New England Meeting House and Church: 1630-1850.* Boston, Mass. and Manchester, New Hampshire: Boston University and The Currier Gallery of Art for the Dublin Seminar for New England Folklife, 1979.

Cutting, Alfred Wayland, *An Historical Address: Delivered in the First Parish Church, Wayland, Mass., Sunday, June 25, 1911.* Boston, Mass: Press of Geo. H. Ellis Co., Printers, 1911.

Emery, Helen Fitch. *The Puritan Village Evolves, a history of Wayland, Massachusetts.* Canaan, New Hampshire: Phoenix Publishing, 1981. (Published for the Wayland Historical Commission)

Federal Writers Project of W. P.A., *A Brief History of the Towne of Sudbury in Massachusetts 1639-1939.* Sudbury Historical Society, 1968. Revised edition.

Gormley, Ken. *Archibald Cox: Conscience of a Nation.* Reading, MA: Addison-Wesley, 1997.

Grieve, Mrs. M.. *A Modern Herbal.* In Two volumes. New York: Dover Publications, Inc., 1971.

Hudson, Alfred Sereno. *The History of Sudbury, Massachusetts, 1638-1889.* Sudbury, Mass: The Town of Sudbury, 1889.
.... *The Annals of Sudbury, Wayland, and Maynard, Middlesex County, Massachusetts.* By the author, 1891.

League of Woman Voters of Wayland, Massachusetts. *Wayland, a Community Handbook.* 1968. Revised edition.

Powell, Sumner Chilton. *Puritan Village: The Formation of a New England Town.* New York: Doubleday and Company, 1965.

Reid, Gene B. *Michael Simpson: The Saxonville Mills & The Roxbury Carpet Co.* Framingham, Ma.: Framingham Historical Society, 1982.

Russell, Howard S. *A Long, Deep Furrow: Three Centuries of Farming in New England.* Hanover, New Hampshire: University Press of New England, 1982.

Sudbury Plantation 1640: Essays in Celebration of the 350th Anniversary of the Gathering of Wayland's First Parish. Wayland, First Parish in Wayland, 1990.

Temple, Josiah H. *History of Framingham, Massachusetts 1640-1885.* Framingham: New England History Press, 1997. (Centennial Year reprinting of the 1887 edition.)

The Boston & Maine Railroad Historical Society, Inc., *The Central Mass.,* 1975.

The Commonwealth of Mass. Historical Data relating to Counties, Cities and Towns in Mass. Prepared by Kevin H. White, Secretary of the Commonwealth, 1966.

The Parmenter Story, published by Harvard Trust Company 1960.

INDEX

209

210